Global Debt Report 2024

BOND MARKETS IN A HIGH-DEBT ENVIRONMENT

OECD
BETTER POLICIES FOR BETTER LIVES

Please cite this publication as:
OECD (2024), *Global Debt Report 2024: Bond Markets in a High-Debt Environment*, OECD Publishing, Paris, https://doi.org/10.1787/91844ea2-en.

ISBN 978-92-64-56736-8 (print)
ISBN 978-92-64-32369-8 (PDF)
ISBN 978-92-64-86611-9 (HTML)
ISBN 978-92-64-92591-5 (epub)

Photo credits: Cover © gyn9038/Getty Images.

Corrigenda to OECD publications may be found on line at: www.oecd.org/about/publishing/corrigenda.htm.

Foreword

This is the first edition of the annual Global Debt Report, which examines sovereign and corporate bond markets, providing insights into current market conditions and associated policy considerations. It consolidates the Sovereign Borrowing Outlook, previously a standalone OECD publication, with chapters on corporate bond markets and sustainable bonds. The report draws from original OECD survey data provided by national authorities as well as OECD analysis of both commercial and public data sources.

Chapter 1 analyses sovereign debt developments for the period 2008-2024 with a focus on the OECD countries. It explores borrowing requirements and funding strategies; debt-to-GDP ratio dynamics; borrowing costs and yield curve shapes; interest payments and refinancing risks; and the effects of quantitative tightening on the investor base and market liquidity. This chapter draws on responses received to the OECD 2023 Survey on Primary Market Developments, the OECD 2023 Survey on Liquidity in Government Bond Secondary Markets, and the annual survey on the borrowing needs of OECD governments, all circulated in 2023. It also benefits from the direct contributions of members of the OECD Working Party on Debt Management (WPDM). This chapter does not cover supranational or sub-sovereign bond markets.

Chapter 2 explores how global corporate bond markets have evolved during a time of accommodative financial conditions in terms of credit quality, investor universe, and geographic and sectoral composition with a view to identifying the build-up of possible vulnerabilities. It then examines the implications of a changing macrofinancial landscape with sharp shifts in monetary policy for these markets, seeking to identify possible financial stability risks.

Chapter 3 focuses on the key characteristics of and trends in the sustainable bond market. It aims to inform policy discussion on the goals of investors when acquiring sustainable bonds, how these instruments may alter corporate and official sector issuers' decisions, and what could be done to further develop the market for sustainable bonds.

Comments and questions should be addressed to the Capital Markets and Financial Institutions Division of the OECD Directorate for Financial and Enterprise Affairs (e-mail: GlobalDebtReport@oecd.org).

Acknowledgements

The Global Debt Report 2024 was prepared by the Capital Markets and Financial Institutions Division within the OECD Directorate for Financial and Enterprise Affairs (DAF), under the general supervision of Serdar Çelik, Head of Division.

Chapter 1 "Sovereign borrowing outlook" is one of the activities of the OECD Working Party on Debt Management (WPDM), supported by the Financial Markets Unit of the Capital Markets and Financial Institutions Division within DAF. This Outlook was prepared by Pietrangelo De Biase and Luca Policino, with the support of Sam Foxall, under the supervision of Fatos Koc, Head of the Unit. The following members of the WPDM provided valuable feedback: Grahame Johnson (Chair of the WPDM, Assistant Deputy Minister, Financial Sector Policy Branch, Department of Finance, Canada); Anthony Linehan (Vice-Chair of the WPDM, Deputy Director, Funding and Debt Management, NTMA, Ireland); Antoine Deruennes (Director General, Agence France Trésor); Davide Iacovoni (Director General; Ministry of Economy and Finance, Italy); Frederick Pietrangeli (Director, Office of Debt Management, US Treasury); Sir Robert Stheeman (Chief Executive; UK Debt Management Office); Rui Arase (Director for Debt Management and Investor Relations Office Financial Bureau; Ministry of Finance of Japan); and Tammo Diemer (Managing Director of Germany's Finance Agency). Several OECD colleagues provided valuable feedback: Nigel Pain, Alvaro Pina, Carl Magnus Magnusson, Ono Nobukazu and Ane Kathrine Christensen.

Chapter 2 "Corporate debt markets in a changing macrofinancial landscape" was prepared by Carl Magnus Magnusson, Tugba Mulazimoglu, Caroline Roulet and Yun Tang, under the supervision of Alejandra Medina, Acting Head of the Financial Economics Team, all from the Capital Markets and Financial Institutions Division within DAF. An initial draft of this chapter was discussed by the OECD Committee on Financial Markets and incorporates comments from delegates.

Chapter 3 "Sustainable bonds: State of the market and policy considerations" was prepared by Pietrangelo De Biase, Adriana De La Cruz, Caio de Oliveira and Giulio Mazzone with the support of Valentina Cociancich and Luca Policino, all from the Capital Markets and Financial Institutions Division within DAF. An initial draft of the chapter was discussed by the OECD Committee on Financial Markets and the Corporate Governance Committee and incorporates comments from delegates.

Flora Monsaingeon-Lavuri, Greta Gabbarini and Meral Gedik supported the team with publishing, editorial guidance and with communication expertise. Several OECD colleagues provided feedback on all three chapters; Flore-Anne Messy, Oliver Garrett-Jones, Sam Foxall, Catriona Marshall, John-David Tochon, and Juan Pavajeau.

Table of contents

FIGURES

INFOGRAPHICS

TABLES

BOXES

Editorial

Sovereign and corporate bond markets are at the centre of the global financial system. At a combined value of almost USD 100 trillion, they are similar in size to global GDP. Following decades of expansion, a rapidly changing macrofinancial landscape is now presenting the most significant test to these markets in a generation.

The extended period of historically low interest rates that enabled the widespread growth of global debt and the expansion of riskier market segments has come to an end. Higher policy rates, quantitative tightening and heightened geopolitical tensions are having substantial impacts. Refinancing needs are considerable. Today's bond markets are also characterised by a growing universe of more price sensitive investors.

These dynamics combine to form a key consideration: making sure that debts that were manageable in a low-interest rate environment, where central banks were buyers, are not rendered unsustainable in this new reality.

At the same time, borrowing needs are higher than ever. Demographic changes, slowing economic growth and decarbonisation will require the mobilisation of tens of trillions of dollars. Successfully managing this might be the defining issue facing the global economy.

It is against this backdrop that the OECD is launching this new annual report, which examines key challenges policy makers face in working to safeguard the functioning of bond markets and financial stability.

Over three separate chapters, this first edition paints a comprehensive picture of how global bond markets have developed in the last two decades and seeks to identify the build-up of risks and vulnerabilities. Recognising the high overall levels of indebtedness and the inherent interlinkages, it covers both sovereign and corporate bond markets. In addition, it studies the rapid growth of sustainable bond markets and the associated policy implications.

The global economy, and indeed the world at large, are facing great challenges. Bond markets will play a critical role in providing the funding needed to overcome them. Ensuring that they continue to function efficiently is essential, but it is also a considerable task that calls for shrewd and effective policy making.

One of the most important tools at our disposal in that endeavour is knowledge: navigating a difficult terrain is significantly easier with a good map. The overarching ambition of this report is to provide part of that map.

Carmine Di Noia

Director for Financial and Enterprise Affairs, OECD

Abbreviations and acronyms

ATM	Average Term-to-Maturity
ATR	Average Term-to-Refixing
BoC	Bank of Canada
BoE	Bank of England
BoJ	Bank of Japan
BTP	Buono del Tesoro Poliennale
CBI	Climate Bonds Initiative
CB	Central Bank
CBS	Climate Bonds Standard
COVID	Coronavirus disease (COVID-19)
CPI	Consumer Price Index
DMO	Debt Management Office
ECB	European Central Bank
EBITDA	Earnings Before Interest, Taxes, Depreciation, and Amortisation
EMDEs	Emerging Markets and Developing Economies
EO	OECD Economic Outlook
ESG	Environmental, Social and Governance
ETFs	Exchange Traded Funds
EU	European Union
EUR	Euro
FRN	Floating Rate Note
FX	Foreign Exchange
GBP	Great Britain Pound
GDP	Gross Domestic Product
GFC	Global Financial Crisis
GHG	Greenhouse Gases
GSS	Green, Social and Sustainability
HICs	High-Income Countries
ICMA	International Capital Market Association
IMF	International Monetary Fund
ISAE	International Standard on Assurance Engagements
ISIN	International Securities Identification Number
JGB	Japanese Government Bond
KPI	Key Performance Indicator
LAC	Latin America and the Caribbean
LICs	Low-Income Countries
LMICs	Lower-Middle Income Countries

LSEG	London Stock Exchange Group
MENA	Middle East and North Africa
MMFs	Money Market Funds
NA	OECD National Accounts
OATs	Obligations Assimilables au Trésor
OECD	Organisation for Economic Co-operation and Development
OEFs	Open-Ended Funds
PDM	Public Debt Management
PEPP	Pandemic Emergency Purchase Programme (ECB)
PSPP	Public Sector Purchase Programme (ECB)
QE	Quantitative Easing
QT	Quantitative Tightening
SBO	OECD Sovereign Borrowing Outlook
SLB	Sustainability-Linked Bond
SDRs	Special Drawing Rights
SNA	System of National Accounts
SPT	Sustainable Performance Target
SSA	Sub-Saharan Africa
TBAC	Treasury Borrowing Advisory Committee
TRBC	The Reference data Business Classification
UK	United Kingdom
UMICs	Upper-Middle Income Countries
UN	United Nations
UNEP	United Nations Environment Programme
US	United States
USD	United States Dollar
WPDM	OECD Working Party on Debt Management
YTM	Yield-to-Maturity

Executive summary

Both sovereign and corporate bond market borrowing have grown significantly around the world

Bond financing has grown alongside expansionary monetary policies, in particular quantitative easing, since the 2008 global financial crisis. This trend is broad-based, from sovereign issuers responding to increased public spending needs in both advanced and emerging economies, to financial and non-financial corporations across the world. A favourable funding environment post-2008 has opened bond markets to a wider range of issuers, including lower-rated governments and companies, expanding into riskier market segments. It has also contributed to the emergence of the sustainable bond market. The total volume of sovereign and corporate bond debt globally at the end of 2023 was almost USD 100 trillion, similar in size to global GDP.

At the end of 2023, OECD governments' total bond debt stood at USD 54 trillion, an increase of USD 30 trillion since 2008. This is projected to increase further to USD 56 trillion in 2024. The United States will represent roughly half of this debt, twice its share in 2008. The share of People's Republic of China's (China) debt in Emerging Markets and Developing Economies has also doubled, reaching nearly 30% of the total outstanding amount.

The total global outstanding corporate bond debt has increased from USD 21 trillion to USD 34 trillion over the same period. Over 60% of this increase came from non-financial corporations. Structurally low yields have enabled lower-rated corporates to access the market, with an expansion of the non-investment grade market and a sharp decrease in the value-weighted average corporate credit rating globally. The outstanding debt of the non-investment grade segment totalled USD 3.4 trillion at the end of 2023, almost twice the 2008 figure.

The post-2008 environment has also seen the emergence of sustainable bond markets. This is still a nascent market segment but one that has been growing rapidly. At the end of 2023, the outstanding amount of sustainable corporate and official sector bonds totalled USD 2.3 trillion and USD 2.0 trillion respectively.

Bond issuance reached record levels during the pandemic and remains elevated for sovereigns

Bond markets play a critical role in allowing both governments and corporations to respond to periods of financial distress. During the COVID-19 crisis, sovereign and corporate bond issuance reached record levels. However, in some segments of bond markets this rapid growth has halted and even reversed from 2022 as monetary policy began tightening sharply in response to elevated levels of inflation.

The economic and financial disruption which resulted from the onset of the COVID-19 pandemic prompted a further easing of already accommodative monetary policies, with the substantial expansion of asset purchase programmes. During the period 2020-21, sovereign bond issuance in the OECD area peaked at USD 15.4 trillion in 2020, and sovereign issuance in Emerging Market and Developing Economies reached a then-record of USD 3.2 trillion in 2021, as governments provided large, mostly blanket fiscal support to businesses and households. Similarly, corporate issuance peaked in 2020 at USD 6.9 trillion, almost 50% above the 2008-19 average.

However, the sharp reversal in monetary policy starting in 2021-22 to tackle higher inflation has halted, and even reversed, this trend for certain market segments. Significantly tighter financial conditions have caused corporate issuance in particular to contract. While sovereign issuance by OECD countries fell somewhat in 2022, down approximately 16% from 2021, it remained substantially higher than pre-pandemic levels, and is projected to reach a new record high in 2024. Corporate issuance, however, fell by 25% in 2022, bringing it close to the pre-pandemic average. Non-investment grade corporate issuance contracted by as much as 74%. Both total and non-investment grade issuance remained around 2022 levels in 2023.

Central banks absorbed large parts of the increases in borrowing but have begun withdrawing from bond markets

Central banks have purchased large amounts of sovereign debt from markets. While corporate debt purchases have been much smaller, sovereign debt purchase programmes have also had a significant indirect effect on corporate bond markets by lowering borrowing costs. However, as central banks have begun withdrawing from bond markets through quantitative tightening, a more price sensitive investor base is emerging.

At the end of 2023, the aggregate central government debt-to-GDP ratio in the OECD was approximately 83%, an increase of 30 percentage points compared to 2008, even though higher inflation, which boosted nominal GDP growth, has contributed to a decrease in this ratio of more than 10 percentage points over the past two years. Central bank holdings of sovereign bonds in the OECD area is currently equivalent to nearly 30% of GDP. The gradual withdrawal of central banks from bond markets globally will therefore not simply result in a return to the pre-quantitative easing market structure. Despite the surge in borrowing since 2008, the level of sovereign bonds held by the market as a percentage of GDP has remained largely unchanged. As central banks begin to shrink their balance sheets through quantitative tightening, the net supply of bonds to be absorbed by the broader market will increase to record levels. This will result in a growing share of bonds being held by more price sensitive investors, such as the non-bank financial sector and households.

The withdrawal of central banks from global sovereign bond markets will also affect corporate markets. Quantitative easing has had a strong effect on corporate bond markets, driving down yields and making issuance cheaper. Quantitative tightening will have the opposite effect, further contributing to the tightening of financial conditions. In addition, while much smaller than their sovereign holdings, certain central banks, notably the ECB and the Bank of Japan, hold considerable amounts of corporate bonds as well.

The expansion of the non-bank financial sector is particularly visible in the corporate bond market, where investment funds have substantially increased their activity. In the United States, investment funds quadrupled their ownership share of outstanding non-financial corporate bonds from 8% in 2008 to 34% in 2021, before falling sharply to 23% in 2022, illustrative of the price sensitivity of this investor category. Globally, open-ended funds invested in corporate bonds have an aggregate size of USD 8.9 trillion. They have increased their average net holdings of corporate bonds from 38% in 2005 to 51% in 2023.

Favourable funding conditions have enabled high-grade issuers to extend the maturities of their borrowing

Many governments and companies have locked in the benefits of the favourable funding conditions post-2008, by extending debt maturities and increasing the share of fixed-rate issuance. This has mitigated the immediate impact of the steep increases in policy rates since early 2022.

OECD area sovereigns have increased the average maturity of their borrowing from around 6 years in 2008 to approximately 8 years in 2023. As a result, more than half of the total outstanding stock will mature after 2027, reducing the near-term impact of the current tightening cycle on interest payments. For example, average sovereign yields in the OECD area rose from 1% in 2021 to 4% in 2023, whilst interest expenses only rose from 2.3% to 2.9% of GDP in the same period. The average maturity of investment grade corporate bonds has also been extended in most regions. In the United States, for example, maturities have more than doubled since 2000, and stood at above 10 years in 2023.

In addition, the vast majority of both sovereign and corporate bonds have fixed rate coupon structures, further reducing immediate exposure to interest rate fluctuations. On aggregate, both financial and non-financial companies in advanced as well as emerging economies have increased the fixed rate share of their borrowing over time.

Considerable amounts of debt will need to be refinanced in the near-term

The partial insulation from increasing interest rates is only transitory. Even if inflation is brought down to target and remains low, yields will likely remain higher than when most of the debt was originally issued. As the amount of debt maturing in the next three years remains considerable, this will add significantly to financing pressures, especially in emerging economies.

Around 40% of sovereign bonds will mature by 2026 globally. While this will entail further borrowing from the markets, the impact on interest payments is limited due to short-term, floating rates, and inflation-linked instruments already having been re-fixed at higher rates. Pressure on future interest payments will largely arise from new borrowings and the refinancing of fixed-rate debt, projected to lead to an increase in interest payments amounting to 0.5% of GDP in the OECD area by 2026. That is equivalent, for example, to OECD government's average annual expenditure on environmental protection.

Owing to the extension of maturities, the corporate refinancing profile in advanced economies has improved over time. The share of debt due in the following three years is equivalent to 32% of the total outstanding amount in 2023, compared to 37% in 2008. However, considering the increase in borrowing, this still represents a substantial amount totalling USD 8 trillion.

In emerging economies, the situation for corporates is more challenging. Debt coming due in the next three years has grown significantly in both absolute terms and as a share of total outstanding debt, representing 51% in 2023 (USD 4.4 trillion). This increase is driven to a large extent by the growth of the Chinese market, where maturities have been shortening. When looking at emerging markets excluding China, the share of debt maturing in the next three years is more stable, but was still 48% at the end of 2023.

Key risks are currently concentrated in some market segments

Market risks are especially present in certain advanced economies with higher debt-to-GDP ratios, low-income countries experiencing credit downgrades and very high spreads, and low-quality corporate issuers in particular sectors, notably real estate.

Inflation has reduced debt-to-GDP ratios, but it does not improve the fundamentals of debt sustainability. It may have the initial effect of lowering debt-to-GDP ratios, but the medium-term impact of elevated inflation is to put upward pressure on debt-to-GDP ratios, due to high inflation premiums. This leaves several highly indebted OECD countries facing the potential negative feedback loop of rising rates, slow growth and expanding deficits unless they take steps to enhance fiscal resilience.

Rapid monetary tightening in major economies has also affected the credit ratings of low-income and lower middle-income countries, which together have seen a total of 24 downgrades compared to 6 upgrades in 2023. This figure is almost twice the annual average of downgrades and about half the average number of upgrades observed from 2010 to 2019 for countries in these income groups. In sub-Saharan Africa, the average 10-year sovereign yield spread over the US Treasury benchmark is above 10%, which is a key threshold for considering whether a country is in debt distress.

Amongst corporates, sector-specific risks are particularly visible among real estate companies. The aggregate leverage in the sector has more than tripled since 2005, with the debt to EBITDA ratio reaching 13.5 in 2022. Globally, real estate companies have increased their use of bond markets; their share of total issuance is around three times what it was in 2000.

Risk-taking has increased substantially in the non-financial corporate sector

Indications of decreased credit quality for non-financial corporate bonds merit attention. An increasingly large share of non-financial investment grade bonds is just above the non-investment grade threshold. At the same time, the characteristics of these issuers have changed over time. The average leverage of companies issuing BBB rated bonds is substantially higher today than it was 15 years ago. The potential for fire sale dynamics in the event of widespread downgrades is a key aspect to consider.

The decrease in corporate credit quality is not just an effect of the expansion of the non-investment grade market, but also of an increasing concentration of lower-rated issuance within the investment grade segment. At the end of 2023, 53% of all investment grade issuance by non-financial companies was rated BBB, the lowest investment grade rating, more than twice the share in 2000. In addition, bonds rated BBB-minus have grown as a share of total BBB issuance over time.

Another component adds further complexity to this deterioration in investment grade credit quality: the average leverage of a BBB rated bond issuer was 44% higher in 2023 than in 2008 in advanced economies, and 162% higher in emerging economies. Globally, 42% of BBB rated bonds were issued by non-financial companies with debt-to-EBITDA ratios over 4 in 2023, compared to 11% in 2008.

Historically, BBB-minus bonds have had the lowest probability of being downgraded. In addition to companies paying particular attention to their credit quality metrics, it is possible that rating agencies exercise particular caution when it comes to downgrading these bonds to non-investment grade. Given the increase in within-rating leverage, the implications of this possibility should be considered.

Owing to the sheer size of the non-financial BBB market – USD 4.3 trillion at the end of 2023 – even a relatively small transition rate to non-investment grade of 5% would be equivalent to 58% of 5-year average non-investment grade issuance globally. The non-investment grade market's capacity to absorb these quantities needs to be considered.

The risk of widespread downgrades is especially relevant given the changing investor structure of corporate bond markets. Open-ended funds categorised specifically as investment grade funds hold USD 651 billion worth of BBB rated securities. In a scenario where there are a higher number of downgrades from investment grade to non-investment grade, the potential for fire sale dynamics in illiquid secondary markets by price sensitive investors such as these, and others with rating-based mandates, is a key risk.

There is no clear evidence that issuers systematically benefit from a "greenium" for issuing sustainable bonds

Despite the rapid growth of the sustainable bond market, there is no clear evidence that companies systematically benefit from a premium for issuing sustainable bonds.

At the end of 2023, the outstanding amount of sustainable bonds globally reached USD 4.3 trillion, up from USD 641 billion just five years prior. Europe has been the most active region in the sustainable bond market in both the corporate and official sectors. From 2014 to 2023, 45% of the global amount issued through corporate non-financial sustainable bonds was raised by European companies.

In terms of pricing, investors may not be willing to pay a premium for sustainable bonds either because they do not value the potential sustainability impacts of their investments or, while investors may value such impacts, sustainable bond contracts might not create credible commitments by the issuer. It may also be the case that investors would be willing to pay a small premium for sustainability impacts, but that liquidity-related discounts and the transaction costs involved in the investment process may offset this.

An analysis of a sample of green, social and sustainability (GSS) bonds prospectuses shows that two-thirds mention that refinancing existing eligible projects with the proceeds is allowed, and no prospectus explicitly mentions that proceeds would not be used for refinancing. This effectively means that proceeds of many GSS bonds may not be used to finance a new green or social project. Additionally, no GSS bond prospectus in the sample refers to a contractual penalty in case the issuer does not use all proceeds to finance or refinance eligible projects, which may undermine investor confidence in issuers' compliance with the sustainability-related commitments.

The share of sustainable bonds being assured by second party opinion providers has grown from less than half in 2019 to three-quarters in 2023. These service providers verify whether the bond contract is aligned with a specific sustainable bond standard, and these verifications may help assure sustainability-conscious investors that their investment will have a positive impact on the environment and society.

The new funding environment requires a prudent policy response

A new macroeconomic landscape of higher inflation and more restrictive monetary policies is transforming global bond markets at a pace not seen in decades. This has profound implications for debt markets and financial stability at a time of renewed financing needs. Vigilant monitoring and appropriate policy responses are needed to ensure that sovereign and corporate bond markets continue to function effectively.

Public debt managers face a range of challenges, including a continued growth in borrowing needs in the context of a changing investor base and shifts in demand for securities across different maturities. Strategic debt management decisions are needed to ensure the long-term sustainability of government debt. These should be implemented with great care and by adhering to the key principles of debt management, including providing transparency and predictability while maintaining flexibility in market operations. Monitoring and, where possible, actively supporting market liquidity will also be vital.

Market supervisors should closely monitor the evolution of corporate debt sustainability indicators. The exposure of investment funds to corporate bonds at the lower end of the investment grade category warrants particular attention. Given the sharp growth in the outstanding amount of BBB rated bonds, even a relatively small transition rate to non-investment grade would represent a large share of average non-investment grade issuance. A limited market capacity to absorb significant new quantities of non-investment grade bonds could lead to fire sale dynamics with implications for market stability.

Meanwhile, further improvements are needed to the sustainable bond market to enhance its efficiency, safeguard investor interests, and ensure that these bonds can be an effective tool in combatting climate change. Market regulators can support these goals by adopting sustainable bond standards that effectively commit issuers to investing in new sustainable projects that help drive additionality (new funding for the climate, not repackaged existing funding); and by requiring external reviews of such standards to ensure that sustainable bonds deliver the intended positive impacts for society and the environment.

Infographic 1. Key facts and figures

Sovereign and corporate bond markets have grown significantly since 2008 and have a current value of approximately USD 100 trillion

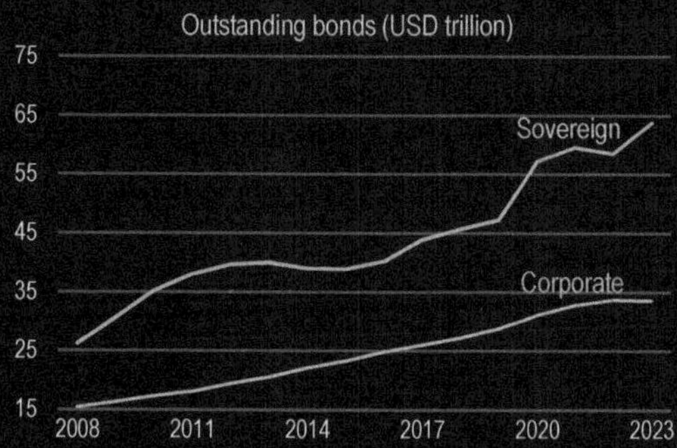

A considerable amount of bonds will mature over the next three years, and will mostly be refinanced at higher rates than when they were originally issued

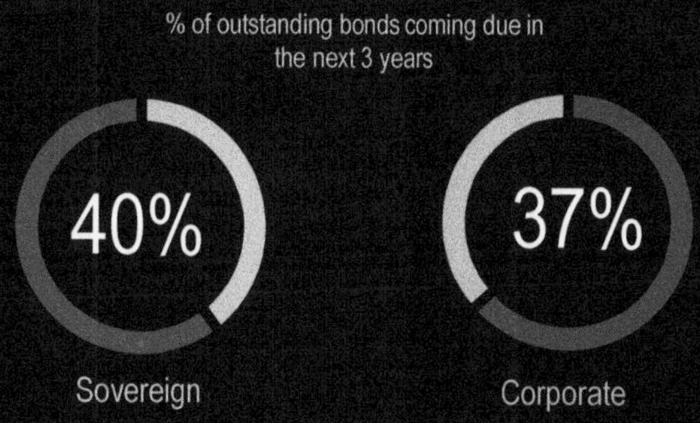

Central banks are shrinking their balance sheets through QT, unwinding their huge holdings of bonds

This increases the level of supply for the market to absorb, leading to a more price sensitive investor base

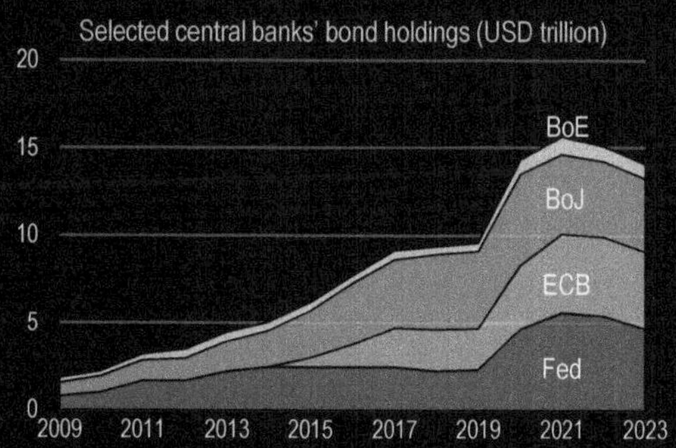

Credit ratings have deteriorated in recent years

There has been a rise in lower-rated investment grade issuances in the corporate bond market and multiple credit downgrades of low and lower-middle income countries

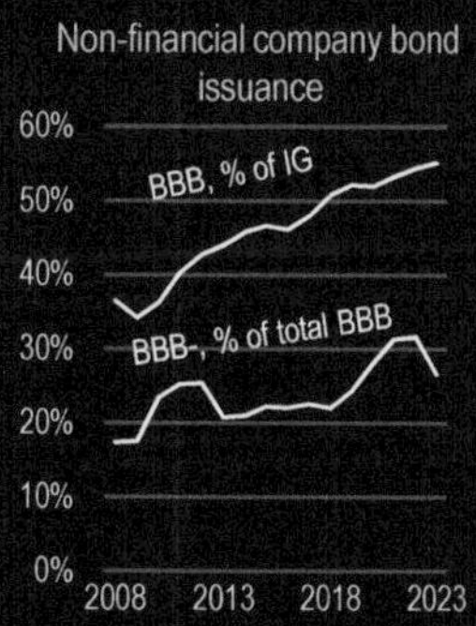

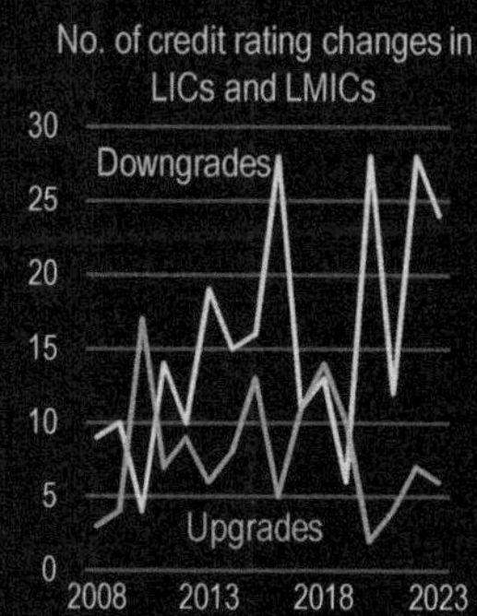

Sustainable bond issuance has been growing and diversifying rapidly

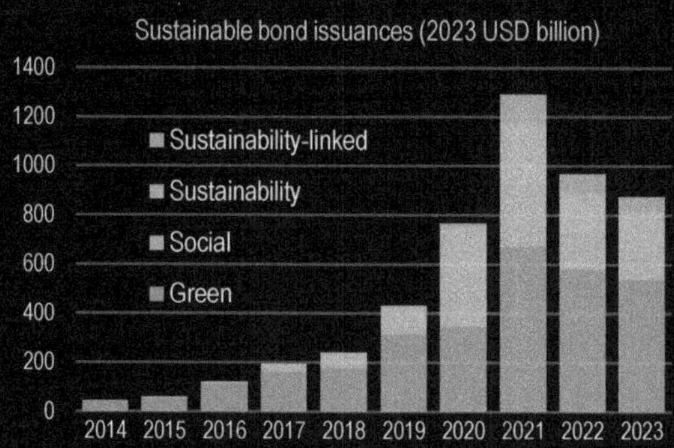

...but further improvements are needed to enhance the sustainable bond market's efficiency and safeguard investor interests

GSS bond contracts often enable refinancing of concluded projects and have no penalties for the partial use of proceeds for sustainable projects

25% of issuance in 2023 was not assured by second-party opinion providers

There is no clear evidence that issuers systematically benefit from a premium for issuing a sustainable bond

1 Sovereign borrowing outlook

Gross borrowing in the OECD area increased in 2023, having fallen in the previous two years, and is projected to reach a record high in 2024, surpassing the previous peak during the height of the COVID-19 pandemic. This has pushed outstanding sovereign debt to unprecedented levels, yet debt-to-GDP ratios have remained relatively stable, as borrowing increases have been largely offset by the impact of inflation on nominal GDP.

Despite the cost of borrowing increasing for the third consecutive year, the public finances of OECD countries are partially insulated from higher rates because of the lengthening of maturity profiles since 2008. At the same time, as central banks begin reducing their holdings of sovereign bonds, the net supply for the market to absorb has reached record levels.

1.1. Introduction

This chapter analyses sovereign debt developments for the period of 2008-24 with a focus on the OECD area. It explores borrowing requirements and funding strategies; debt-to-GDP ratio dynamics; borrowing costs and yield curves; interest payments and refinancing risks; and the effects of central banks' balance sheet reduction on the investor base and market liquidity. This chapter draws mainly on responses received to an annual survey on the marketable debt of central governments. It provides data up to 2022, with 2023 estimates and 2024 projections. Details on the methodology can be found in Annex 1.A.

Key findings

- **Gross borrowing in the OECD area rose from USD 12.1 trillion in 2022 to 14.1 trillion in 2023** and is projected to rise further to USD 15.8 trillion in 2024, which would be the highest level ever, surpassing the previous record in 2020. The US accounted for nearly two-thirds of the 2023 figure, mostly through new borrowing.
- **Short-term borrowing through treasury bills accounted for 50% of gross borrowing in 2023 and is projected to reach a historical high of 51% in 2024.** This increase is predominantly driven by a small group of issuers.
- **OECD governments' outstanding marketable debt increased from USD 40 trillion in 2019 to USD 54 trillion in 2023 and is expected to reach a new record of USD 56 trillion in 2024.** The debt-to-GDP ratio held steady at around 83% in 2023, still well above the pre-pandemic level of 73%, even though inflation, which boosted nominal GDP growth, reduced this by more than 10 percentage points in 2022-23.
- **The cost of new borrowing in the OECD area increased on average from 1% in 2021 to 4% in 2023, while interest expenses rose from 2.3% to 2.9% of GDP over the same period**. The longer average maturity of OECD government debt partially insulates public finances from yield hikes. However, the reprieve is only temporary, and by 2026, refinancing fixed-rate debt alone is projected to result in an increase of 0.5% of GDP in interest payments compared to 2023.
- **The average term spread in the OECD area reached nearly zero in 2023, a historical low**, and yield curves are exhibiting varying levels of inversion. This affects sovereign issuers' cost and risk trade-off: fixed rates might seem economical but could result in locking in higher yields.
- **Central banks have been reducing their holdings of sovereign bonds which increases the level of supply for the market to absorb and is changing the investor base for sovereign debt,** leading to a growing share being held by more price sensitive investors. Additionally, losses incurred by central banks due to monetary tightening are either diminishing their remittances to treasuries or triggering calls for indemnification, leading to higher borrowing requirements.
- **Liquidity in government bond markets remained mostly unchanged in 2023, having deteriorated in 2022**. It continues to be impacted mostly by primary dealers' warehousing capacity, changes in the investor base, and macroeconomic and geopolitical uncertainty. Sovereign issuers put in place various measures to support market liquidity, with the most effective being taps of existing securities, buybacks and switch operations, and securities lending facilities.
- **Sovereign bond issuance in Emerging Market and Developing Economies rose from USD 3.0 trillion in 2022 to USD 3.9 trillion in 2023, exceeding the 2021 peak.** China's share of borrowing surged from 15% in 2021 to 37% in 2023.
- **The credit ratings of low-income and lower-middle income countries deteriorated in 2023**, with countries in these groups receiving 24 downgrades against 6 upgrades.

1.2. Higher gross borrowing has pushed debt stocks to record levels in 2023

The decline in gross borrowing by OECD governments in 2021 and 2022 halted in 2023. After reaching a high of USD 15.4 trillion in 2020, it reduced to USD 12.1 trillion in 2022, with estimations indicating a rise to USD 14.1 trillion in 2023 (Figure 1.1, Panel A). The 2024 projection of USD 15.8 trillion would surpass the peak reached during the pandemic, and mark a nearly 45% and 25% rise in real terms from the 2019 and 2022 levels, respectively. Box 1.1 explores these trends for Emerging Market and Developing Economies (EMDEs).

Gross borrowing needs consist of net borrowing and refinancing requirements, with the former driving the increase in the gross figure in 2023. Net borrowing peaked in 2020 at USD 7.3 trillion but declined to roughly USD 2.1 trillion in 2022, close to pre-pandemic levels. However, rising spending, notably on social security and cost-of-living-related measures, has reversed this two-year downward trend (OECD, 2023[1]) with net borrowing estimated to rise to around USD 3.6 trillion in 2023 then decline slightly to USD 3.2 trillion in 2024. That net borrowing levels are now more closely aligning with fiscal deficits suggests cash balances have normalised somewhat, after surging during the pandemic.[1]

Refinancing requirements are anticipated to be the primary driver of higher gross borrowing in 2024. These amount to approximately USD 7 trillion before the pandemic but have been above USD 10 trillion since 2021, with a projected peak of USD 12.6 trillion in 2024. This projected record high is attributed to the rise in short-term borrowing, which needs to be refinanced within a year, during 2023-24.

Driven by higher net borrowing, the OECD debt stock is expected to reach USD 54 trillion in 2023 and is projected to climb further to USD 56 trillion in 2024 (Figure 1.1, Panel B). In terms of issuers, the United States' portion of the OECD debt stock has risen notably in recent years, constituting nearly half of the total in 2023. The EU's share is 20%, Japan's 16%, the United Kingdom's 6%, with the remaining OECD countries combined accounting for 9%. Significant shifts have occurred over time, with the United States' share increasing by 7 percentage points (pp) since 2019 and doubling since 2008. This increase is attributed not just to the growth in US debt but also to the appreciation of the US dollar.[2]

Figure 1.1. Borrowing, fiscal and debt outlook in OECD countries

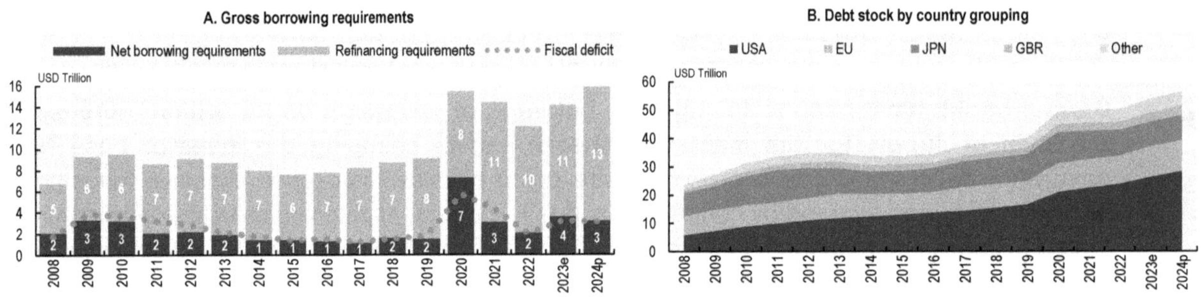

Note: '2023e' denotes estimations and '2024p' indicates projections.
Source: 2023 OECD Survey on Central Government Marketable Debt and Borrowing; LSEG; (OECD, 2023[1]); (IMF, 2023[2]); national authorities' websites; and OECD calculations.

The rise in gross borrowing in the OECD was mainly driven by a few large issuers, with a decrease in the gross borrowing to GDP ratio estimated in more countries than an increase. In only 10 OECD countries, there is an increase exceeding 1pp estimated for 2023; this includes large issuers such as Italy, the United Kingdom and the United States. Meanwhile, a decline exceeding 1pp is estimated for 12 countries, including France, Germany, and Japan (Figure 1.2, Panel A). Compared to their 2015-19 averages, increases above 5 pp in this ratio are estimated for Austria, Finland, Germany, and the United States.

Figure 1.2. Gross and net borrowing, and refinancing requirements as a share of GDP

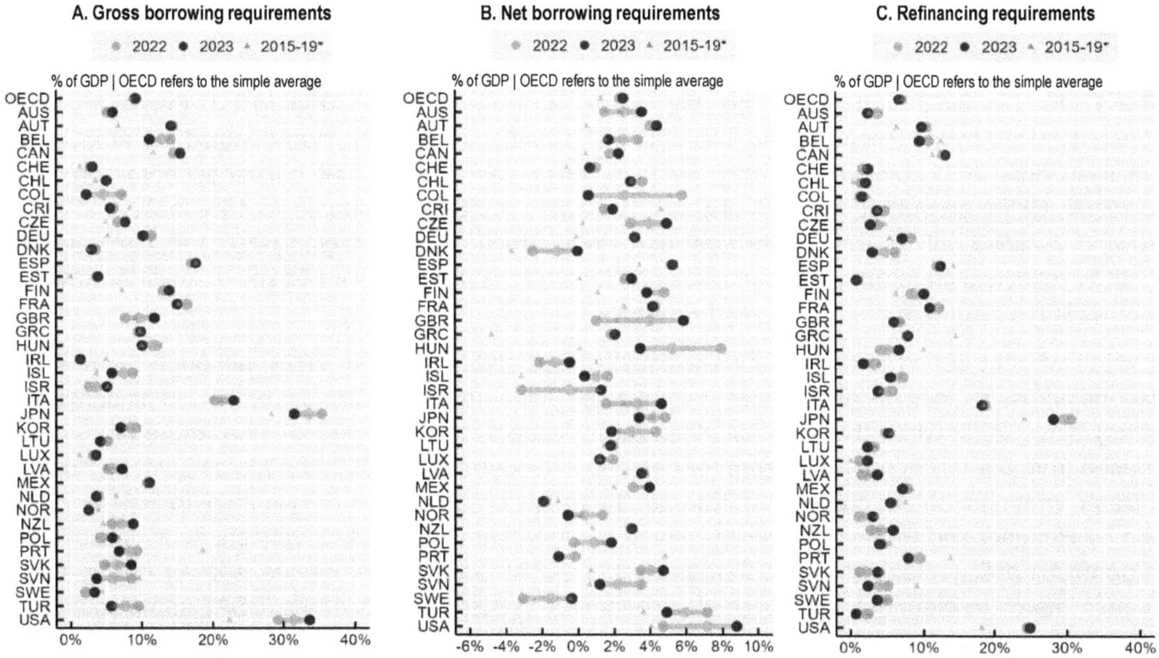

Source: 2023 OECD Survey on Central Government Marketable Debt and Borrowing; LSEG; (OECD, 2023[1]); (IMF, 2023[2]); national authorities' websites; and OECD calculations.

Net borrowing levels have varied widely across countries, with the OECD average remaining stable at around 2.5% of GDP in 2023, around 1 pp higher than the 2015-19 averages (Figure 1.2, Panel B). Notable increases in net borrowing to GDP ratios in 2023 are estimated for the United Kingdom, where a 5pp rise will be largely due to the funding of cost-of-living-related measures; Israel, with a 4pp increase driven in part by the conflict in the Middle East; and Italy, with a 3pp rise driven mainly by tax cuts and new expenditures. Fiscal consolidation led to the steepest falls in Colombia and Hungary (OECD, 2023[1]).

While sustained increases in net borrowing pose fiscal challenges, low and persistent fiscal surpluses may raise certain concerns such as government access to debt funding and the long-term viability of the government securities market. In recent years, countries such as Denmark, Ireland, Norway, and Sweden have run persistent fiscal surpluses (Figure 1.2, Panel B), which may pose challenges in developing credit risk-free yield curves and supporting liquidity in government bond markets. When the supply of government bonds is limited due to diminishing government debt, they could become less liquid and more expensive. A deterioration in the liquidity and efficiency of government securities implies a less useful benchmark for the risk-free interest rate and for pricing and hedging positions in other markets. Additionally, the government's funding needs, which might temporarily disappear, may resurface, leading to market access challenges in periods of heightened borrowing needs (Bjellerup and Rådahl, 2023[3]). Finally, lower market volumes can affect the viability of the primary dealer business models, which can be crucial for market access.

Refinancing requirements in the OECD area overall have remained largely stable in 2023 but have risen significantly in some countries since the pandemic (Figure 1.2, Panel C). Unlike new borrowing, refinancing requirements are not subject to immediate fiscal fluctuations but rather linked to the size and composition of debt portfolios. In 2023, OECD refinancing to GDP ratios remained broadly in line with 2015-19 averages. The United States and Japan individually stand out and are projected to contribute to a USD 5.0 trillion surge in OECD refinancing requirements from 2019 to 2024.

Box 1.1. Sovereign debt issuance trends in emerging and developing market economies

Debt issuance by central governments in EMDEs increased from USD 3.0 trillion in 2022 to USD 3.9 trillion in 2023, surpassing the 2021 peak of USD 3.2 trillion (Figure 1.3, Panel A). This increase is driven by the People's Republic of China (China), which more than doubled the amount of bonds it issued in 2023 compared to 2022 due to increasing spending to help bolster economic growth. As a result, China accounted for 37% of gross borrowing in 2023, compared to 15% in 2021. Gross borrowing declined only in the Middle East and North Africa (MENA) region (-10%) in 2023, which potentially reflects a preference for (concessional) loans, as is the case with Egypt, or lower borrowing needs, as is the case with the United Arab Emirates.

The share of debt issued in foreign currencies remained stable at 5% in 2023, although there were variations across regions. In Asia, values were stable: China has issued almost entirely in its domestic currency since 2002 while the ratio for other Asian issuers is 2%. In MENA, the aggregate share increased from 5% to 7% but it was zero for high-income countries (HIC) in the region such as Kuwait and Qatar. Amongst EMDE countries in Europe, the ratio increased from 17% in 2022 to 20% in 2023 driven by Hungary and Poland, for which issuing foreign-denominated debt was cheaper because of high domestic policy rates, whilst the foreign exchange risk on their Eurobonds is lower due to their economic interconnectedness with eurozone economies. In Sub-Saharan Africa (SSA), some countries have difficulties accessing international markets; as a result, bond issuance in foreign currencies fell from 5% in 2022 to 1% in 2023.

Figure 1.3. Gross borrowing and refinancing risks in EMDEs

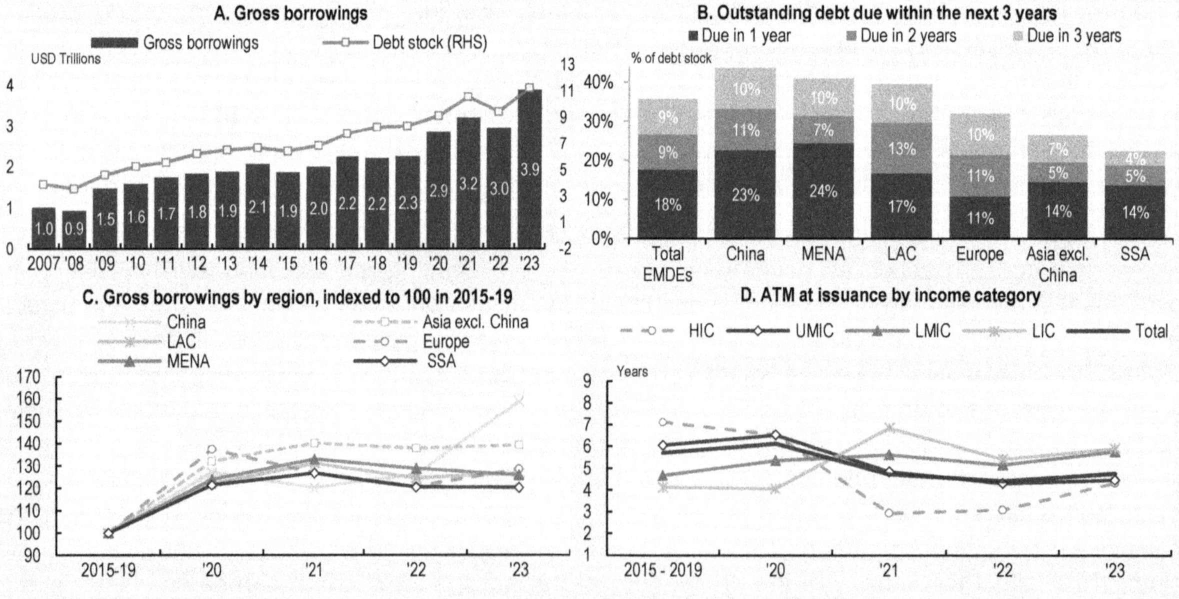

Note: Annex 1.D provides a detailed methodology. Averages presented in Panel D are weighted by issue size, total refers to aggregate data. Country groupings are consistent with the IMF classification.

Source: LSEG; and OECD calculations.

The average term-to-maturity (ATM) for sovereign bonds issued by EMDEs in 2023 increased among all income groups, rising on aggregate from 4.4 to 4.8 years, (Figure 1.3, Panel D), although there were significant differences between individual countries. ATM at issuance increased the most for high-income countries, from 3 to 4.3 years, driven by Chile and Poland. For low-income countries (LIC), it increased from 5.4 in 2022 to 5.9 in 2023, although it actually declined for all countries in this group except Tanzania and Uganda, perhaps revealing investors' concerns about most LIC economies in the current environment. One of the issuers whose ATMs decreased the most was Ukraine (from 7.8 to 1.6 years), which is having difficulties in accessing market funding because of the war.

Despite the average spread of EMDEs' sovereign bond yields over the benchmark 10-year US Treasury yield decreasing in 2023 across all regions except Europe[1], it remains above 1 000 basis points (bps) in Sub-Saharan Africa, which is a critical threshold for considering whether a country is in debt distress. This reveals the challenge faced by SSA countries, most of which are LICs: funding their borrowing needs at such rates can be prohibitively costly, forcing them to rely on other funding means such as concessional or bilateral loans. Amongst European EMDEs, the rise in the average spread was largely accounted for by Türkiye, where it almost doubled to 1 500 bps. Excluding Türkiye, the spread of these issuers declined (Figure 1.4, Panel A). Notable declines in spreads can also be seen in Zambia (-350 bps), which made progress in its debt restructuring negotiations, and Brazil (-300 bps), which started to reduce monetary policy rates amid further global monetary tightening.

More than one-third of EMDE sovereign bonds will mature by 2026, presenting refinancing risk, which is especially problematic for low- and lower-middle income countries (LICs and LMICs) given their higher current borrowing costs (Figure 1.3, Panel B). Among them is Ethiopia, which defaulted in December, 100% of whose marketable debt matures in 2024 (around USD 1 billion). Myanmar also has 100% of its marketable debt (around USD 2.7 billion) maturing in the next 2 years, and Malawi has 62% (around USD 441 million) maturing in the same period.

Refinancing risk can be a source of concern for economies belonging to other regions and income categories. For example, more than 60% of Moldova's marketable debt (equivalent to 8% of GDP) matures in 2024. This figure is 45% for Argentina (equivalent to 10% of GDP) and Egypt (equivalent to 26% of GDP). A high share of short-term borrowing in recent years exacerbated refinancing risk amidst a worsening sovereign credit outlook in these countries.

Changes in credit ratings have been mixed in 2023, with almost the same number of upgrades (27) and downgrades (29) but with most of the downgrades occurring in LMICs (Figure 1.4, Panel B and C). This highlights the challenges faced by LMICs amidst the global tightening in monetary policy and volatility in commodity prices. No country lost its investment grade status, but Argentina, Ethiopia and Ukraine joined the group of countries with an average rating corresponding to (or near) default. This group also includes Ghana, Grenada, Laos, Lebanon, Sri Lanka, Suriname, Venezuela, and Zambia. Cameroon and El Salvador temporarily obtained technical default ratings before regaining non-investment grade status.

Figure 1.4. Yield spreads and credit ratings in EMDEs

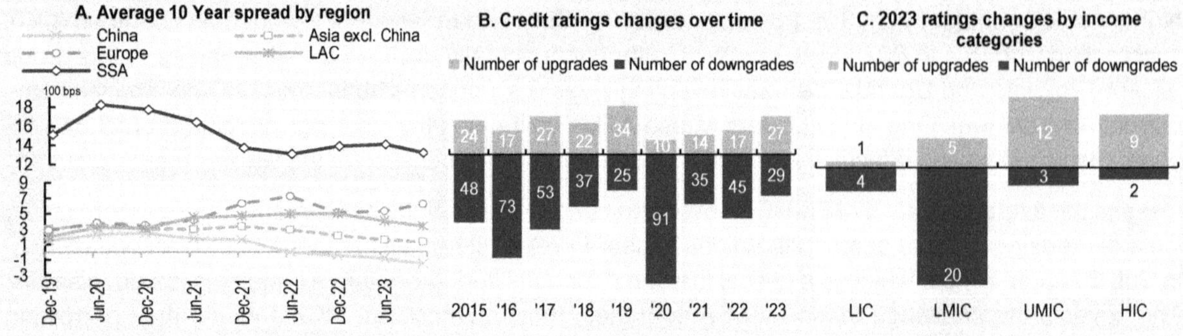

Note: Annex 1.D provides a detailed methodology. Panel A displays by group simple averages of the spreads over the 10-year US benchmark yield for all countries for which this measure is available on LSEG. They are Bulgaria, Brazil, China, Hungary, Indonesia, India, Kenya, Mexico, Malaysia, Philippines, Poland, Romania, Russian Federation, Thailand, Türkiye, South Africa and Zambia. Values in Panel B and C are computed using the long-term Issuer Ratings (Foreign) assigned by Moody's, Fitch and S&P. If a country has received several ratings in one month from the same agency, the lowest one is used, except when that is a default or technical default rating. The regional and emerging markets definitions are consistent with the IMF's country classification.
Source: LSEG; and OECD calculations.

1. MENA was not included in this analysis due to data availability constraints.

1.2.1. The share of total borrowing accounted for by short-term debt is expected to rise in 2023-24

Short-term debt (securities issued with less than a one-year maturity) accounted for 50% of gross borrowing in 2023 and is estimated to account for 51% in 2024, surpassing the previous peak in 2020 of 43% (Figure 1.5, Panel A). This shift corresponds to a decrease in the issuance share of fixed rate debt, while the shares of inflation-linked and variable-rate instruments are projected to remain stable at 3%, despite large fluctuations in inflation levels and policy rates during 2021-23. Although there has been a rise in short-term borrowing, the ATM for OECD debt has remained largely stable at around 8 years (see Figure 1.20).

The historically high share of short-term borrowing stems largely from macroeconomic and geopolitical uncertainties combined with quantitative tightening (QT) and higher levels of gross borrowing,[3] which made it difficult for some sovereign issuers to issue more fixed rate debt. As a result, short-term debt issuance accounted for more than half of the new borrowing (USD 2.0 trillion out of USD 3.6 trillion) in 2023, further increasing the share of short-term debt in the outstanding debt stock (Figure 1.5, Panel B).

Issuing short-term instruments provides significant operational flexibility to debt managers, aiding in managing uncertainties and temporary shocks by allowing issuers to quickly raise large levels of funding. During periods of heightened uncertainty and/or when gross borrowing is higher, investor demand typically shifts towards the safest, most liquid assets (often short-term instruments). On the supply side, crises introduce uncertainties about the extent and duration of revenue shortfalls and costs associated with government support measures; short-term instruments allow for better matching of inflows with these outflows, and faster repayment if the revenue shortfalls subside. For these reasons, short-term instruments were used as shock absorbers at the onset of the COVID-19 pandemic (OECD, 2022[4]).

Figure 1.5. Instrument composition of gross borrowing and funding sources

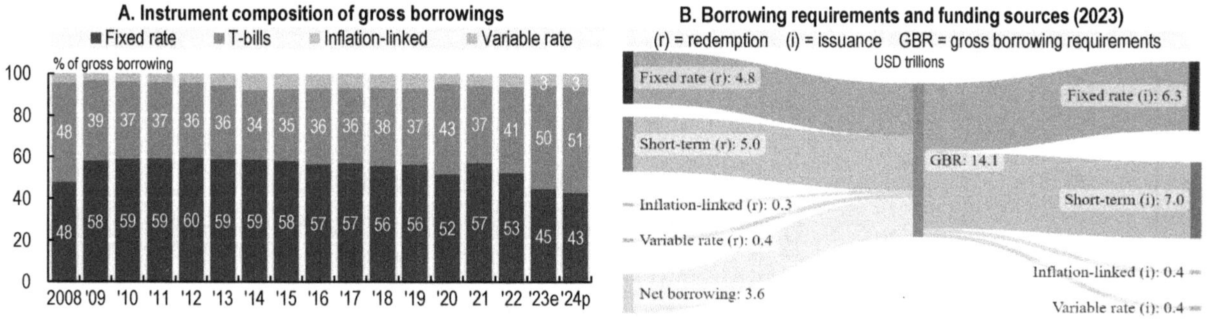

Source: 2023 OECD Survey on Central Government Marketable Debt and Borrowing; LSEG; (OECD, 2023[1]); (IMF, 2023[2]); national authorities' websites; and OECD calculations.

The increased share of short-term borrowing in the OECD in 2023 was predominantly driven by a small group of large issuers. While the share of fixed-rate borrowing in the OECD area declined overall (Figure 1.6, Panel A), it actually increased in 19 individual countries, declined in 14 and remained stable in 5. Increases in the share of short-term borrowing by large issuers, such as Canada, France, Germany and especially the United States (where it jumped from 49% of total issuance in 2022 to 62% in 2023) outweighed the increase in the share of fixed-rate issuance in half of OECD countries.

Short-term borrowing in the United States has risen especially since June 2023, mainly to increase the balance in the Treasury General Account. This declined rapidly in the months prior to the suspension of the debt ceiling rule, leading the US Treasury to, in part, finance the federal government by drawing down this balance. Market conditions in the second half of 2023 were shaped by this increased supply of US treasuries in conjunction with QT, and higher long-term yields, indicative of possible changes in long-run neutral interest rates and term premia. The Treasury Borrowing Advisory Committee (TBAC), in November 2023, suggested that this trend of greater short-term borrowing in the United States might persist until Q2 2025 (TBAC, 2023[5]; TBAC, 2023[6]). Likewise, the United Kingdom reduced the issuance share of long-dated (and inflation-linked) bonds in 2023-24 compared to 2022-23 as pension funds' appetite for such debt wanes as part of a structural change to demand (UK DMO, 2024[7]).

Figure 1.6. Instrument composition of gross borrowing

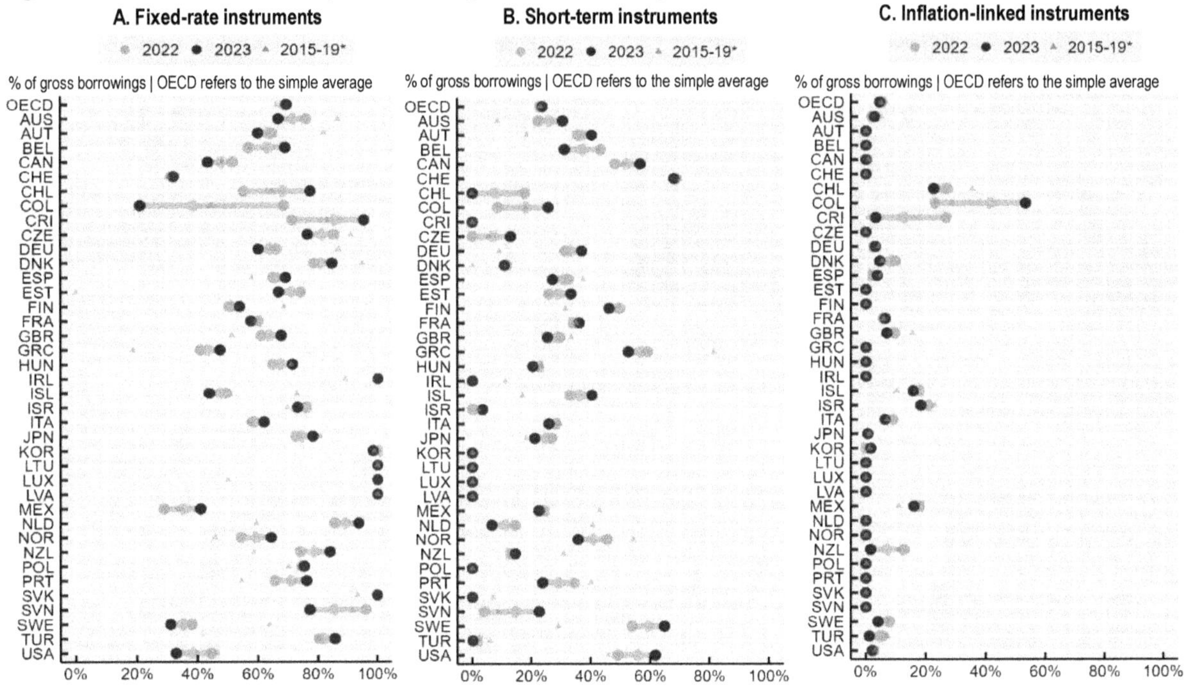

Source: 2023 OECD Survey on Central Government Marketable Debt and Borrowing; LSEG; (OECD, 2023[1]); (IMF, 2023[2]); national authorities' websites; and OECD calculations.

Twenty OECD countries issue inflation-linked securities (linkers) offering a typically much-demanded risk-free product which provides an inflation hedge for investors. This can help to broaden the investor base for government debt and can also represent cost-effective financing for issuers. With inflation higher in 2023, 14 of these countries reduced the share of linkers they issued (Figure 1.6, Panel C). This trend emerged despite stable or increasing market demand for linkers according to survey results, indicating a strategic shift in debt portfolio management.[4] Colombia recorded the highest borrowing share in linkers at 53%, whilst the average amongst all 20 issuers was 9%. In 2023, only Colombia raised its linker issuance share by over 1pp, while the issuance share in countries such as Italy and the United Kingdom declined by more than 1pp. Notably, Germany ceased its linker programme in 2023, as Canada did in 2022 (Government of Canada, 2022[8]).

Owing to higher gross borrowing, and the loss of central banks as net buyers of sovereign debt, several sovereign issuers have placed a greater focus on capturing demand from retail investors. Survey findings show that 13 OECD countries are giving more consideration to the retail sector in 2023-24. Given the higher yields, government bonds are an increasingly attractive investment for typically more price sensitive household investors. Thus, sovereign issuers are attempting to capture this demand through retail products and/or programmes, with retail purchases reaching unprecedented levels in 2023 (Box 1.2).

Box 1.2. Retail debt programmes and products in selected OECD countries

This box outlines the retail programmes and products in Belgium, Italy, Japan, Portugal, the United Kingdom, and the United States. Total issuance in retail debt programmes peaked at USD 222 billion in 2022 driven largely by the United States (Figure 1.7, Panel B), where retail investors can bid on-demand when the US Treasury auctions securities. The previous peak, in 2020, was largely due to activity in the United Kingdom, where the cut in policy rates was not initially reflected in the rates of retail products to help support government funding.

The share of borrowing accounted for by retail programmes reached a record high in recent years in all selected countries except Japan (Figure 1.7, Panel C), where nominal yields remain less than 1%. In Portugal, products offered to retail investors carry attractive interest rates linked to Euribor. In Belgium, the surge in 2023 was due to a 1-year retail note with reduced withholding tax offering the highest coupon since 2011 (Figure 1.7, Panel D). Meanwhile, Italy's retail-dedicated bond issuances reached a high of more than 8% of its total gross borrowing in 2023.

While retail products can offer portfolio and investor base diversification, and help support funding needs, they present a significant operational burden.[1] Managing purchase interfaces, communication channels and back-office processes can be demanding, although technological advancements can help (Boitreau and Secunho, 2020[9]). Sovereign Debt Management Offices also need to consider that issuing retail instruments represents involvement in largely private market activities, where intermediaries already facilitate public access. Moreover, longer-term demand from retail varies more widely than for wholesale investors, while retail does not provide the same relative scale in most markets. Germany, in 2013, and Canada, in 2017, chose to discontinue their retail programmes.

Figure 1.7. Retail debt instruments and programmes

A. Characteristics of selected OECD retail instruments and programmes

Country	Start	Instrument	Issuance	Purchase channel	Instrument type	Maturities (year)
BEL	1996	Retail-dedicated bonds	Subscription	Grands Livres (online), Banks, Financial Institutions	Fixed rate	1, 3, 8, 5, 10
ITA	2012	Retail-dedicated bonds	On-demand	Banks and Post Offices	Fixed rate, Inflation-linked, Step-up rate, Fidelity premium, GDP-linked	4, 5, 6, 8, 10, 12,16
JPN	2003	Retail-dedicated bonds	On-demand	Banks, Post Offices, Financial Institutions	Fixed rate, Floating rate	3, 5, 10
PRT	1960	Retail-dedicated bonds, Saving deposits	Auction, On-demand	AforroNet (online), Post Offices, Banks, Financial Institutions	Floating and Step-up rate	7, 15
GBR	1957	Saving deposits, saving certificates	On-demand	National Savings & Investments (online)	Fixed and Floating rate	3
USA	1935	Saving deposits, regular bonds	Auction, On-demand	TreasuryDirect (online)	Fixed rate, Floating rate, Inflation-linked	All

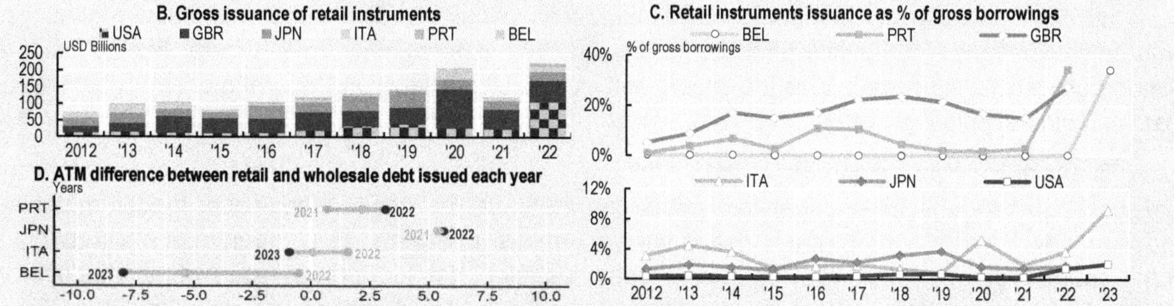

Notes: Panel A is as of November 2023. The start dates of the GBR programme are those of the first Premium Bond issuance. Panel B is ordered by 2022 issuance size. US data includes all debt securities and saving bonds sold through TreasuryDirect. Japan's data includes only Japanese Government Bonds (JGB) for Retail Investors. The UK data refers to gross inflows to NS&I. Panel D shows the ATM at issuance of retail debt minus those of wholesale debt, weighted by issue size.

1. Tax benefits for retail bonds can be an additional source of costs.

Source. (Italian Ministry of Economy and Finance, 2023[10]; Ministry of Finance of Japan, 2023[11]; National Savings & Investments, 2023[12]; Belgian Debt Agency, 2023[13]; US Treasury Department, 2023[14]; Portuguese Treasury and Debt Management Agency, 2023[15]); 2023 OECD Survey on Central Government Marketable Debt and Borrowing; LSEG and OECD calculations.

1.2.2. Issuance strategies must strike the right balance between predictability and flexibility in an uncertain funding environment

Sovereign Debt Management Offices (DMOs) predominantly operate as price takers, acting as intermediaries to align gross borrowing with market funding. Both the borrowing levels and market conditions are largely outside the control of DMOs. Consequently, their primary role is to decide the instrument and maturity composition under the constraints of the level of borrowing and the timing of government cash flows and market access. The decision involves selecting from various debt instruments, each with its own investor demand profile, limiting the operational deliverability of certain debt portfolios.

Sovereign issuers select an issuance composition with the purpose of lowering borrowing costs over the long-term, while maintaining manageable risk levels. This decision requires navigating a trade-off between cost and risk: short-term instruments, while less costly, carry higher refinancing and interest rate risk, whereas long-term instruments typically help mitigate against these risks but often at a higher cost to the issuer. Thus, to meet their long-term mandate, sovereign issuers typically opt to issue at a range of maturities, with programmatic issuance patterns.

The issuance strategy will always be somewhat constrained by uneven demand across maturities and the need to support market liquidity. Long-dated securities, typically bought by pension funds and insurance companies, face lower overall demand, limiting sovereign issuers' strategic flexibility. To enhance market liquidity, DMOs often re-open individual lines multiple times, building them up to a benchmark size, but this can also be costly. This is particularly the case with long-dated securities, where the greater duration reduces the bond market value more significantly during periods of higher rates, resulting in relatively lower cash proceeds raised for the same amount of debt issued.

In 2023, most DMOs in the OECD identified market volatility, rising yields and cash flow forecasting as primary concerns (Figure 1.8, Panel A). Inflation, though on a downward trend, remained above target, with higher services price inflation proving particularly sticky. Economic growth has been dampened by tighter monetary policies and subdued global trade (OECD, 2023[1]; OECD, 2024[16]). Geopolitical tensions, including the war in Ukraine and the conflict in the Middle East, are contributing to market volatility. Despite improved cash flow stability compared to the pandemic period, funding needs still show higher-than-average fluctuations, with public finances particularly under strain due to structural factors such as demographic shifts and decarbonisation efforts, and as a result of the current environment of higher interest costs and slower output growth.

Macro-financial conditions significantly impact the costs of risk minimisation. In uncertain economic times, investors' reluctance to take longer-term risks can increase the cost of issuing at longer maturities. Consequently, low risk portfolio costs rise in such scenarios. Furthermore, in the current environment of higher interest rates, committing to long-term maturities might risk locking in these higher rates over an extended period (regret risk), underscoring that cost and risk considerations extend beyond the current shape of yield curves. In 2022-23, cost-efficient risk curves took a parallel shift higher.

Issuance strategies remain flexible across all OECD countries in an uncertain environment. All DMOs use flexible strategies to handle risks, with 81% using liquidity buffers and 73% adapting their communication strategies (Figure 1.8, Panel B and C). The value of liquidity buffers lies in ensuring the availability of cash during unpredictable market conditions, without the need to match issuances so closely to outflows. This supports a more flexible issuance approach. Communication strategies are also crucial to finding the right balance between flexibility and predictability.

Flexibility has limits, with large issuers often favouring a programmatic approach to issuance. Sudden shifts in issuance strategies by major issuers can immediately impact the yield curve. This can increase volatility and complicate their ability to meet their mandates and ensure market access at all times. When strategic alterations are necessary, issuers will look to provide as much advance notice as possible. For instance, in 2023, the United States was the sole large issuer to alter the instrument composition of its issuance plan (towards shorter-dated instrument), and they provided a timeline with this shift (US Treasury, 2023[17]).

Smaller issuers typically follow a more flexible approach to debt management, given that strategy changes typically have less impact on their markets. This explains why large-scale annual changes in issuance strategies are more frequently undertaken by smaller issuers (Figure 1.6). It also accounts for why, aside from the United States, all twelve countries that modified the instrument composition of their initial issuance strategy are relatively small issuers (Figure 1.8, Panel C).[5]

Flexibility also includes adaptability of issuance techniques and changes to the auction calendar and announcements. In 2023, this included changes in the frequency of auctions, use of switches, use of syndications, private placements, buybacks and post-auction facilities (Figure 1.8, Panel D). Other examples include the use of dual/triple-tranche transactions, allowing an issuer to offer multiple debt securities with varied terms within a single issuance, catering to diverse investor preferences and market conditions; and announcing in advance the total issuance volume but delaying the instrument composition announcement until closer to the operation. These methods allow the DMO to better match volatile funding needs with demand for certain securities.

These changes are balanced with practices that boost predictability. Examples include having a stated minimum target size for the outstanding amount of benchmark securities; being transparent in market consultations, feedback and adjustments to avoid unexpected supply movements; keeping an issuance calendar with weekly issuances of various securities; and opting wherever possible for incremental adjustments to the pre-scheduled auction sizes and calendar, allowing for some fine-tuning to the very latest market conditions.

Figure 1.8. Recent issuance challenges and measures employed by sovereign issuers

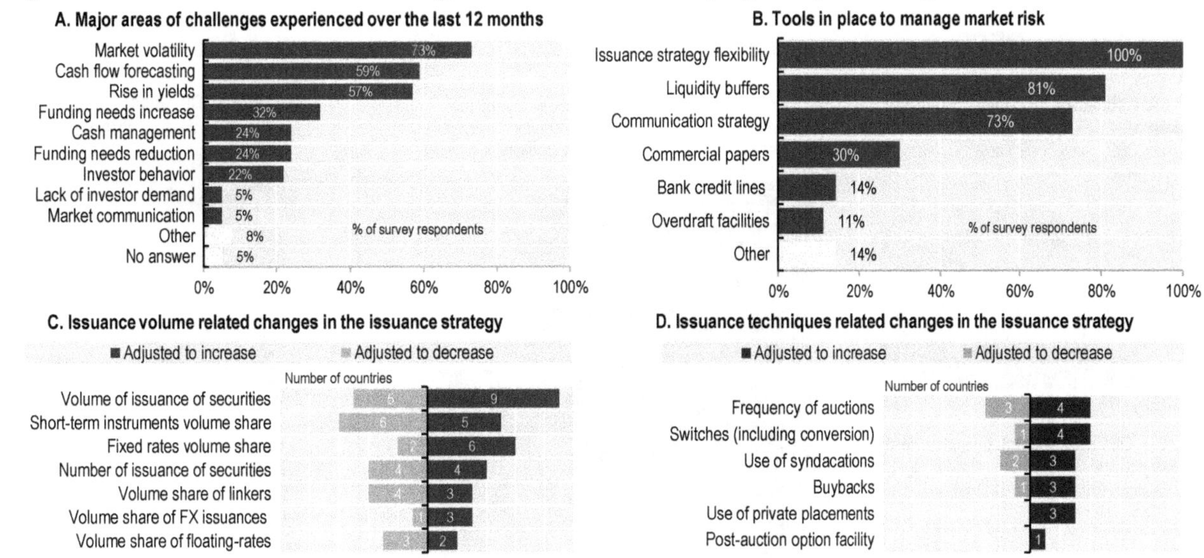

Source: OECD Survey on Primary Market Developments 2023.

1.3. Debt-to-GDP ratios remained largely stable in 2023, after declining in 2021 and 2022, and are projected to increase again in 2024

The aggregate debt-to-GDP ratio in the OECD, measured using central government marketable debt, is estimated to remain largely stable through 2022-23 at 83% and is projected to increase slightly to 84% by 2024 (Figure 1.9, Panel A). This figure masks the high variability in debt-to-GDP ratios across countries (Figure 1.9, Panel D). An increase of over 1pp is projected in nine countries, led by the United States, where it is projected to increase by 3pp. In contrast, 12 countries' debt-to-GDP ratios are projected to fall by over 1pp, with Japan, Portugal, and Spain, where it is projected to fall by over 5pp.

Debt-to-GDP ratios in 2023 surpassed pre-pandemic levels by roughly 5pp on average and 10pp on aggregate in the OECD area.[6] The ratio is higher in 24 countries and has increased by over 8pp in all the G7 countries. Japan and US debt-to-GDP ratios have risen by over 24 and 22pp, respectively, since 2019. Over the same period, debt-to-GDP ratios decreased in 14 countries, falling by over 10pp in Ireland, Poland, Portugal and Sweden. It is worth noting that debt-to-GDP ratios and movements vary greatly depending on debt assessment methodologies, with the OECD's SBO, National Accounts (NA) and Economic Outlook (EO) using different approaches (see Box 1.3).

The share of short-term debt in the OECD debt stock has grown and is projected to reach 16% by 2024 (Figure 1.9, Panel B), the highest value in 15 years aside from 2020. Concurrently, the proportion of fixed-rate instruments is estimated to have fallen from 79% in 2022 to 76% in 2023 – aside from 2020, this is the lowest figure since 2010, a period during which central banks' bond holdings were negligible.

Despite this decline, fixed rate debt continues to constitute over half of the outstanding debt in all OECD countries in 2023. The share of short-term debt ranges from 0% in 9 OECD countries to 22% in the United States, while the share of linkers ranges from 0% in 17 countries to 32% in Chile (Figure 1.9, Panel C).

Figure 1.9. The OECD central government debt stock, debt-to-GDP ratios and debt composition

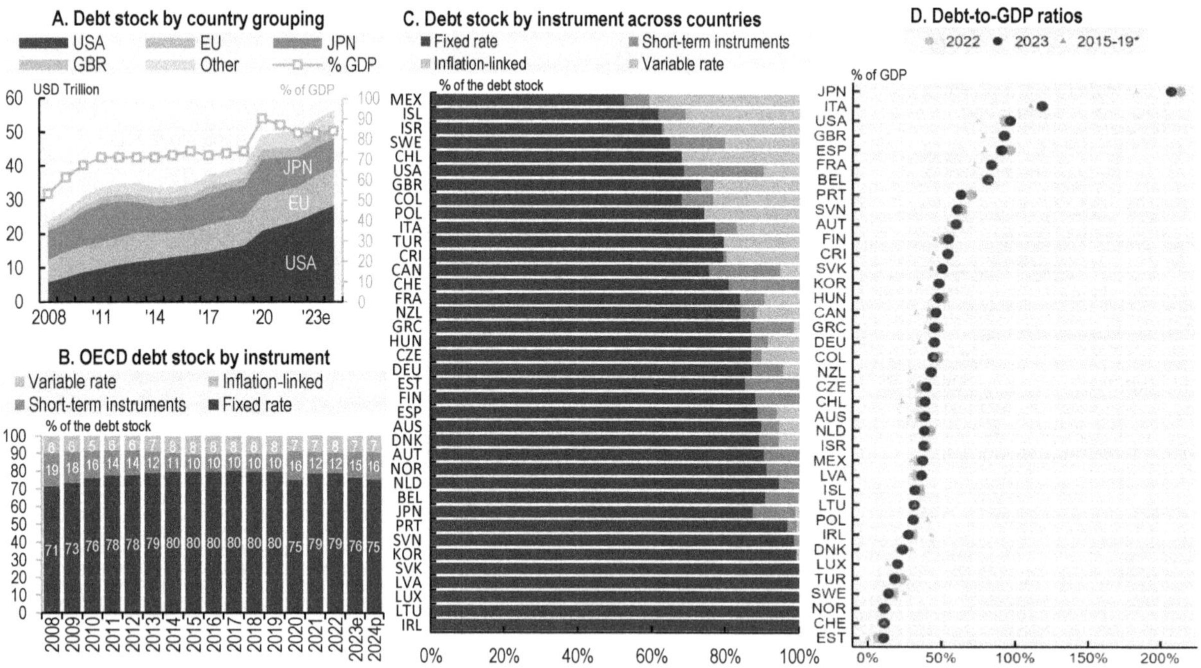

Source: 2023 OECD Survey on Central Government Marketable Debt and Borrowing; LSEG; (OECD, 2023[1]); (IMF, 2023[2]); national authorities' websites; and OECD calculations.

Box 1.3. Sovereign debt calculation methodologies

Gross debt calculation methods differ mainly in the scope of government units, instrument liability coverage, and financial instrument valuation (Figure 1.10, Panel A). In 2022, debt-to-GDP ratios were 83% in the SBO, compared to 113% for the EO and 114% for the NA (Figure 1.10, Panel B). Subnational debt accounts for roughly two-thirds of this discrepancy, while the central government's non-marketable debt liabilities account for the other third. Countries with high subnational debts, like Canada, or significant non-tradeable debts, such as Greece, will have larger discrepancies between the different methodologies (Figure 1.10, Panel C).

Valuation methods can greatly amplify movements in debt-to-GDP ratios. The SBO's use of nominal value ensures yield fluctuations do not impact its debt figures, unlike the EO's and NA's market value approach.[1] In 2022, rising interest rates contributed to debt-to-GDP ratios falling by over 20pp in nine countries under the NA and EO methodologies, but by no more than 10pp in any country by the SBO methodology (Figure 1.10, Panel D). While market value method is beneficial for practices such as debt buybacks, it is essential to note that bonds are redeemed at their outstanding nominal value at maturity. Therefore, debt managers need to refinance based on this value.

Figure 1.10. Methodological differences and debt-to-GDP ratio figures

A. Methodological differences in gross debt calculations between the SBO, NA and EO

Method	Scope of government units	Liability coverage	Valuation method
SBO	Central government	Marketable debt securities	Nominal value
National Accounts (NA)	General government (i.e. central government, social security funds, state and local governments)	Debt securities; loans; currency and deposits; special drawing rights (SDRs); insurance, pension and standardised guarantee schemes; and other accounts payable	Market prices: Tradeable financial instruments; Nominal value: All remaining liabilities
Economic Outlook (NA with adjustments)		The same liability coverage as the NA but excluding insurance, pension and standardised guarantee schemes.	Market prices: Debt securities (excl. US), equity and investment fund shares, financial derivatives and employee stock options; Nominal value: All remaining liabilities

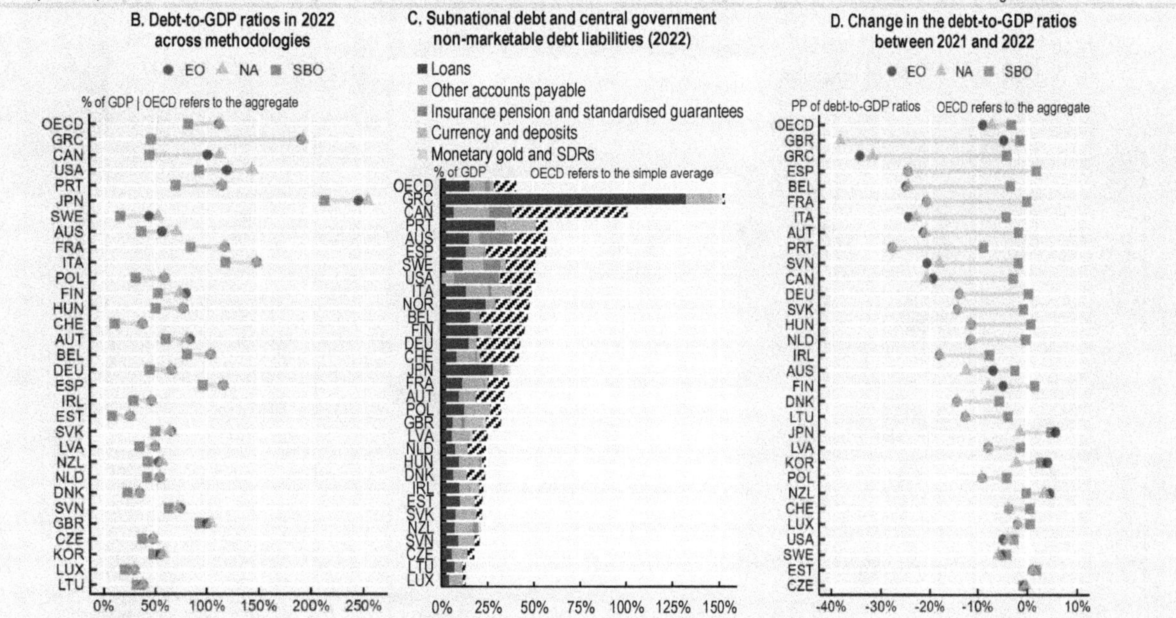

Source: 2023 OECD Survey on Central Government Marketable Debt and Borrowing; (OECD, 2023[1]); (OECD, 2023[18]); (Rawdanowicz et al., 2021[19]) national authorities' websites; OECD Fiscal Decentralisation Database; and OECD National Accounts.

1. The OECD Economic Outlook generally follows the NA with adjustments (as shown in Figure 1.10, Panel A). Still, it also provides alternative debt figures, especially for EU countries, using the Maastricht debt definition, which uses nominal values for financial instrument valuation.

1.3.1. Inflation outweighed higher borrowing costs in debt-to-GDP trajectories in 2022-23

The decrease in debt-to-GDP ratios between 2021 and 2023 is driven mostly by higher inflation, which boosted nominal GDP growth, and partly by real GDP growth (Figure 1.11). Since 2021, inflation contributed to a decrease of 13pp in these ratios while real GDP growth accounted for an 8pp decrease.[7] The real yield, which combines the impact of nominal rates and inflation, was negative in nearly all OECD countries.[8] Most of the OECD debt was issued when inflation and interest rates were lower, carrying lower costs (Figure 1.19). Thus, the current level of nominal GDP growth exceeded the effective interest rates (i.e. the ratio of interest expenses to the debt stock), helping to reduce debt-to-GDP ratios.

With falling inflation and an increasing amount of debt issued under higher rates, the declining trend in debt-to-GDP ratios in 2021-23 is set to reverse in 2024. While inflation's effect on the nominal GDP is immediate and short-lived, the effects of higher borrowing costs on interest expenditure are gradual and long-lasting. Inflation has the initial effect of lowering debt-to-GDP ratios but, if persistent, its impact in the medium to long run is to increase the inflation premium and debt financing costs.

Inflation does little to improve debt sustainability, as debt-to-GDP trajectories are mainly driven by fiscal balances in the long-term, with unexpected inflation providing only a short-term impact. Historical data indicates the crucial role of primary balances in shaping these trajectories and suggests caution in overinterpreting recent declines (Rawdanowicz et al., 2021[19]; Acalin and Ball, 2023[20]). To avoid an adverse feedback loop of rising interest rates, slow growth and expanding deficits, prudent fiscal policies supported by credible medium-term budget frameworks are essential. Due to these potential feedback loops, for example, the EU is considering incorporating debt sustainability analysis in its new fiscal rules framework.[9]

Figure 1.11. Decomposition of the OECD debt-to-GDP ratio movements

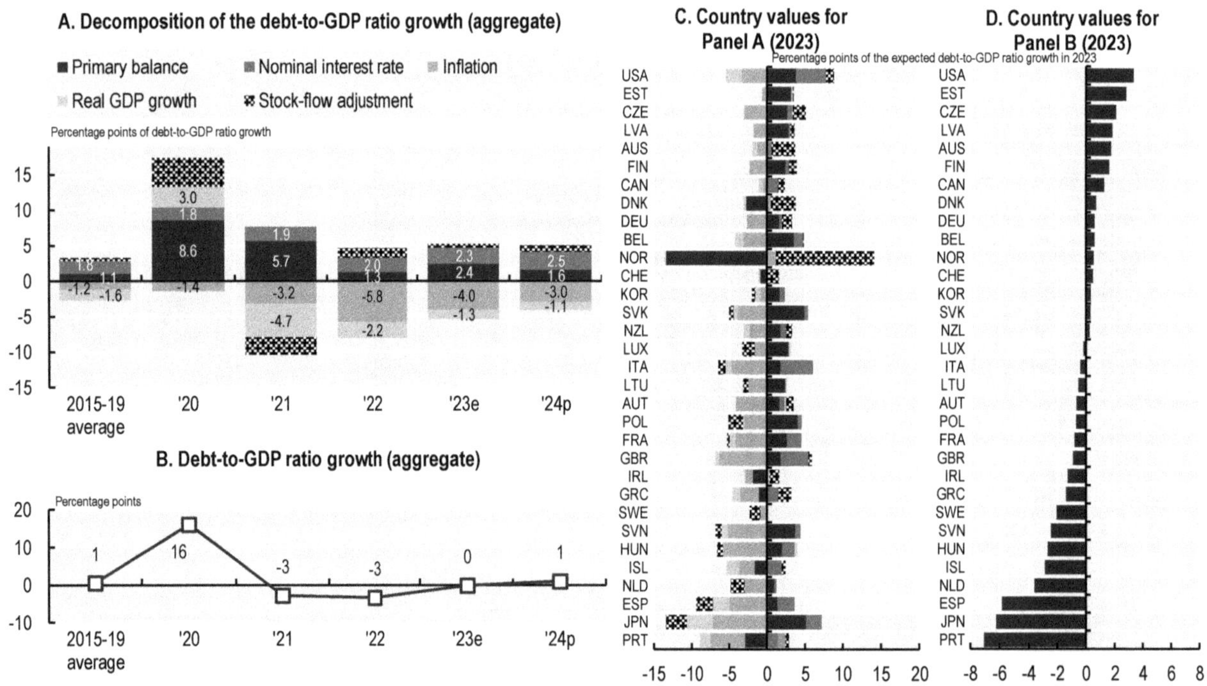

Note: The decomposition of debt-to-GDP ratios combined central and general government information. Details can be found in Annex 1.B.
Source: 2023 OECD Survey on Central Government Marketable Debt and Borrowing; LSEG; (OECD, 2023[1]); (IMF, 2023[2]); national authorities' websites; and OECD calculations.

1.4. Borrowing costs rose more slowly in 2023 than in 2022

Borrowing costs for new debt, measured by the yield to maturity at issuance (YTM), rose from approximately 3% in 2022 to 4% in 2023 on average across OECD countries. This increase is about half of the almost 2pp rise seen in 2022, taking borrowing costs in 2023 to nearly twice their 2015-19 average (Figure 1.12). Moreover, unlike in 2022, when all countries experienced an increase, five countries saw a reduction in their average YTM in 2023, with some central banks lowering rates last year (e.g. Chile, Czechia and Poland). This suggests that the rise in YTM is slowing, with further increases unlikely as policy rates are expected to fall in most countries in 2024 (OECD, 2024[16]).

Negative nominal rates, common in many European countries in 2020 and 2021, were only present in Japan in 2023 (Figure 1.12, Panel B). Additionally, the percentage of debt issued at borrowing costs below 2% fell sharply from nearly 40% in 2022 to 15% in 2023, whereas the proportion of debt issued with a yield exceeding 4% more than tripled, from 11% in 2022 to 37% in 2023.

The rise in average YTM during 2023 was more pronounced in European countries. Of the 20 countries experiencing the highest increases in YTM at issuance, 13 belonged to the euro area and 5 were non-Euro European nations. This pattern reflects the ECB's intensified monetary tightening in 2023, a shift from 2022 when euro area nations had some of the smallest yield and policy rate increases (Figure 1.13, Panel A). Concurrently, 2023 saw a narrowing of the spread over German bonds in 12 European countries, while only 3 witnessed a widening, possibly reflecting a perception of lower risk, and the mix of the ECB's reinvestments under their asset purchase programmes.

Figure 1.12. Borrowing costs of the new debt issuances

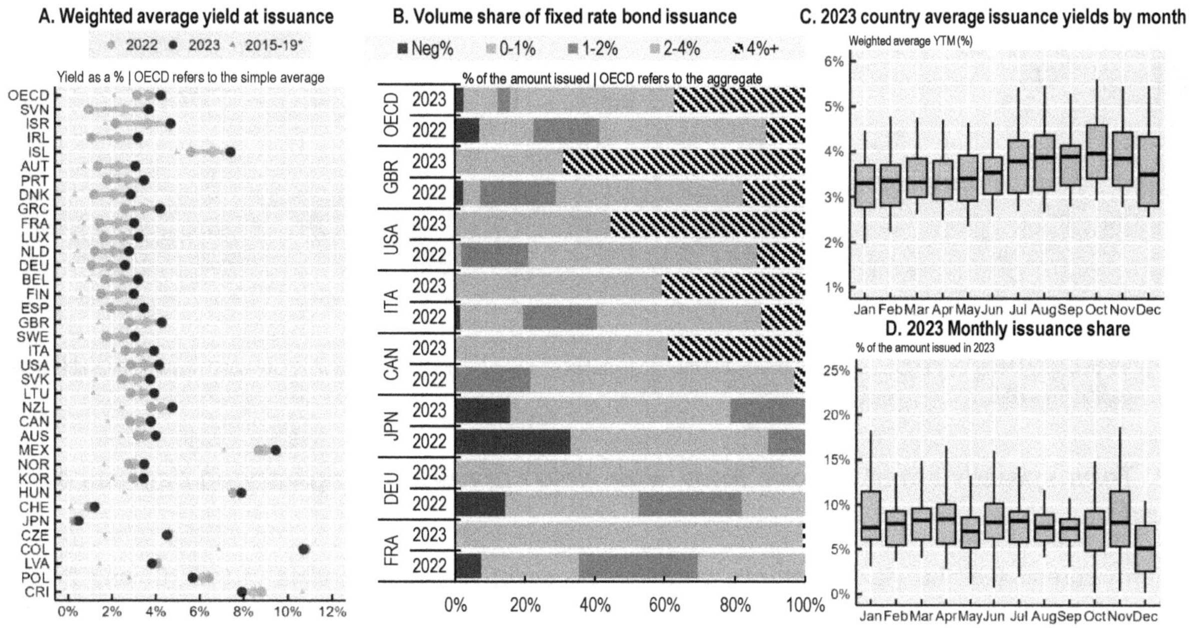

Note: Panels A, B, and C include only fixed rates instruments in domestic currency, while Panel D includes all issuances.
Source: LSEG and OECD calculations.

The key driver of the rise in yields is expectations for central bank policy rates, with the average policy rate in the OECD rising from 5% in 2022 to 6% in 2023 (Figure 1.13, Panel A). In 2023, 15 out of 20 OECD central banks raised their policy rates. Notably, the ECB raised policy rates by 2.0pp, the second largest increase in the OECD behind the Icelandic central bank. The BoJ has kept policy rates near zero since 2016 while central banks in Chile, Czechia, Hungary, and Poland began to lower rates in 2023.

Nominal rates are typically determined by three factors: real interest rates, inflation expectations and a risk premium. Real interest rates refer to the real returns that consumers and savers demand in exchange for postponing consumption, being an estimation of the real returns on investments and largely determined by real economic growth expectations and volatility. Inflation expectations are incorporated into nominal interest rates to offset savers' anticipations of changing price levels. The risk premium compensates investors for the uncertainty around future inflation levels. This premium tends to be higher for bonds with longer maturities due to the increasing uncertainty of longer-term expectations, whereas short-term bonds are more directly affected by prevailing policy rates and more immediate inflation expectations.

In 2023, there was a consistent rise in the average yields across the OECD, coinciding with a decline in breakeven inflation rates and an increase in real yields (Figure 1.13, Panel B, C and D).[10] According to the no-arbitrage principle, which posits that securities with the same cash flows should have identical prices, the spot rate of a bond is equivalent to the spot rate of a shorter-term bond and the series of forthcoming short-term forward rates until the bond's maturity. This implies that market pricing reflects expectations that future short-term forward rates will stay high, suggesting policy rates will not return to the near zero level of much of the last decade in the medium-term – the implication being that rates will be kept higher for longer.[11]

Figure 1.13. Drivers of the increase in borrowing costs

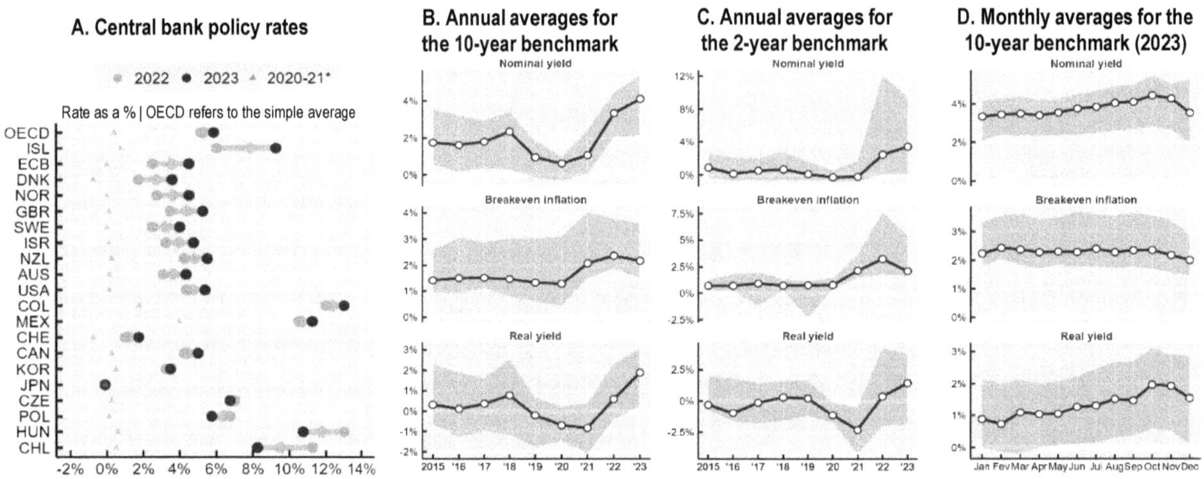

Note: Panels B, C and D display the OECD simple mean and the range between the 10% and 90% percentiles for countries with available data.
Source: Adapted from (BIS, 2023[21]) and LSEG.

1.4.1. Term spreads are at historic lows, with yield curves showing varying degrees of inversion

The term spread (i.e. the yield difference between the secondary market yield of the 10- and 2-year benchmark bonds) is a key indicator for sovereign issuers to consider when balancing cost and risk. This typically positive spread arises from the term premium, the extra return demanded by investors for the risk of buying longer-term bonds. The term spread varies, influenced by factors such as the supply and demand of bonds across the curve, inflation and interest rate expectations, the business cycle and output growth. DMOs can use this spread to help assess the trade-off between short-term debt, typically with lower cost and higher liquidity and refinancing risk, and long-term debt, typically with lower refinancing risk and liquidity but higher cost.

The average term spread in the OECD reached historical lows, approaching zero in 2023 (Figure 1.14, Panel A). This figure has been trending downwards since 2009, largely driven by increased demand for longer maturities in search of positive yields due to central banks taking interest rates to at or near zero and QE programmes; expectations for lower levels of future inflation; and subdued growth, which diminishes expected returns on future investments (Cohen, P. and Xia, 2018[22]). This downward trend halted in 2021 amid heightened uncertainty about the trajectory of policy rates and inflation but has continued over 2022-23 with inflation easing and markets anticipating declining policy rates in 2024.

Figure 1.14. Term spreads expressed as the difference between 10- and 2-year benchmark yields

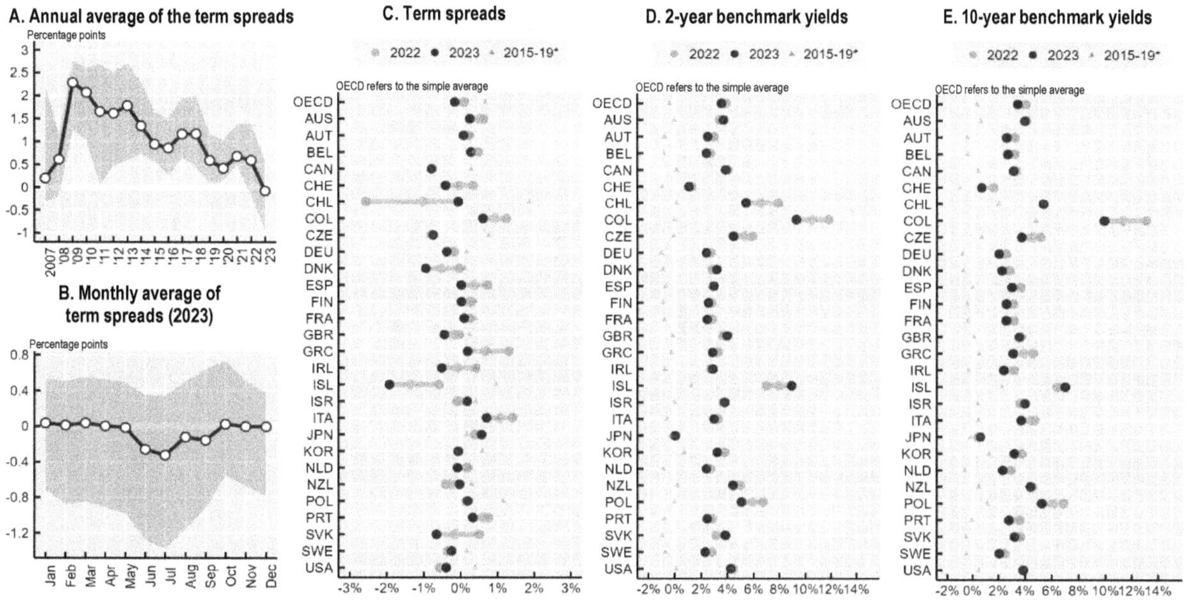

Note: Panels A and B display the OECD simple mean and the range between the 10% and 90% percentiles.
Source: LSEG and OECD calculations.

Throughout 2023, the term spread moved in different directions, mirroring changing conditions throughout the year (Figure 1.14, Panel B). It remained stable from January through May before dipping in June and July, influenced by easing inflation in the United States and Europe and growing recession concerns. From July to December, there was a reversal, with the spread increasing once again due to supply-demand imbalances triggered by higher borrowing needs, especially in the United States, and QT.

The term spread declined overall in more than two-thirds of countries in 2023, but the dynamics varied between euro area and non-euro area economies (Figure 1.14, Panel C). In the euro area, all countries experienced a decline in term spreads, by an average of 0.5pp, mirroring the widespread decrease in 10-year yields in the region. Outside the euro area, term spreads moved in both directions, with half of the countries experiencing a rise in 10-year yields and the other half a decline. Compared to 2015-19 levels, term spreads rose only in Japan, reflecting the increased flexibility of the BoJ's yield curve control (BoJ, 2023[23]).

Nominal yield curves in G7 countries remained largely unchanged and inverted in 2023, contrasting the pre-pandemic period when all G7 countries had mostly upward-sloping curves (Figure 1.15). Canada, Japan and the US nominal yield curve remained largely unchanged in 2023. In the same period in the United Kingdom, nominal yields increased at the short end but slightly declined in the 5, 7 and 10-year benchmarks, leading to further inversion. Short-end yields also rose in France, Germany and Italy in 2023, while their nominal yield curves displayed varying degrees of inversion.

Yield curves typically slope upwards, reflecting risk premiums that align with bond duration, whereas downward slopes suggest anticipated reductions in policy rates. The effect of current monetary policy on long-term rates is often limited, given that the market always expects policy rates to converge to the neutral rate in the long run. Given the cyclical nature of high short-term rates during periods of high inflation, yield curves often invert in these periods.[12]

Figure 1.15. Shapes of the nominal and real yield curves in G7 countries

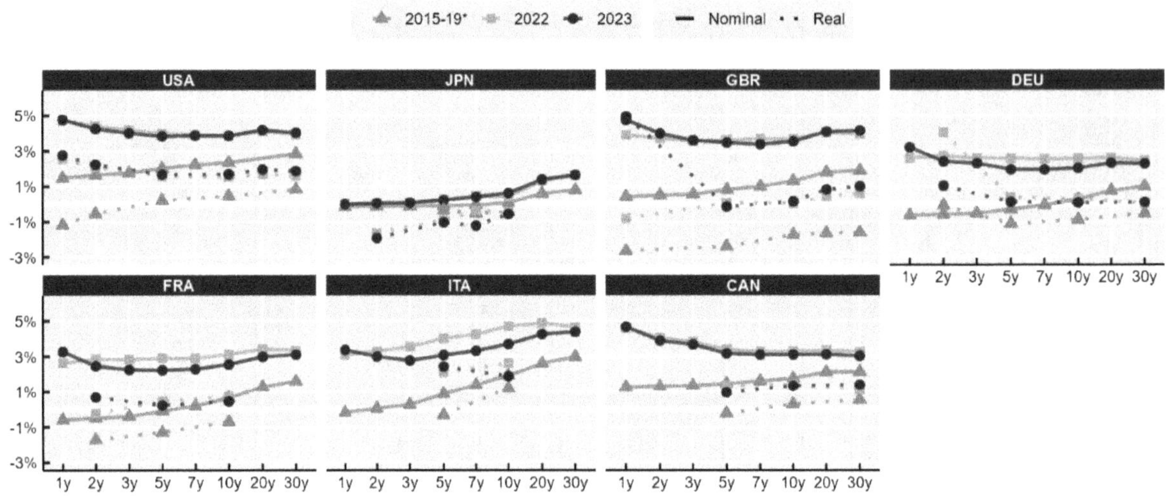

Note: Data gaps indicate limited data availability. Real yields are the nominal yield minus the breakeven inflation for the same maturity.
Source: LSEG and OECD calculations.

Inverted yield curves can impact the cost-risk trade-off between alternative borrowing strategies. They imply that longer maturities bear lower costs and carry fewer risks compared to shorter maturities, as rates are fixed for a longer period at a lower rate. However, as inverted curves anticipate falling interest rates, locking into a certain yield level in a longer term when interest rates may be about to fall can lead to regret risk. Thus, some DMOs are opting to issue more at shorter maturities. Additionally, issuance strategies should factor in demand patterns across the maturity spectrum, with certain investors persistently favouring specific parts of the curve, such as pension funds' preference for longer-term investments and money market funds' (MMF) preference for shorter-dated instruments. Thus, a well-balanced issuance strategy, with regular supply at key benchmark maturities across the curve, is often the norm regardless of the shape of the curve.

Similar to nominal yield curves, real yield curves in G7 countries remained largely unchanged in 2023, with all G7 nations, aside from Japan, having displayed largely positive real yield curves. Real yield curves finished 2023 inverted at the short end in all G7 countries aside from Canada and Japan.

The main implication of positive real yields is the pressure it puts on primary balances, raising the risk of a vicious cycle of increasing deficits through higher interest payments and debt. The disparity between real interest rates and GDP growth is a key factor in debt-to-GDP dynamics. Most government debt in the OECD was accumulated when GDP growth exceeded real rates, allowing governments to run primary fiscal deficits and still have falling debt-to-GDP ratios. Now, with OECD debt at record levels and being refinanced with positive real interest rates, most governments must achieve primary balance surpluses to stabilise debt-to-GDP ratios. However, achieving primary balance surpluses in the current context of heightened spending pressures may be harder than in the past (OECD, 2023[1]). DMOs, acting as intermediaries between governments and markets, can only determine the timing and terms under which the debt matures, without significantly impacting debt-to-GDP trajectories.

1.5. Interest payments rose in 2023 and are expected to rise further in 2024

Interest expenditures in the OECD are expected to have risen gradually from 2.3% in 2021 to 2.9% of GDP in 2023 (Figure 1.16, Panel A). Estimates show an increase in this ratio in 20 countries, a negligible change in 9, and a decline in 4.[13] Notably, this ratio is expected to rise by more than 0.5pp of GDP in 2023 in Czechia, Greece, Hungary, New Zealand and the United States. Against this overall upward trend, Italy and the United Kingdom are expected to see interest payment-to-GDP ratios reduce in 2023, compared to 2022, due to declining inflation. This will lead to lower expenses on their stock of linkers, which comprise around 10% and 25% of their respective debt portfolios.

The expected interest expenditure-to-GDP ratio in the OECD is just 0.3pp higher in 2023 than 2015-19 levels (Figure 1.16, Panel B). Despite the higher yield environment, only 15 countries are expected to have higher interest payments as a percentage of GDP in 2023 compared to pre-pandemic levels. In this period, the United Kingdom has experienced the largest increase, at 1.8pp of GDP, nearly twice the second largest, which is Hungary at 1.0pp, and three times that of France and the United States, both at 0.6pp. This increase amounts to almost two-thirds of the UK's annual investment expenditure (OECD, 2023[18]).

Figure 1.16. OECD general government interest expenditure trends

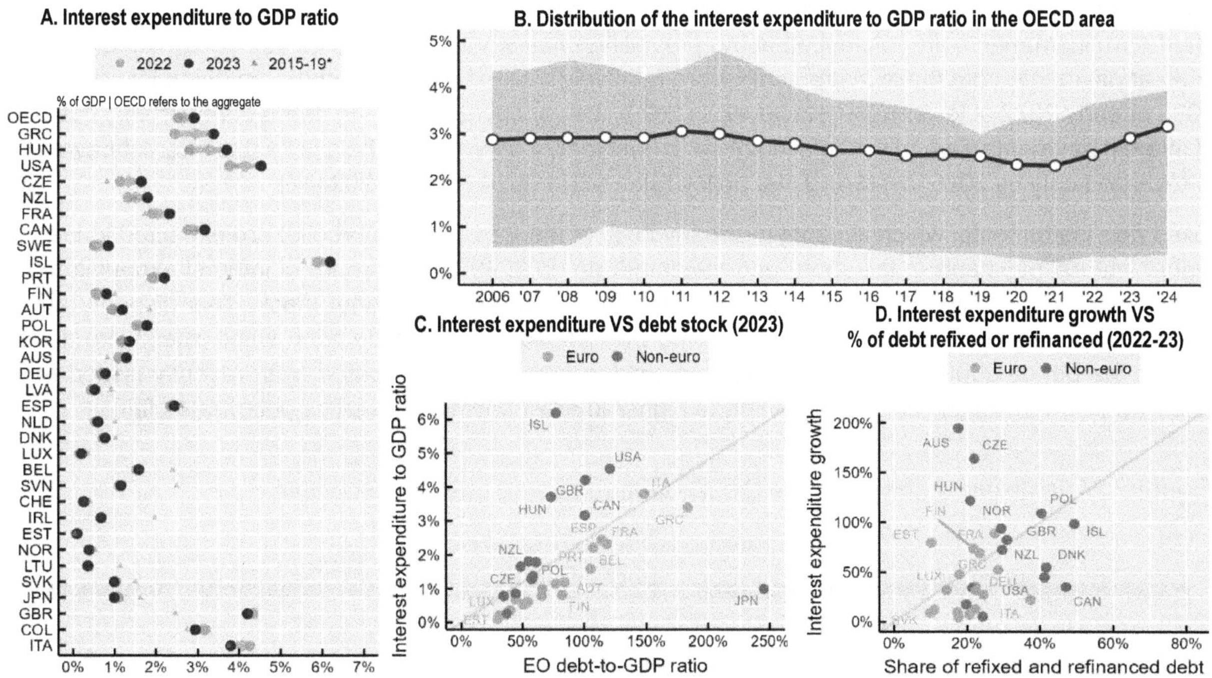

Note: Interest expenditures are the gross general government interest payments sourced from the OECD Economic Outlook. Values for 2023 are estimates and 2024 projections. Panel B's shaded area displays the range between the 10% and 90% percentiles. Refixing debt refers to the debt that matures or refixes (inflation-linked or floating rates) in the period.

Source: 2023 Survey on Central Government Marketable Debt and Borrowing; LSEG; (OECD, 2023[1]); (IMF, 2023[2]) national authorities' websites; and OECD calculations.

Euro area countries have experienced relatively lower interest payment levels and less movement in these levels. In the euro area, the share of interest expenditure to GDP typically remains lower than in countries with comparable debt-to-GDP ratios, with the exception of Italy and Greece, reflecting the ECB's lower policy rates, and expectations for lower inflation in the future (Figure 1.16, Panel C). Additionally, euro area countries have seen a comparatively smaller rise in interest expenditure due to their debt profiles (Figure 1.16, Panel D).

The increase in the interest expenditure-to-GDP ratio in 2023 is smaller than the jump in the average cost of issuance of 1pp (Figure 1.12, Panel A), as changes in the interest expenditure of OECD countries are typically gradual, largely due to the predominance of fixed-rate debt in their portfolios. Under accrual accounting, the predominant method in the OECD area, interest payments accrue every year proportionally to their yield at issuance and outstanding amounts.[14] As it is rare for an OECD country to refinance more than a quarter of its debt annually, shifts in interest payments tend to be incremental (Figure 1.16, Panel B). Linkers and floaters differ as their costs follow the prevailing inflation and interest rates, respectively.

Interest payments on inflation-linked bonds were significantly impacted by the sudden increase in inflation in 2022-23 but are expected to fall going forward. In 2022, these bonds made up about 8% of the OECD's total debt stock but accounted for around 30% of the interest payments (Figure 1.17). In 2023, even though the share of inflation-linked debt in the total stock stayed relatively unchanged, the share of interest payments it accounts for has halved. However, this is still roughly twice the proportion of these instruments in the debt stock.

Interest payments on floating-rate instruments are anticipated to decline along with policy rates in 2024. As they only represent roughly 2% of the OECD debt stock and 4% of the interest payments in 2022-23, the reduction in interest payments from floaters will be minor compared to those from linkers.

Short-term instruments exhibit a similar pattern to floaters, although there is a time lag, and they constitute a far greater share of the debt. While the borrowing costs of floating rates quickly align with policy rates, short-term instruments are refinanced at the prevailing rates when they mature. This meant that, in 2022, interest payments from these instruments were relatively modest, with many of them being issued in late 2021 or early 2022 at lower rates. However, in 2023, they accounted for 15% of the debt portfolio but 23% of interest payments. Due to the time lag of up to one year, a decrease in the associated interest payments is expected only by 2025, assuming that policy rates fall in 2024 (OECD, 2024[16]).

Fixed rate instruments, which account for nearly 80% of the OECD debt portfolio, are expected to lead to higher interest payments in the short- and medium-term. In 2009-20, the share of interest expenditure for fixed rates was, on average, nearly 10% higher than its share of the debt stock. This disparity arose because much of the fixed rate debt outstanding was issued in the decade prior, when rates were higher than in the period 2009-20. Moving forward, a similar dynamic is anticipated, with recently issued fixed rates launched at higher rates, contributing to higher interest payments even as policy rates fall.

Figure 1.17. Instrument shares of the OECD debt stock and interest expenses

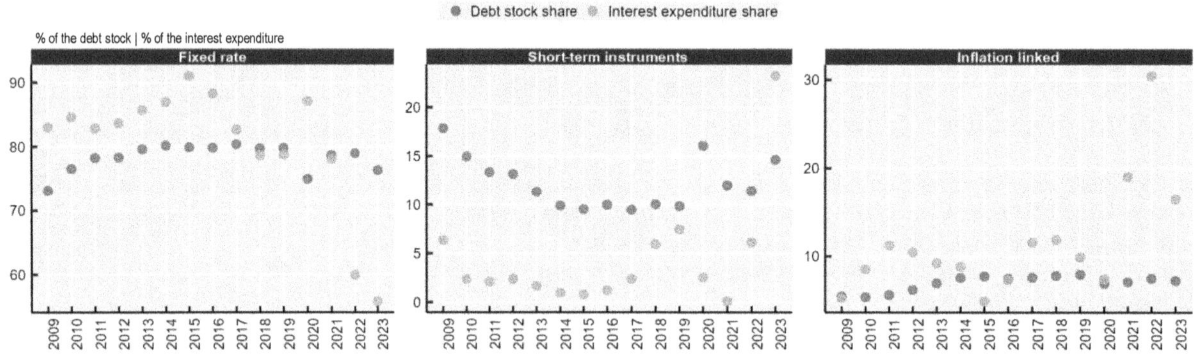

Note: The interest expenditure share is computed assuming accrual accounting. Methodological details are in Annex 1.C.
Source: 2023 Survey on Central Government Marketable Debt and Borrowing; LSEG; and OECD calculations.

1.5.1. Inflation-linked bonds can offer longer term advantages in terms of cost and risk management even against a backdrop of higher interest costs

In theory, fixed-rate debt is associated with higher issuance costs due to duration risk, while inflation-linked debt is typically less costly for the issuer, as investors are willing to pay a premium for inflation protection. However, in 2022-23, with inflation way significantly above target, linkers were more expensive to issue than fixed rate debt. It is important to note that the true cost-effectiveness of an inflation-linked bond can only be assessed at maturity by comparing it with a fixed-rate counterpart. If the average inflation rate over the bond's lifetime is lower than the breakeven rate at issuance, the linker was cost effective, and vice versa if it is higher.

An analysis of matched pairs of inflation-linked and fixed-rate bonds shows that linkers are typically cost-effective. In 66% of the matched pairs maturing between 2011-21, linkers incurred lower costs than their fixed-rate counterparts (Figure 1.18, Panel A). Conversely, in 85% of the matched pairs that matured between 2022-23, fixed rates were more cost-effective. When analysing bonds based on their issuance year, linkers issued between 2011-15 tended to be cost-efficient but the opposite can be said for those issued between 2016-18 (Figure 1.18, Panel B). Looking forward, as inflation falls back towards target and linker payments decline, fixed rates are expected to be the main driver behind higher interest payments.

Beyond potential cost efficiencies, inflation-linked bonds can provide several advantages to DMOs (OECD, 2023[24]). From a fiscal perspective the correlation between the interest payments on linkers and government revenues can stabilise the ratio between these variables.[15] Also, the market for linkers differs from that of conventional bonds, enabling sovereign issuers to diversify their investor base and to extend the maturity of their debt portfolio, as buyers of linkers often prefer longer maturities.[16] Finally, they can contribute to price stability by signalling the government's commitment to controlling inflation.[17]

Inflation-linked instruments can also come with other considerations for issuers. These considerations include the potential for high volatility in the level of interest payments, since the benefits of lower costs associated with linkers accrue gradually, in contrast to the sharp increases in payments during periods of higher inflation. This dynamic can result in asymmetrical reputational risk for the product, with the cost-effectiveness of linkers being realised incrementally over many years, while the cost of financing them surges and is very visible when inflation spikes.

Figure 1.18. Difference in the effective interest rates of matched real rate and nominal bonds

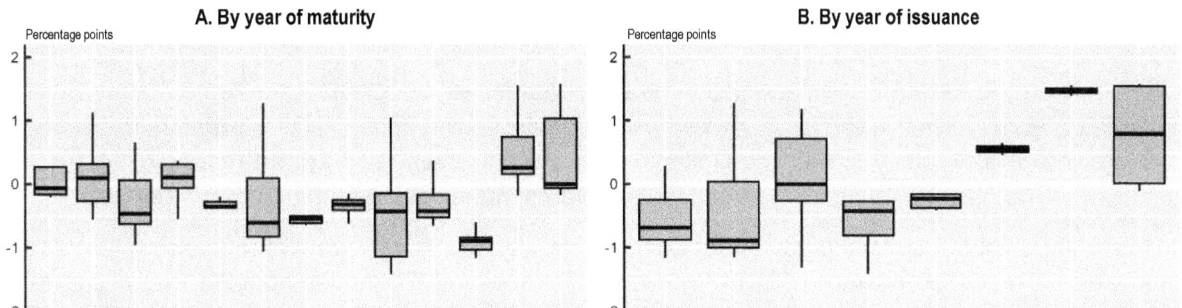

Note: 91 inflation-linked bond issuances from Australia, Chile, Denmark, France, Germany, Italy, Korea, Spain, Sweden, Türkiye, the United Kingdom and the United States were matched with the nearest fixed-rate counterpart in terms of maturity and issuance date. All matched pairs' issuance and maturity dates fall within a 60-day window. For issuances from Spain, the United Kingdom, and Türkiye, a relaxed criterion allowing up to 180 days difference was employed as closer matches were nearly non-existent. Cost calculations were conducted following the methodology outlined in Annex 1.C.
Source: 2023 Survey on Central Government Marketable Debt and Borrowing; LSEG; and OECD calculations.

1.5.2. Debt refinancing could raise interest payments by 0.5% of GDP in 2024-26

About 60% of the outstanding OECD debt stock has coupons fixed at pre-2022 yield levels and is likely to be refinanced at higher rates in the future (Figure 1.19, Panel A). Roughly 30% of OECD debt was issued in 2022-23, when rates had already begun increasing, and a further 10% of the debt stock consists of linkers and floaters, for which interest has already been adjusted to higher rates and inflation. Thus, in the short- to medium-term, higher interest payments are likely to result from the refinancing of fixed rate issuances and new borrowing.

The current tightening cycle has had a significant impact on borrowing costs, with 30% of OECD debt issued in 2022-23 accounting for around 40% of interest expenses. This marks the first occasion since the data series began in 2009 that the proportion of interest payments from debt issued in the current and preceding year exceeds the share of the debt stock issued in that same period (Figure 1.19, Panel B).

Concurrently, debt issued during the peak of the pandemic in 2020-21 amounts to nearly the same 30% of the current OECD debt stock, yet it represents less than 15% of the interest payments. In addition, around 7% of the debt stock that was issued before 2012 accounts for 13% of the interest payments, due to the relatively higher yields prevalent during and right after the GFC.

Figure 1.19. Reverse maturity structure of the OECD debt stock and interest payments

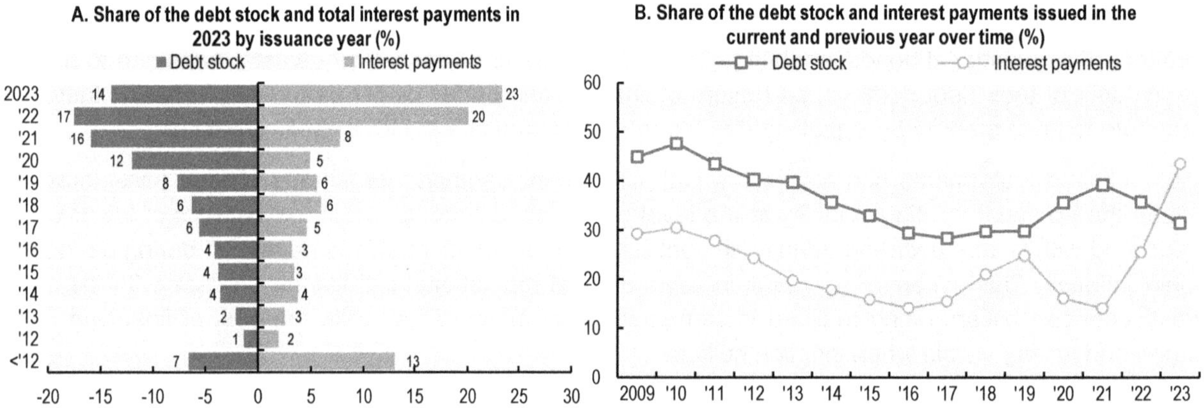

Note: The "reverse maturity structure" of debt refers to the array of years in which the existing debt was issued, contrasting with the standard forward-looking maturity structure. Interest payment calculations were conducted following the methodology outlined in Annex 1.C.
Source: 2023 Survey on Central Government Marketable Debt and Borrowing; LSEG; and OECD calculations.

Looking forward, fixed-rate instruments worth nearly a quarter of OECD GDP are set to mature by 2026 (Figure 1.20, Panel A). In five OECD countries, fixed rates exceeding 20% of GDP will mature in this period, including Japan (52%), Italy (33%), the United States (27%), Spain (27%) and France (20%).[18] These countries face heightened refinancing risks if higher interest rates persist for much of this period.

The lower the YTM at issuance on maturing debt, the greater the fiscal impact of refinancing that debt at higher yields. The OECD average YTM of fixed-rate debt due by 2026 ranges from 2% to 3%, compared to fixed-rate issues in 2023 which on average were yielding around 4% (Figure 1.20, Panel B). Costa Rica and Slovenia, which issued fixed rates in 2023 with a YTM below that of the debt that matures between 2024 and 2026 might see reduced interest payment pressures upon refinancing in the next three years. Conversely, 19 OECD countries, including all G7 nations except Japan, issued fixed rate debt in 2023 at a YTM that was more than 1pp higher than their fixed rate debt that matures by 2026.

Reflecting these disparities between the YTM of the maturing fixed-rate debt and that of new issuances, OECD government interest expenses are estimated to climb by 0.5pp of GDP by 2026, solely due to fixed-rate refinancing (Figure 1.20, Panel D).[19] This projected increase is the same as the average OECD government's annual expenditure on environmental protection (OECD, 2023[18]) and is relatively higher for a few large issuers including the United States, Italy, France and the United Kingdom.

Figure 1.20. ATM, Average term-to-refixing (ATR) and refinancing risks in the OECD area

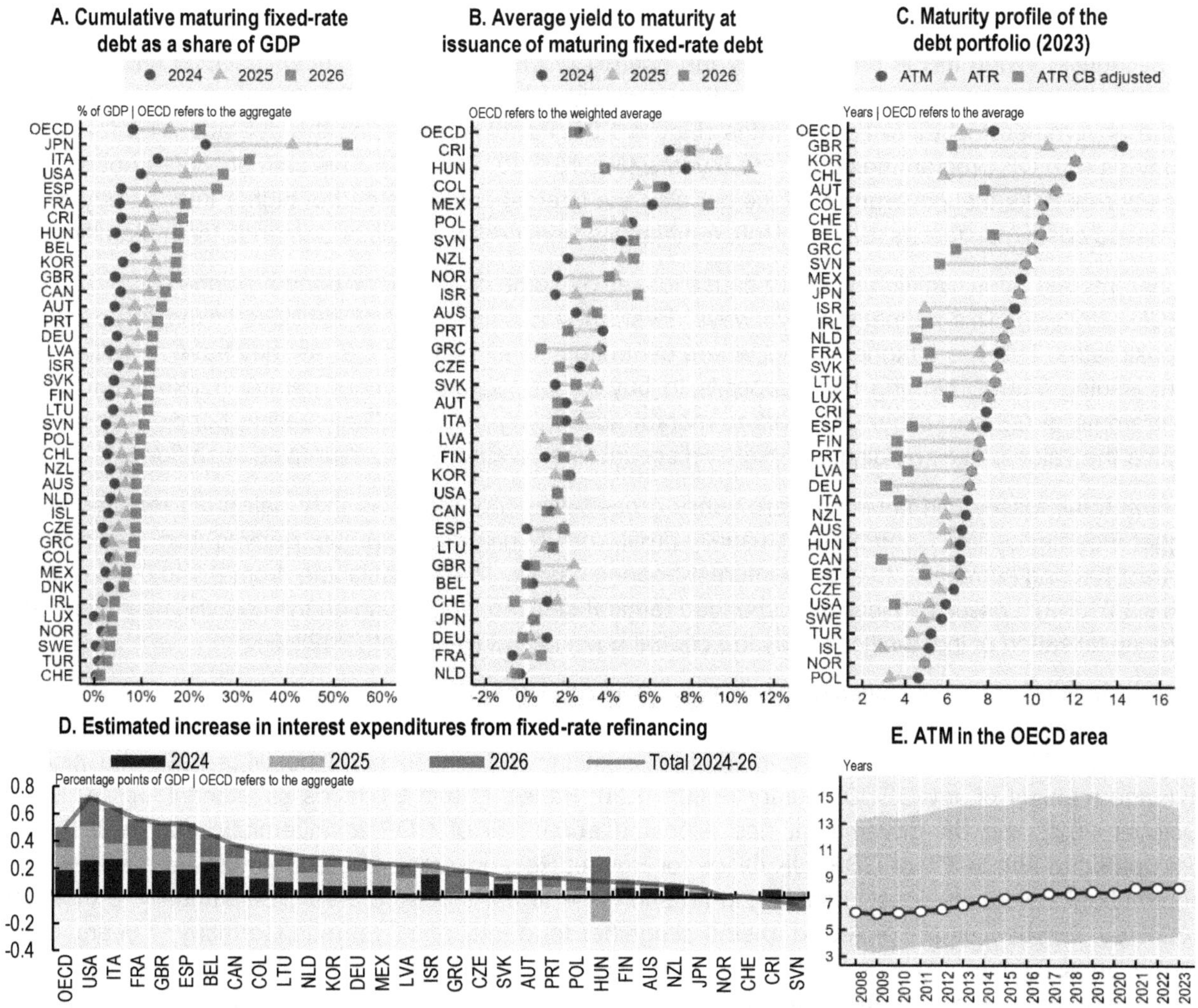

Note: ATM and ATR refer respectively to the average term to maturity and refixing, both as a weighted average of the outstanding amount. Panel C displays ATR CB adjusted figures only for countries in which their respective central banks report the maturity profile or the ATM of their government bond holdings. Panel E excludes Estonia in the average computation due to the high variability of the country's ATM.
Source: 2023 Survey on Central Government Marketable Debt and Borrowing; LSEG; (OECD, 2023[1]); national authorities' websites; and OECD calculations.

Compared to the increase in yields, the projected growth in interest payments due to debt refinancing is relatively small, thanks to the average maturity in OECD member's debt portfolios being approximately 8 years as of 2023 (Figure 1.20, Panel C). Over the last two decades, sovereign issuers have generally lengthened the maturity profile of their debt portfolios (Figure 1.20, Panel E), largely to help reduce refinancing risk. Thus, more than half of the current OECD debt matures or refixes beyond 2027, partially insulating countries from the impact of the current tightening cycle on interest payments, revealing the benefit of longer maturity profiles.

1.6. Quantitative tightening increases borrowing needs and the net supply of bonds to markets, affecting the investor base and market liquidity

The combination of central banks' large sovereign bond holdings and monetary tightening significantly impacts government security markets and sovereign debt portfolios. The large-scale purchases of government securities by central banks were executed through the issuance of bank reserves in exchange for securities. When this is considered in the context of the entire public sector balance sheet, central banks' bond holdings essentially act as floating rates with private creditors. This transforms about one third of the government debt into floating rates (Figure 1.20, Panel A), reducing the average ATR for OECD countries with QE programmes from 8 to 5 years (Figure 1.20, Panel C). This shift obscures not only the interest rate risks that governments face but also the interest costs; instead of higher interest payments, increased costs manifest as reduced profit remittances from central banks or demands for indemnification.

Higher interest rates diminish profits or cause losses on some central bank bond holdings (ECB, 2023[25]; OECD, 2023[26]). This happens in two ways. First, they raise the cost of liabilities linked to policy and deposit rates. This has a higher impact where central banks engaged in QE, as they have more liabilities from issuing interest-bearing bank deposits to buy bonds. Second, where central banks conducted a programme of QE and either use mark-to-market accounting or are actively selling bonds, higher rates reduce the value of their holdings, as higher discount rates are applied to their fixed cash flows.[20]

Central bank losses can impact government's gross borrowing needs as they halt profit remittances or trigger indemnification. Central banks usually profit from seigniorage revenue, derived from issuing non-interest-bearing currencies to acquire interest-bearing assets. These profits vary from 0.1 to 0.9% of GDP (Reis, 2013[27]). Losses can lead to suspended remittances and, depending on the country, may even lead to recapitalisation or indemnification by the central government (Bell et al., 2023[28]).[21]

Central bank losses in the United Kingdom have resulted in direct indemnification by the government whilst there has been a halt in the remittances in the United States and in some EU countries. The Bank of England (BoE), which uses mark-to-market accounting, and whose bond holdings have the highest average maturity of any OECD country (Figure 1.20, Panels C and E), faces substantial losses. Since October 2022, the UK government has allocated about 1% of GDP to indemnification, with losses anticipated to rise to 5% of GDP (UK Office for Budget Responsibility, 2023[29]). In the euro area where central banks were previously transferring around 0.1% to 0.2% of euro area GDP annually to member countries, remittances are projected to stop altogether for a total of 11 years in Germany, 4 years in the Netherlands, 3 years in France and 2 years in Spain (Belhocine, Bhatia and Frie, 2023[30]). The US Federal Reserve, after a decade of annual remittances paid to the US federal government which rose to as high as 0.5% of GDP in 2020, ceased to make a profit on its holdings in 2022 Q3 and is not expected to resume paying remittances until 2027 (Castro and Jordan-Wood, 2023[31]).

In 2023, central banks' average government bond holdings as a percentage of the national government debt decreased from 37% to 33% in 21 selected OECD countries (Figure 1.21, Panel A).[22] Notable declines occurred in Canada, Finland, and Baltic countries.

The four largest central banks that engage in QT – the Federal Reserve, ECB, BoE, and Bank of Canada (BoC) – reduced their government security holdings from USD 11.5 trillion in 2021 to USD 10.0 trillion in 2023 (Figure 1.21, Panel B). An additional decrease of USD 1.0 trillion is projected for 2024. This corresponds to an annual decrease of around 7% in their government security holdings over 2021-24.

Figure 1.21. Central banks' government security holdings and quantitative tightening

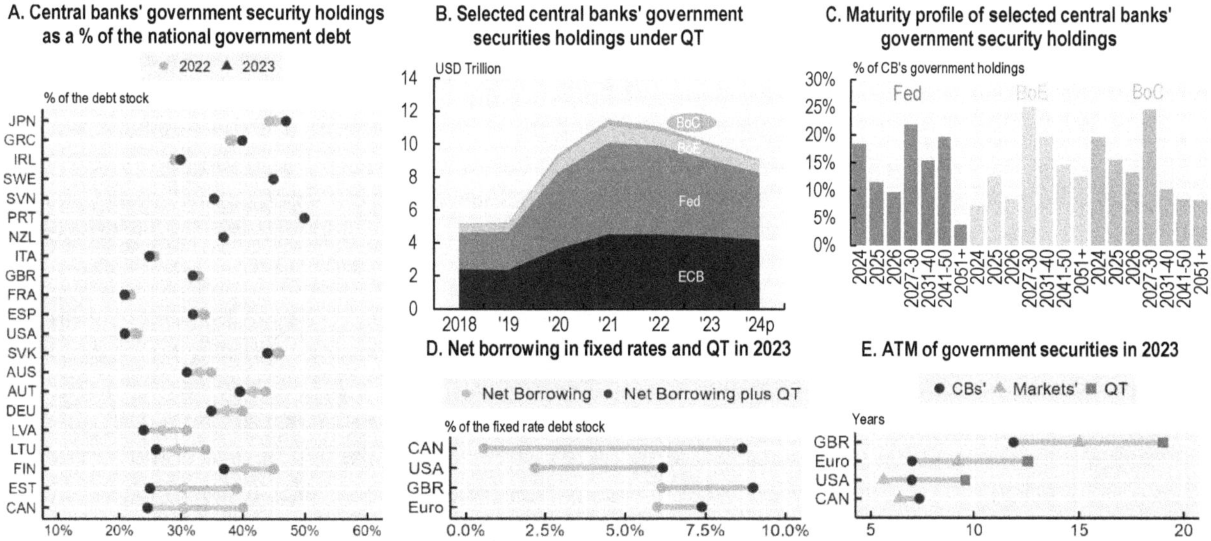

Note: Panel A uses OECD survey data as of end 2022 and June 2023. 2024 values are forecasted based on the pace published on central banks' websites and their maturity profile. The ECB does not disclose the maturity profile of its government securities and thus is excluded from Panel C. Panels D and E include data from central banks' websites available as of the end of December 2023. ECB holdings include only those under PSPP and PEPP.

Source: 2022 and 2023 Survey on Liquidity in Government Bond Secondary Markets; 2023 Survey on Central Government Marketable Debt and Borrowing; LSEG; (OECD, 2023[1]); and national authorities' websites.

QT can be achieved by central banks not or only partially reinvesting the proceeds from their maturing bond holdings, known as passive QT, or through a combination of not reinvesting and directly selling some of their outstanding bond holdings, known as active QT. The ECB and central banks of Canada and the United States are adopting a passive QT approach (BoC, 2022[32]; ECB, 2023[33]; OECD, 2023[34]; BIS, 2023[35]; Fed, 2022[36]). Meanwhile the Bank of England is adopting an active QT approach. (BoE, 2022[37]). Conversely, the BoJ has an ongoing QE programme due to Japan's low inflation levels (BIS, 2023[35]).[23] Among these central banks, the BoC is forecasted to see the largest decline in government security holdings over 2021-24, of 50%. This compares to a roughly 25% reduction for the Federal Reserve, 40% for the BoE, and 7% in the ECB. The ECB, adopting a slower pace of balance sheet reduction, is projected to surpass the Federal Reserve in having the largest holdings of government securities during 2024.

The pace of QT programmes will tend to align with the maturity profile of central banks' bond holdings (Figure 1.21, Panel C). Nearly 50% of the BoC's government holdings mature by 2026, compared to 40% for the Fed and 30% for the BoE. In contrast, about 50% of the BoE's government security holdings mature beyond 2031, whereas for the Fed this figure is 40%, and for the BoC, it is 30%.

As central banks' government bond holdings are predominantly fixed-rate, QT has significantly increased the supply of these securities to the market. New borrowing in fixed rates as a share of their respective outstanding amounts in 2023 was 1% for Canada, 2% for the United States and 6% for the euro area and the United Kingdom. Due to QT, the extra supply to the market rose to 9% of this figure in Canada, 6% in the United States, 7% in the euro area and 9% in the United Kingdom (Figure 1.21, Panel D).

QT implies more debt for the market to absorb, and unless debt managers alter their issuance strategy, there is also more net duration for the market to absorb.[24] The ATM of central bank holdings is 1 year longer than the ATM of the bonds in the market in Canada and the United States (Figure 1.21, Panel E). The United Kingdom faces additional pressure in terms of duration supply to the market, as the BoE's active QT has led to the sale of bonds with an ATM of close to 20 years.[25]

1.6.1. The investor base of sovereign debt is becoming more price sensitive

In addition to defining the instrument and maturity composition of issuances, another crucial task of public debt management (PDM) is developing a diverse investor base (OECD, 2019[38]). This diversity is key, due to the varying behaviour and investment needs of different investors. It lessens the probability of uniform buying or selling movements, contributing to deeper and more liquid markets. It also enables sovereign issuers to better balance cost and risk trade-offs, with some investors seeking high returns through risk-taking and others preferring more conservative and programmatic strategies. Geographical diversification can further support demand, leaving an issuer less reliant on the macro-financial conditions of specific regions.

Sovereign issuers engage in many activities to develop a stable investor base, including enhancing transparency in debt operations transparency, frequently engaging with investors, diversifying their product offerings, and taking measures to boost market liquidity. A consistent and predictable issuance strategy can play a crucial role in building a stable investor base. Additionally, sovereign issuers from more than 50 countries, of which nearly 30 are in the OECD area, have issued sustainable bonds, with one of their main objectives for doing so being the diversification of the investor base (as discussed further in Chapter 3).

In the past 15 years, the investor base for OECD general government debt has shifted significantly as a result of the greater role of domestic central banks in these markets. Their share of sovereign bond holdings jumped from 5% in 2008 to 27% in 2022 (Figure 1.22, Panel A), reflecting their increased purchases of new and existing government bonds against a backdrop of growing supply. Simultaneously, other domestic investors' shares were reduced, with domestic banks' holdings dropping from 46% to 33% and the holdings by the non-banking sector declining from 20% to 14%.

Foreign investors' shares fluctuated between 28% and 31% during 2008-19, but fell in 2020 as central banks accelerated or re-introduced QE programmes in response to the pandemic. Foreign official investors' shares dropped from a high of 17% in 2013 to 12% in 2022. This coincides with diverging growth rates between the OECD government debt stock and global foreign exchange (FX) reserves (Figure 1.22, Panel D); Although both grew at a similar rate between 2008-15, FX reserves rose by 9% in 2015-23, while the OECD debt stock surged by 57% in the same period (Figure 1.22, Panel C).[26]

Compared to the period 2008-22, survey responses indicate that in 2023 there was a partial reversal in the investor base composition trends, with a decrease in the share of domestic central banks and a rise in the non-bank financial sector's share (Figure 1.22, Panel B). In 2023, the share of domestic central banks' sovereign debt decreased in 16 countries, while it increased for domestic asset managers and hedge funds in 11 countries, for institutional investors increased in 9, and for of other investors increased in 10. This indicates a growing absorption of government bond supply by the non-banking financial sector in times of monetary tightening and rising yields (Figure 1.22, Panel D).

Figure 1.22. Composition of OECD sovereign debt investor base

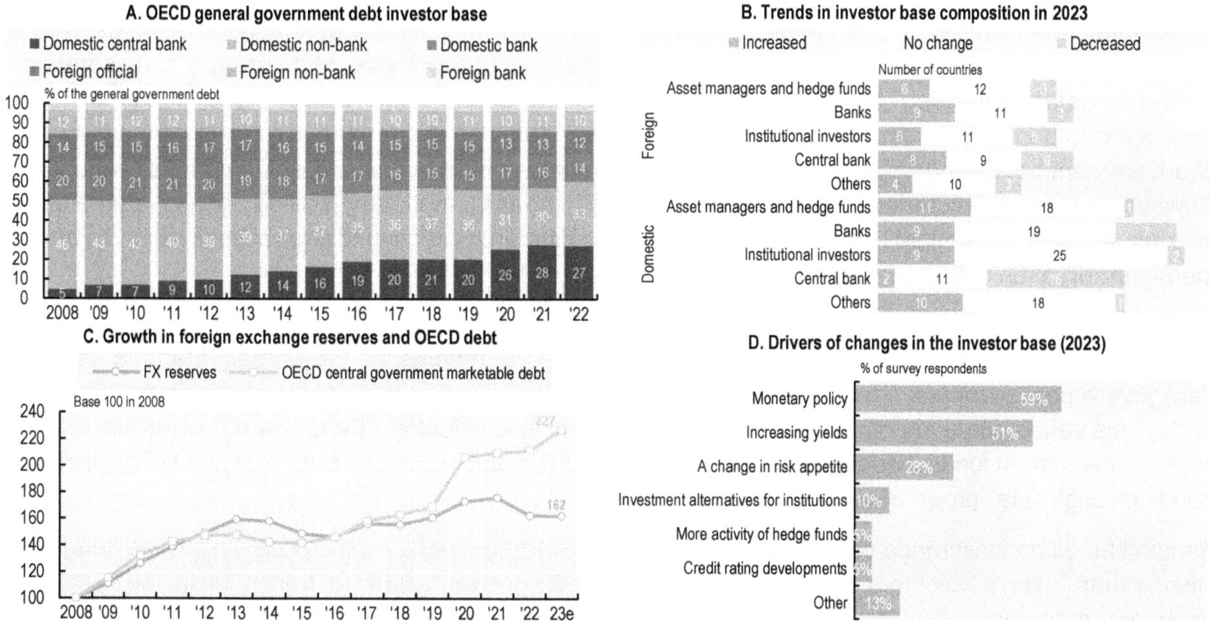

Note: Panel A refers to the average across OECD countries weighted by their debt stock from the SBO.
Source: 2023 OECD Survey on Secondary Market Developments; 2023 Survey on Central Government Marketable Debt and Borrowing; LSEG; (OECD, 2023[1]); (IMF, 2023[39]; IMF, 2023[40]; IMF, 2023[2]); national authorities' websites.

As QT progresses, it remains unclear which investors will absorb the additional supply of government bonds and how maturity structures and yields will evolve. This will affect the cost and risk profiles of sovereign debt portfolios. The change will not simply be a shift back to the investor base before the major QE programmes which began in 2008. Currently, the OECD central government marketable debt stock, as a share of GDP, stands at around 83%, compared to 53% in 2008, with the 30pp increase largely accounted for by central banks' bond holdings. As a result of QT and continued high borrowing, the market will have to absorb a record level of net supply, with potential consequences for borrowing costs and maturity profiles.

The composition of sovereign debt investors is expected to increasingly include more price sensitive investors, which could put upward pressure on yields. This contrasts with central banks, whose acquisition of government bonds is largely detached from the current bond prices as they are guided by mandates for price stability. Likewise, under QT, central banks tend to be price insensitive sellers, ready to sell if required by their mandates, irrespective of market prices.[27]

Foreign investors' medium-term demand may rise as the current high FX hedging costs decline, but their demand for hard currency could decrease if economies perform more robustly and avoid a downturn. Tightening cycles typically elevate FX hedging costs, as investors need to hedge against a stronger currency amid growing interest rate differentials and heightened FX volatility. Furthermore, if a soft economic landing materialises, it might boost the appeal of government securities in weaker currencies compared to hard currencies, reducing the demand for the sovereign debt of most OECD countries. Conversely, a downturn would likely result in "safe havens", such as Germany and the United States, benefitting from a "flight to safety", which can translate into lower borrowing costs.

Domestic banks' demand for government securities is influenced by the relevant regulations. Post-GFC Basel III's enhanced liquidity requirements caused a notable rise in banks' demand for these securities in the last decade but also reduced the likelihood of new regulations, given that the banking sector has largely remained resilient during the ongoing monetary tightening cycle (FSB, 2023[41]). Yet, following the banking turmoil in the first semester of 2023, the United States is contemplating new capital treatment rules, which could elevate the demand for government securities by US-based institutions (CRS, 2023[42]).

Banks often meet liquidity requirements by holding government securities or central bank reserves, basing their choice on yield levels (Eren, Schrimpf and Xia, 2023[43]), duration risk, and currency considerations. During monetary tightening, duration risks prompt banks to opt for bank reserves over bonds, although they revert to bonds under improved funding conditions. Thus, banks are not expected to be major buyers of government bonds under QT, as evidenced by the decrease in their government bond holdings in 2022. However, in the medium-term, with a potential shift towards monetary easing, banks' demand for government securities might rise, provided that the yield differential relative to central bank reserves offsets the higher duration risk.

As foreign investors and domestic banks reduce their holdings of government securities during the tightening cycle, the domestic non-bank sector is expected to emerge as the primary marginal buyer of new government securities. Thus, the trend witnessed in 2022-23 is expected to persist with the tightening cycle. This varied group encompasses the most price sensitive investors (Fang, Hard and Lewis, 2023[44]) such as investment funds, hedge funds, and households. The latter bought a record amount of government bonds through retail programs in 2022-23 (Box 1.2).

Pension funds and insurance companies' demand for government bonds will probably align with long-term yield trends. These investors seek higher yields and longer maturities to match their liabilities. Yet, uncertain macroeconomic conditions in 2023 impacted demand for long-duration bonds in some countries.[28] Regulatory mandates for pension funds to maintain minimum government bond holdings can also influence their holdings, but any such regulatory changes are not planned in the near future (OECD, 2023[45]).

Among investment funds, MMFs, open-ended funds (OEFs), and hedge funds contribute to market liquidity, but can also be the cause of instability. MMFs, who are often major investors in short-term government securities, may quickly sell assets to fulfil investor redemptions in periods of market stress. OEFs face liquidity mismatches due to their daily redemption promises and holding of bonds, which can result in fire sales at the onset of crises to avoid selling later and sustaining large losses. Hedge funds, which may be required to rapidly unwind their leveraged positions in times of heightened volatility, can also exacerbate selling pressures.[29]

Sovereign issuers regard the non-bank financial sector's involvement in bond markets as a contributor to liquidity but note its potential to amplify market shock sensitivity.[30] These entities invest in government bonds under a different regulatory framework than banks. Moreover, as they are not primary dealers, they are not obligated to maintain liquidity, and they offer two-way pricing at all times. Thus, in times of heightened volatility, they can sometimes add to market instability. This became apparent in 2020, when central banks stepped in to purchase a large number of government securities, and during the UK 'mini-budget' crisis in Autumn 2022, which was exacerbated by the leveraged positions of pension funds.[31]

If the non-bank financial sector becomes an even more significant holder of government bonds, supporting continued liquidity in times of heightened market stress is crucial. These liquidity challenges can also create financial stability concerns, with central banks and regulators considering steps to prevent the need for direct interventions to stabilise markets, as was required in 2020.[32] This is vital for sovereign issuers, as fire sales of government securities could result in higher cost of borrowing or more drastically prevent them from accessing liquidity during crises.

1.6.2. Market liquidity has improved in 2023 but volatility remains high

Liquidity in the secondary market for government bonds is essential to support primary market access and minimise sovereign borrowing costs over the long run. Therefore, liquidity conditions are among the most important factors that are actively monitored by sovereign DMOs (OECD, 2018[46]). The share of DMOs that reported a decline in liquidity fell from its record high level of 63% in 2022 to 19% in 2023 (Figure 1.23). Sovereign issuers assessed geopolitical risks and the slowdown in global trade as the main factors negatively impacting liquidity in 2023. Unlike 2022, geopolitical risks outweighed macroeconomic uncertainties in terms of their impact on liquidity (Figure 1.23, Panel B).

Figure 1.23. Recent liquidity trends and their driving factors

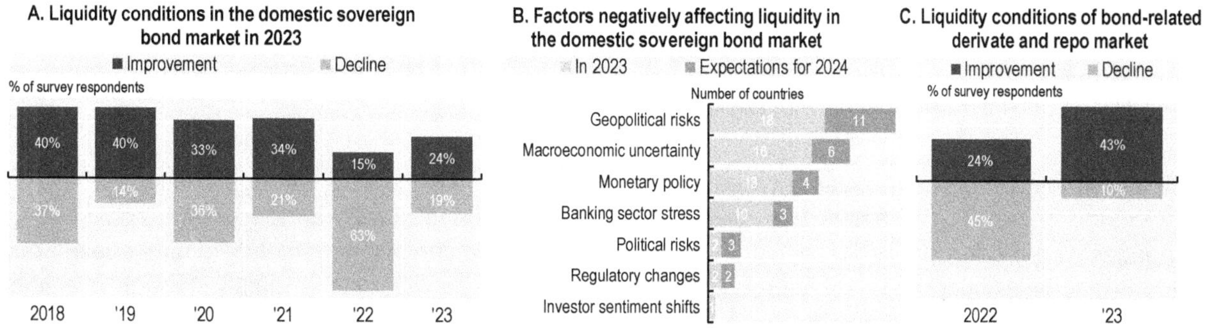

Note: Panels A and B cover all OECD countries with a single answer while Panel C only cover the countries that answered the respective survey question with the respective liquidity movement.
Source: 2023 OECD Survey on Secondary Market Developments.

Liquidity in the repo and derivative bond markets in 2023 improved in a larger number of OECD countries compared to those experiencing a decline, a notable shift from the pattern for 2022 (Figure 1.23, Panel C). These markets experienced increased liquidity mainly due to QT, increasing the free float (i.e. the share of debt held by the market) and therefore the availability of government securities for use in repo and derivative hedging. However, some issuers with negative net borrowings did not report improvements in liquidity in their markets, implying that their reduced borrowings may have offset the increase in collateral released by central banks into the market for repo and derivative transactions.[33]

DMOs assess market liquidity using multiple indicators such as bid-ask spreads, market turnover, volatility, and auction-related metrics. In 2023 these data points have presented somewhat conflicting signals (Figure 1.24).

Bid-ask spreads have nearly returned to pre-pandemic levels. In the US, bid-ask spreads have been stable, but are still slightly wider than pre-pandemic levels; in the euro area, the bid-ask spreads of the 30-year benchmark tightened significantly; in Japan, they widened in 2023, particularly at the long end of the curve with the BoJ's more flexible approach to yield curve control; whilst in the UK they tightened at the long end.

Volatility in the OECD area remains above pre-pandemic levels, notably at the long end of the yield curve. Many OECD countries noted that structural changes in markets have contributed more to higher volatility, as well as ongoing macroeconomic and geopolitical uncertainties, and a more price sensitive investor base. Despite this heightened volatility and greater borrowing needs, bond auctions in the OECD were predominantly oversubscribed, indicating robust investor interest.[34]

Figure 1.24. Recent changes in liquidity indicators

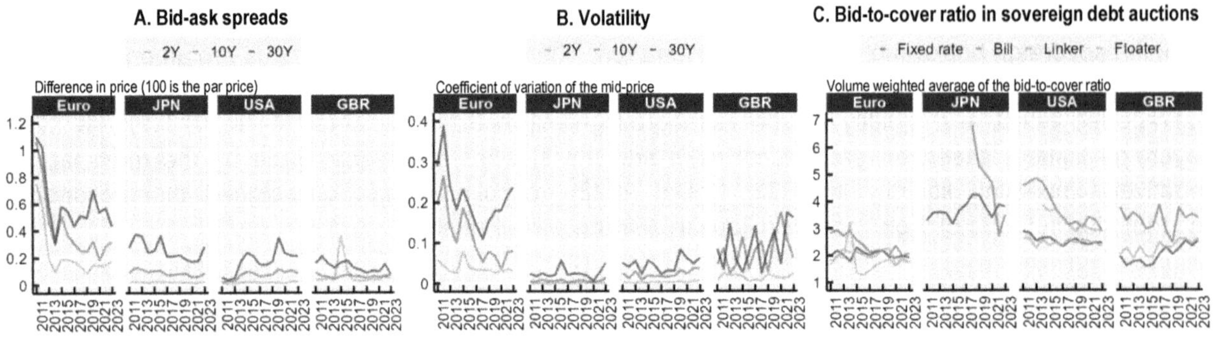

Note: The bid-ask spreads denote the annual average for each benchmark. Volatility is measured as the annual average coefficient of variation (i.e., the ratio of standard deviation to the mean) of the mid-price by benchmark. The bid-to-cover ratio is an average weighted by issuance volume – for the euro area, this ratio represents the median of weighted averages across countries to remove outlier effects.
Source: LSEG and OECD calculations.

Auction metrics are of great importance as sovereign issuers mainly borrow through auctions where, in most cases, only primary dealers can directly participate.[35] This structure contrasts with conventional exchanges where participants directly trade, as seen in equity and derivative markets. Primary dealers buy bonds in auctions, operate in the interdealer market, and engage with clients mainly through over-the-counter operations.[36]

Thus, the role of primary dealers in buying and distributing bonds is vital for liquidity. As they are mostly banks (Figure 1.25, Panel A),[37] they face stricter post-GFC regulations under Basel III, leading to increased balance sheet constraints that could impact their warehousing capability (Figure 1.25, Panel B). With the obligation to maintain capital against settlement risk, a rise in trading volume elevates capital requirements. In scenarios where dealers lack adequate capital or cannot promptly secure it, their ability to trade is constrained. This is evidenced in the United States, where liquidity dropped when the balance sheets of primary dealers in treasuries were heavily utilised (Duffie et al., 2023[47]).[38] Under the previous QE regime, these constraints were less of a factor, but they are exacerbated when volatility is higher, and in particular, when having to absorb the extra supply created by QT.

Figure 1.25. Primary dealers' eligibility and factors affecting their profitability

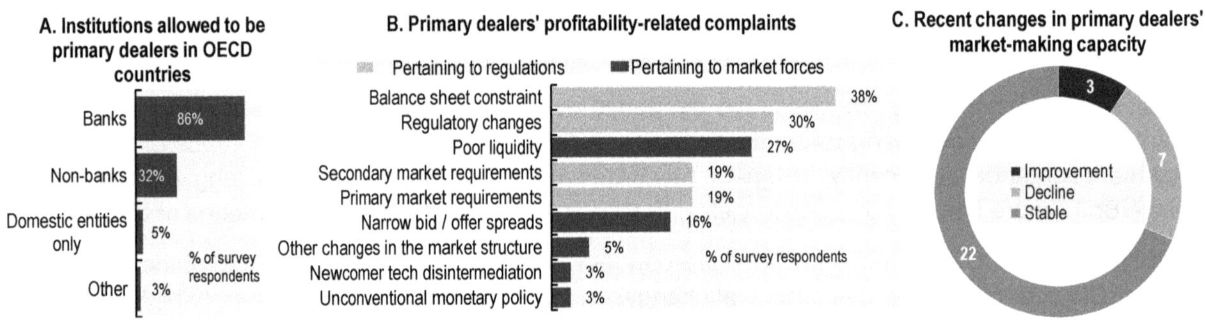

Note: Chile, Costa Rica, Estonia and Switzerland don't have primary dealership systems.
Source: 2023 OECD Survey on Secondary Market Developments.

Despite heightened volatility and borrowing requirements, primary dealers have remained able to fulfil their roles. Most OECD countries reported stability in primary dealers' market-making capacity (Figure 1.25, Panel C), with downturns reported only in periods of heightened market stress. The approach of selecting dealers to promote competition and enhance market activities has proven effective.[39] To address the current demanding context, DMOs in 8 OECD countries are adjusting dealers' performance evaluation standards, increasing their privileges in 4 countries, and reducing their obligations in 2.

Common measures adopted to help support market liquidity include regular taps of existing securities, securities lending facilities, enhanced market communication and buyback/switch operations (these were deemed the most effective measures – Figure 1.26).[40] Recent initiatives include the US's new buyback program which starts in 2024 (US DMO, 2023[48]),[41] and the Swiss DMO's plan to build a government bond portfolio for collaterised money markets.

Tapping lines when rates are higher brings immediate cost but accrues longer-term benefits. In periods of higher rates, tapping bonds trading below par means that the government accrues more debt than the funds it raises, increasing net debt levels. However, tapping leads to lower interest expenses due to depressed liquidity premiums, fulfilling DMOs' long-term mandates of aiming for low borrowing costs under controlled risks.

Security lending enables DMOs to stabilise yield curves, standardise repo rates, supply collateral and cash for market making, reduce bid-ask spreads, and access the repo market for their own cash management purposes. The main objective is to aid the market without becoming a dominant player, with large issuers often being more active. Large interventions are generally limited to exceptional cases. The benefits of these facilities are widely considered to outweigh their operational costs (e.g. IT, human resources and accounting).

Figure 1.26. Measures to support market liquidity

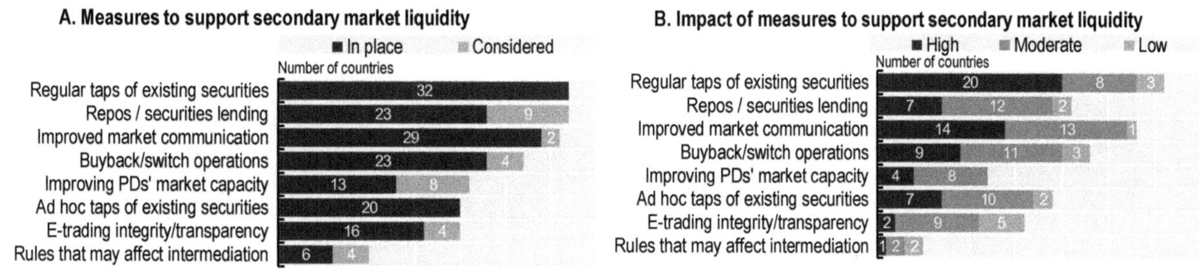

Source: 2023 OECD Survey on Secondary Market Developments.

Anticipating possible market changes due to QT, some sovereign issuers are discussing a wider adoption of central clearing in government bond markets. This involves a Central Clearing Counterparty (CCP) acting as the intermediary to both buyers and sellers. Currently, government bond markets, unlike their repo and derivative counterparts, are mostly not centrally cleared. In France, Germany, the United Kingdom and the United States, only a negligible volume of transactions are centrally cleared; in Italy and Japan, transactions are centrally cleared for inter-dealer trades, but not for dealer-to-client trades (FSB, 2022[49]).

Central clearing offers the benefits of decreasing the pressure on primary dealers' balance sheets and ensuring access to central bank aid in the event of a crisis. By netting opposing transactions, a CCP can reduce settlement obligations, evidenced by the potential reductions of up to 53% in the United Kingdom (Baranova et al., 2023[50]), and up to 70% in both the United States (Fleming and Keane, 2021[51]) and Canada (Chen et al., 2022[52]) during the pandemic. CCPs' ability to utilise central bank reserves and security lending facilities further enables effective trading during such periods, acting as a backstop for defaults and transaction clearing. Additionally, higher pre- and post-trade transparency in combination with central clearing can enable all-to-all trading in government bond markets. This framework is currently only present in Israel (Kutai, Nathan and Wittwer, 2023[53]) but it could further increase liquidity in other markets (Chaboud et al., 2022[54]).

However, structural changes in government bond markets, such as greater central clearing and all-to-all trading, require careful consideration due to the potential risks they pose to the current system. Firstly, some market participants often prefer direct dealer relationships for advantageous pricing and discreet handling of large-scale trades, with primary dealers incentivised to engage even in times of acute stress due to customer loyalty. Secondly, these reforms could lead to a concentration of risks in CCPs. Thirdly, while reforms could enhance dealers' intermediation capacity, this additional balance sheet room might be diverted to other business areas, potentially affecting government bond market liquidity. Thus, structural reforms should be approached cautiously, incrementally, with long-term aims and with comprehensive market consultation, as is the current practice of sovereign issuers. The recent announcement in the US by the SEC that all trading in US Treasuries should be centrally cleared by 2026 is a huge development in the largest and most important bond market in the world.

Against the backdrop of changing market conditions and investor dynamics, particular attention needs to be given to monitoring and supporting the liquidity in government securities markets. Sovereign debt management offices should monitor market conditions closely and remain vigilant in using a variety of tools to support liquidity, including through enhanced market communication, tapping existing securities and conducting buyback and switch operations, as well as providing security lending facilities,

References

Acalin, J. and L. Ball (2023), "Did the U.S. really grow out of its World War II debt?", *National Bureau of Economic Research*, Vol. Working Paper No. 31577, http://www.nber.org/papers/w31577. [20]

Bank of England (2022), "Asset Purchase Facility: Gilt Sales", *Market Notice 1 September 2022*, https://www.bankofengland.co.uk/markets/market-notices/2022/september/apf-gilt-sales-market-notice-1-september-2022 (accessed on 16 January 2024). [66]

Baranova, Y. et al. (2023), "The potential impact of broader central clearing on dealer balance sheet capacity: a case study of UK gilt and gilt repo markets", *BoE Staff Working Paper No. 1,026*, https://www.bankofengland.co.uk/-/media/boe/files/working-paper/2023/the-potential-impact-of-broader-central-clearing-on-dealer-balance-sheet-capacity.pdf. [50]

Belgian Debt Agency (2023), *Bons d'Etat*, https://www.debtagency.be/fr/productsbeinfo. [13]

Belhocine, N., A. Bhatia and J. Frie (2023), "Raising Rates with a Large Balance Sheet: The Eurosystem's Net Income and its Fiscal Implications", *IMF Working Paper 23/145*, https://www.imf.org/en/Publications/WP/Issues/2023/07/07/Raising-Rates-with-a-Large-Balance-Sheet-The-Eurosystems-Net-Income-and-its-Fiscal-535549. [30]

Bell, S. et al. (2023), "Why are central banks reporting losses? Does it matter?", *BIS Bulletin 68*, https://www.bis.org/publ/bisbull68.htm. [28]

BIS (2023), "Central bank asset purchases in response to the Covid-19 crisis", *Committee on the Global Financial System Papers No. 68*, https://www.bis.org/publ/cgfs68.pdf. [35]

BIS (2023), *Central bank policy rates*, https://www.bis.org/statistics/cbpol.htm (accessed on 20 December 2023). [21]

Bjellerup, M. and J. Rådahl (2023), "Debt Office Commentary: Long-term conditions for debt management", *Swedish National Debt Office*, Vol. 2023 Number 3, https://www.riksgalden.se/contentassets/ea257dc12453430186b47e2bcfe20376/debt-office-commentary-long-term-conditions-for-debt-management.pdf. [3]

Blanchard, O., Á. Leandro and J. Zettelmeyer (2021), "Redesigning EU Fiscal Rules: From Rules to Standards", *Economic Policy*, Vol. 36/106, https://doi.org/10.1093/epolic/eiab003. [68]

BoC (2022), "Understanding quantitative easing", *Bank of Canada*, https://www.bankofcanada.ca/2022/06/understanding-quantitative-easing/#:~:text=QE%20helps%20stabilize%20the%20economy,interest%20they%20pay%20to%20bondholders. [32]

BoE (2022), "Asset Purchase Facility: Gilt Sales – Market Notice 20 October 2022", *Bank of England*, https://www.bankofengland.co.uk/markets/market-notices/2022/october/asset-purchase-facility-gilt-sales-market-notice-20-october-2022. [37]

Boitreau, S. and L. Secunho (2020), "Retail investors in government debt: Can fintech bring about cheaper, more inclusive programs?", *World Bank Blog*, https://blogs.worldbank.org/psd/retail-investors-government-debt-can-fintech-bring-about-cheaper-more-inclusive-programs. [9]

BoJ (2023), “Statement on Monetary Policy October 31”, https://www.boj.or.jp/en/mopo/mpmdeci/mpr_2023/k231031a.pdf. [23]

Castro, M. and J. Jordan-Wood (2023), “The Fed’s Remittances to the Treasury: Explaining the 'Deferred Asset”, *Federal Reserve Bank of ST. Louis*, https://www.stlouisfed.org/on-the-economy/2023/nov/fed-remittances-treasury-explaining-deferred-asset. [31]

Chaboud, A. et al. (2022), “All-to-All Trading in the U.S. Treasury Market”, *New York Fed Staff Report No. 1036*, https://www.newyorkfed.org/research/staff_reports/sr1036. [54]

Chen, J. et al. (2022), “Potential netting benefits from expanded central clearing in Canada’s fixed-income market”, *Bank of Canada Staff Analytical Note 2022-8*, https://www.bankofcanada.ca/2022/06/staff-analytical-note-2022-8/. [52]

Cohen, B., H. P. and D. Xia (2018), “Term premia: models and some stylised facts”, *BIS Quarterly Review, September 2018*, https://www.bis.org/publ/qtrpdf/r_qt1809h.htm. [22]

CRS (2023), “Bank Capital Requirements: Basel III Endgame”, *Congressional Research Service*, https://crsreports.congress.gov/product/pdf/R/R47855. [42]

Duffie, D. et al. (2023), “Dealer Capacity and U.S. Treasury Market Functionality”, *New York Fed Staff Report No. 1070*, https://doi.org/10.59576/sr.1070. [47]

EC (2023), “Commission adopts report on the functioning of the Money Market Funds Regulation (MMF)”, *News Article*, https://finance.ec.europa.eu/news/commission-adopts-report-functioning-money-market-funds-regulation-mmf-2023-07-20_en. [62]

ECB (2023), “Overall amount of unrealised losses in euro area banks’ bond portfolios contained”, *Press Release*, https://www.bankingsupervision.europa.eu/press/pr/date/2023/html/ssm.pr230728_1~4d466b8b80.en.html. [25]

ECB (2023), “Quantitative tightening: rationale and market impact”, *European Central Bank Speech*, https://www.ecb.europa.eu/press/key/date/2023/html/ecb.sp230302~41273ad467.en.html. [33]

Eren, E., A. Schrimpf and F. Xia (2023), “The demand for government debt”, *BIS Working Paper No. 1105*, https://www.bis.org/publ/work1105.htm. [43]

Escolano, J. (2010), “A Practical Guide to Public Debt Dynamics, Fiscal Sustainability, and Cyclical Adjustment of Budgetary Aggregates”, *IMF Technical Notes and Manuals*, https://www.imf.org/external/pubs/ft/tnm/2010/tnm1002.pdf. [55]

European Parliament (2023), “Debt sustainability analysis as an anchor in EU fiscal rules”, *Economic Governance and EMU Scrutiny Unit*, https://www.europarl.europa.eu/RegData/etudes/IDAN/2023/741504/IPOL_IDA(2023)741504_EN.pdf. [60]

Fang, X., B. Hard and K. Lewis (2023), “Who holds sovereign debt and why it matters”, *BIS Working Papers No. 1099*, https://www.bis.org/publ/work1099.pdf. [44]

FCA (2022), “Resilience of Money Market Funds”, *UK Financial Conduct Authority*, https://www.fca.org.uk/publications/discussion-papers/dp22-1-resilience-money-market-funds. [63]

Fed (2022), “Plans for Reducing the Size of the Federal Reserve’s Balance Sheet”, *Board of Governors of the Federal Reserve System*, https://www.federalreserve.gov/newsevents/pressreleases/monetary20220504b.htm. [36]

Fleming, M. and F. Keane (2021), “The Netting Efficiencies of Marketwide Central Clearing”, *New York Fed Staff Report No. 964*, https://www.newyorkfed.org/research/staff_reports/sr964. [51]

FSB (2023), “Promoting Global Financial Stability”, *2023 FSB Annual Report*, https://www.fsb.org/wp-content/uploads/P111023.pdf. [41]

FSB (2023), “Thematic Peer Review on Money Market Fund Reforms: Summary Terms of Reference and request for public feedback”, *Annoucement*, https://www.fsb.org/2023/08/thematic-peer-review-on-money-market-fund-reforms-summary-terms-of-reference-and-request-for-public-feedback/. [64]

FSB (2022), “Enhancing the Resilience of Non-Bank Financial Intermediation”, *Progress report*, https://www.fsb.org/2022/11/enhancing-the-resilience-of-non-bank-financial-intermediation-progress-report-2/. [65]

FSB (2022), “Liquidity in Core Government Bond Markets”, *Report*, https://www.fsb.org/2022/10/liquidity-in-core-government-bond-markets/. [49]

Garcia-Macia, D. (2023), “The Effects of Inflation on Public Finances”, *IMF Working Paper WP/23/93*, https://www.imf.org/en/Publications/WP/Issues/2023/05/05/The-Effects-of-Inflation-on-Public-Finances-533099. [67]

Government of Canada (2022), *Update on the 2022-23 Debt Management Strategy*, https://www.budget.canada.ca/fes-eea/2022/report-rapport/anx2-en.html. [8]

IMF (2023), “Foreign Exchange Reserves”, *IMF Data*, https://data.imf.org/?sk=e6a5f467-c14b-4aa8-9f6d-5a09ec4e62a4. [39]

IMF (2023), “IMF Sovereign Debt Investor Base for Advanced Economies”, *IMF Data*, https://www.imf.org/-/media/Websites/IMF/imported-datasets/external/pubs/ft/wp/2012/Data/_wp12284.ashx. [40]

IMF (2023), *World Economic Outlook (October 2023)*, https://www.imf.org/external/datamapper/NGDP_RPCH@WEO/OEMDC/ADVEC/WEOWORLD (accessed on 1 December 2023). [2]

Italian Ministry of Economy and Finance (2023), “Press releases”, *MeF Website*, https://www.mef.gov.it/en/ufficio-stampa/comunicati/2023/index.html. [10]

Kutai, A., D. Nathan and M. Wittwer (2023), “Exchanges for Government Bonds? Evidence during COVID-19”, *Bank of Israel*, https://papers.ssrn.com/sol3/papers.cfm?abstract_id=3882548. [53]

Lybek, T. (2023), “Hungarian Monetary Policy Operations Before, During, and After the Pandemic: Hungary”, *IMF*, https://www.elibrary.imf.org/view/journals/018/2023/005/article-A001-en.xml. [59]

Ministry of Finance of Japan (2023), “Debt management report”, *MoF website*, https://www.mof.go.jp/english/policy/jgbs/publication/debt_management_report/index.htm. [11]

National Savings & Investments (2023), , *Annual report*, https://nsandi-corporate.com/performance/annual-reports. [12]

OECD (2024), *OECD Economic Outlook, Interim Report February 2024: Strengthening the Foundations for Growth*, OECD Publishing, Paris, https://doi.org/10.1787/0fd73462-en. [16]

OECD (2023), *Government at a Glance 2023*, OECD Publishing, Paris, https://doi.org/10.1787/3d5c5d31-en. [18]

OECD (2023), *OECD Economic Outlook, Volume 2023 Issue 1*, OECD Publishing, Paris, https://doi.org/10.1787/ce188438-en. [26]

OECD (2023), *OECD Economic Outlook, Volume 2023 Issue 2*, OECD Publishing, Paris, https://doi.org/10.1787/7a5f73ce-en. [1]

OECD (2023), *OECD Economic Surveys: Israel 2023*, OECD Publishing, Paris, https://doi.org/10.1787/901365a6-en. [34]

OECD (2023), *OECD Sovereign Borrowing Outlook 2023*, OECD Publishing, Paris, https://doi.org/10.1787/09b4cfba-en. [24]

OECD (2023), *Pensions at a Glance 2023: OECD and G20 Indicators*, OECD Publishing, Paris, https://doi.org/10.1787/678055dd-en. [45]

OECD (2022), *OECD Economic Outlook, Volume 2022 Issue 2*, OECD Publishing, https://www.oecd-ilibrary.org/economics/oecd-economic-outlook/volume-2022/issue-2_f6da2159-en. [4]

OECD (2019), *OECD Sovereign Borrowing Outlook 2019*, OECD Publishing, Paris, https://doi.org/10.1787/aa7aad38-en. [38]

OECD (2018), *OECD Sovereign Borrowing Outlook 2018*, OECD Publishing, Paris, https://doi.org/10.1787/sov_b_outlk-2018-en. [46]

Portuguese Treasury and Debt Management Agency (2023), "Government Debt Statistics", *IGCP*, https://www.igcp.pt/en/1-4-399/statistics/government-debt/. [15]

Rawdanowicz, Ł. et al. (2021), "Constraints and demands on public finances: Considerations of resilient fiscal policy", *OECD Economics Department Working Papers*, No. 1694, OECD Publishing, Paris, https://doi.org/10.1787/602500be-en. [19]

RBA (2022), "From QE to QT – The next phase in the Reserve Bank's Bond Purchase Program", *Reserve Bank of Australia Speech*, https://www.rba.gov.au/speeches/2022/sp-ag-2022-05-23.html. [58]

RBNZ (2022), "Reserve Bank details planned sales of New Zealand Government Bonds", *Reserve Bank of New Zealand*, https://www.rbnz.govt.nz/hub/domestic-markets-media-releases/reserve-bank-details-planned-sales-of-new-zealand-government-bonds. [56]

Reis, R. (2013), "The Mystique Surrounding the Central Bank's Balance Sheet", *American Economic Review* 103(3), pp. 135–140, https://doi.org/10.1257/aer.103.3.135. [27]

SRB (2022), "Press Releases", *Sveriges Riksbank*, https://www.riksbank.se/en-gb/press-and-published/notices-and-press-releases/press-releases/2022/policy-rate-raised-by-1-percentage-point/. [57]

TBAC (2023), "Explaining the recent market moves across the Treasury yield curve", *TBAC Presentation*, https://home.treasury.gov/system/files/221/TBACCharge1Q42023.pdf. [5]

TBAC (2023), "Outlook for demand for US Treasuries", *TBAC Presentation*, https://home.treasury.gov/system/files/221/TBACCharge2Q42023.pdf. [6]

UK DMO (2024), "Minutes of annual consultation meetings with GEMMs and gilt investors held at HM Treasury on 29 January 2023", *The UK Debt Management Office's financing remit 2024-25*, https://www.dmo.gov.uk/media/rihkgdsg/sa300124.pdf. [7]

UK Office for Budget Responsibility (2023), "Economic and fiscal outlook", https://obr.uk/efo/economic-and-fiscal-outlook-november-2023/. [29]

US DMO (2023), "Treasury's Current Views on the Operational Design of a Regular Buyback Program", *The Department of the Treasury*, https://home.treasury.gov/system/files/221/TreasurySupplementalQRQ32023.pdf. [48]

US SEC (2023), "SEC Adopts Money Market Fund Reforms and Amendments to Form PF Reporting Requirements for Large Liquidity Fund Advisers", *Press Release*, https://www.sec.gov/news/press-release/2023-129. [61]

US Treasury (2023), *Upcoming Auctions*, https://www.treasurydirect.gov/auctions/upcoming/ (accessed on 1 November 2023). [17]

US Treasury Department (2023), "Securities issued in TreasuryDirect", *Fiscal Data Treasury Website*, https://fiscaldata.treasury.gov/datasets/securities-issued-in-treasurydirect/. [14]

Annex 1.A. Methodology for data collection and classification

Definitions and concepts used in the Sovereign Borrowing Outlook Survey

The Borrowing Outlook survey collects gross borrowing requirements, redemption and outstanding debt amounts with a breakdown of these items by maturity, currency, interest rate types and Environmental, Social and Governance (ESG)-labelling (i.e. sustainable bonds). It also collects data on DMOs' holdings, NextGenerationEU loans and country-specific methodological aspects. It uses the core definition of sovereign debt, called 'central government marketable debt', mainly due to its comparability and collectability. This measure, directly linked to the central government budget financing, enabled the OECD to collect not only for realisations but also for estimates of government borrowing requirements, funding strategies, as well as outstanding debt with instruments, maturity and currency types.

Coverage of institutions: Central Government

The coverage of institutions by debt statistics varies from public sector to central government. Public sector represents the broadest institutional coverage, as it includes local governments, state funds financial and non-financial public corporations as well as central government debt. The general government definition, which is used for example by the OECD System of National Accounts (SNA), consists of central government, state and local governments and social security funds controlled by these units. Central government covers all departments, offices, establishments and other bodies classified under general government, which are agencies or an instrument of the central authority of a country, except for separately organised social security funds or extra-budgetary funds. In terms of layers of coverage of institutions, central government stands out as the core definition. Debt of the central government is raised, managed and retired by the national DMOs on behalf of the central government. Hence, the advantage of this relatively narrow definition of debt is that it enables countries to provide comparable figures, in particular for the purpose of estimations.

Coverage of types of debt: Marketable debt

In terms of instruments, liabilities can be in the form of debt securities, loans, insurance, pensions and standardised guarantee schemes, currency and deposits, and other accounts payable. Debt items can be classified as marketable and non-marketable debt. While marketable debt is defined as financial securities and instruments that can be bought and sold in the secondary market, non-marketable debt is not transferable. For example, bonds and bills issued in capital markets are marketable debt; multilateral and bilateral loans from the official sector are non-marketable debt.

The Borrowing Outlook survey focuses on marketable debt instruments, while most government debt statistics (e.g. OECD SNA, EU Maastricht debt, and IMF Public Sector Debt Statistics) cover both marketable and non-marketable debt items. OECD governments are financed predominantly by marketable debt instruments. This is a central definition for every analysis concerning various issues around debt management including borrowing conditions, portfolio composition, investor preferences and market liquidity. An advantage of using this definition is to indicate to investors which instruments are available to trade in the secondary markets, and which are not. Another reason is to enable the issuer to calculate different characteristics of the debt, such as duration or time to maturity, which in the case of non-marketable debt would present difficulties.

Terminology

- The standardised gross borrowing requirement (GBR) for a year is equal to the net borrowing requirement during that year plus the redemptions of long-term instruments in the same year and the redemptions of short-term instruments issued in the previous year. Therefore, this indicator captures the issuances of all securities excluding those that were issued and redeemed in the same calendar year. In other words, the size of GBR in the calendar year amounts to how much the DMO needs to issue in nominal terms to fully pay back maturing debt issued in previous years plus the net cash borrowing requirement through any issuance mechanism.
- Net borrowing requirement (NBR) is the amount required to finance the current budget deficit. While the refinancing of redemptions is a matter of rolling over the same exposure as before, NBR refers to new exposure in the market, or new borrowing.
- Gross debt, or debt stock, corresponds to the outstanding debt issuance at the end of calendar years. This measure does not take the valuation effects from inflation and exchange rate movements; thus, it is equal to the total nominal amount that needs to be redeemed.
- Redemptions refers to the total amount of the principal repayments of the corresponding debt including the principal payments paid through buy-back operations in a calendar year.

Regional aggregates

- Total OECD area denotes the following 38 countries: Australia, Austria, Belgium, Canada, Chile, Colombia, Costa Rica, Czechia, Denmark, Estonia, Finland, France, Germany, Greece, Hungary, Iceland, Ireland, Israel, Italy, Japan, Korea, Latvia, Lithuania, Luxembourg, Mexico, the Netherlands, New Zealand, Norway, Poland, Portugal, the Slovak Republic, Slovenia, Spain, Sweden, Switzerland, Türkiye, the United Kingdom and the United States.
- OECD accession countries include Bulgaria, Brazil, Croatia, Peru and Romania.
- The G7 includes seven countries: Canada, France, Germany, Italy, Japan, the United Kingdom and the United States.
- The OECD euro area includes 17 Member countries: Austria, Belgium, Estonia, Finland, France, Germany, Greece, Ireland, Italy, Latvia, Lithuania, Luxembourg, the Netherlands, Portugal, the Slovak Republic, Slovenia and Spain. The euro (EUR) is the official currency of 20 out of 27 EU Member countries. These countries are collectively known as the euro area. The euro area countries are Austria, Belgium, Croatia, Cyprus, Estonia, Finland, France, Germany, Greece, Ireland, Italy, Latvia, Lithuania, Luxembourg, Malta, the Netherlands, Portugal, the Slovak Republic, Slovenia and Spain. In this report, the euro area covers only the countries that are simultaneously in the euro area and in the OECD.
- In this publication, from a public debt management perspective, the Emerging OECD group (i.e. OECD emerging-market economies) is defined as including seven countries: Chile, Colombia, Costa Rica, Hungary, Mexico, Poland and Türkiye.

Calculations and data sources

- Estimates that are presented as a percentage of GDP, for consistency reasons, use GDP estimates from the last OECD Economic Outlook in the previous year (so November 2003 for this publication) and are calculated using nominal GDP data.
- Debt is measured as the face value of current outstanding central government debt. Face value, the undiscounted amount of principal to be repaid, does not change except when there is a new

issue of an existing instrument. This coincides with the original promise (and therefore contractual obligation) of the issuer. DMOs often use face value when they report how much nominal debt will mature in future periods. One important reason for using face value is that it is the standard market practice for quoting and trading specific volumes of a particular instrument.

- Currencies are converted into USD using flexible exchange rates, with the data sourced from LSEG.
- All figures use calendar years unless specified otherwise.
- Aggregate figures for gross borrowing requirements (GBR), net borrowing requirements (NBR), central government marketable debt, redemptions, and debt maturing are compiled from answers to the Borrowing Survey. The OECD Secretariat inserted its own estimates/projections in cases of missing information for 2023 and 2024, using publicly available official information on redemptions and central government budget balances. Where government plans have been announced, but not incorporated into financing plans as of the end of December 2023, they are not included in the projections presented in this publication. Also, the latest estimates of government net lending in the OECD Economic Outlook database are used to estimate some missing data.
- Gross and net borrowing requirements presented in the report follow the standardised method and are net of cash management-related issuances.
- Both the 2023 OECD Survey on Primary Market Developments and the 2023 OECD Survey on Liquidity in Secondary Government Bond Markets were carried out in October 2023.

Revised definitions

- Inflation-linked securities are instruments with coupon and/or principal payments which are linked to an inflation index. The data includes accrued inflation for all years up to and including the current year of the survey as of the reporting date.
- Variable rate notes have a floating or variable interest rate or coupon rate. It is a long-dated debt security whose coupon is refixed periodically on a "refix date" by reference to an independent interest rate index such as SONIA or Euribor. For example, medium and long-term floating rate notes (FRNs, colloquially known as floaters) are debt obligations with variable interest rates that are adjusted periodically (typically every one, three, or six months). The interest rate is usually fixed at a specified spread over one of the interest rate indices. For projections of variable rate debt, the rate at the level of the last settled coupon is used.
- Average term-to-maturity (ATM) figures follow the same coverage described at the beginning of this Annex, with country specific methods detailed below:
    - Germany: Calculation excluding holdings in own stock. Inflation-linked securities weighted with 0.75.
    - Hungary: Data excludes retail securities, locally issued FX bonds, loans and since 2020 also excludes the non-marketable bonds issued to municipalities. Data includes cross-currency swaps.
    - Italy: Liabilities under the Support to mitigate Unemployment Risks in an Emergency and Next Generation EU programmes (which would raise the figure at 7.3) are excluded.
    - Japan: The Ministry of Finance announces ATM, based on Fiscal Year, not Calendar Year. Figures from 2006 to 2022 exclude saving bonds. The figure for 2023 is estimated and includes saving bonds.
    - Netherlands: Numbers are based on outstanding T-Bills and bonds and do not include outstanding commercial paper.

- New Zealand: Figures include only marketable securities (excluding non-marketable securities held by the Reserve Bank of New Zealand and the Earthquake Commission). However, it does include securities held by the RBNZ that were purchased under the large asset purchase program and government bond repurchase.
- Sweden: End of year figures. Time to maturity (uplifted amount at current exchange rate) in years. Includes Government bonds; Inflation-linked bonds; Public bonds, foreign currencies; Green bonds; and T-bills.
- United Kingdom: ATM is weighted by the nominal amounts outstanding of gilts and T-bills issued for debt management purposes, as of the reporting date. Nominal amounts of gilts include government holdings; nominal values of index-linked gilts also include accrued inflation as of the reporting date.

Annex 1.B. Debt decomposition model

Single countries

This chapter adopts a variation of the methodology outlined by Escolano (2010[55]) and uses the equation below to capture the change in debt-to-GDP ratio between time t and t-1:

$$d - d_{(t-1)} = \frac{ip}{(1+y)} * d_{(t-1)} - \frac{\pi}{(1+y)} * d_{(t-1)} - \frac{g}{1+g} * d_{(t-1)} - pb + sf$$

Where:

- *d* is the central government debt stock from the Borrowing Survey expressed as a ratio to GDP from OECD countries (2023[1])
- *ip* is the effective interest rate, expressed as general government gross interest expenses from OECD (2023[1]) in time t as a ratio of *d* in time t-1
- *y* is the nominal GDP growth rate from OECD (2023[1]) between time t and t-1
- *π* is inflation, defined as the change in GDP deflator from OECD (2023[1]) between time t and t-1
- *g* is the real GDP growth rate from OECD (2023[1]) between time t and t-1
- *pb* is the general government's primary balance as a ratio of GDP, both from OECD (2023[1])
- *sf* denotes the stock-flow adjustments

OECD area

For the OECD area decomposition, this chapter uses the equation above with the following variables:

- *d* is the sum of each country's central government debt stock divided by the sum of each country's GDP
- *ip* is the sum of each country's general government gross interest payments divided by the sum of each country's *d* at time t-1
- *y* is the growth rate of the sum of each country's nominal GDP
- *π* is the sum of each country's *π*, weighted by GDP
- *g* is the sum of each country's *g*, weighted by GDP
- *pb* is the sum of each country's general government primary balance, divided by the sum of each country's GDP
- *sf* denotes the stock-flow adjustments

Country figures were converted into US Dollars using the year-end exchange rates, sourced from LSEG.

Further specifications

The debt-to-GDP growth rate encompassed all OECD countries, while factor calculations were limited to countries with available data. For example, interest expense computations excluded CHL, COL, CRI, ISR, MEX, and TUR, representing around 3% of OECD central government marketable debt. Stock-flow adjustments absorbed discrepancies arising from the concurrent use of central and general government data, as well as from data gaps.

Annex 1.C. Effective interest rate calculations

Introduction and data sources

Effective Interest Rates (EIR) represent the ratio of interest payments to debt stock and are estimated under accrual accounting using a combination of data sources. Annual inflation and policy rate data up to 2022 and projections for 2023 are sourced from the OECD Economic Outlook (OECD, 2023[1]); bonds' annual yield to maturity at issuance (YTM) and outstanding amounts as well as foreign exchange (FX) rates are sourced from LSEG; and outstanding amount of debt by country and by type of instrument are sourced from the Borrowing Outlook Survey. The annual interest rates, inflation rates, and YTM are converted to daily values to account for the fact that bonds are issued and redeemed throughout the year. This approach ensures that interest payments are accurately apportioned to reflect the actual period during which the bonds remain outstanding.

Instrument specific EIR computations

Fixed Rate and Short-Term Instruments

$$\mathrm{EIR}_{\mathrm{i}}^{\mathrm{y}} = \mathrm{YTM}_{\mathrm{i}}$$

Variable Rate Instruments

$$\mathrm{EIR}_{\mathrm{i}}^{\mathrm{y}} = \frac{\sum_{d=0}^{D^y}\left(S_i^d \times \left(\frac{\mathrm{YTM}_{\mathrm{i}}}{D^y} + F_i^d\right)\right)}{\sum_{d=0}^{D^y} S_i^{\mathrm{d}}}$$

Inflation-linked Instruments

$$\mathrm{EIR}_{i}^{\mathrm{y}} = \frac{\sum_{d=0}^{D^y}\left(\frac{S_i^d}{D^y} \times \left(\mathrm{YTM}_{\mathrm{i}} + I^Y + I^Y \times \mathrm{YTM}_{\mathrm{i}}\right)\right)}{\sum_{d=0}^{D^y} S_i^{\mathrm{d}}}$$

Where:

EIR_t^y: $Effective\ Interest\ Rate\ for\ debt\ instrument\ i\ for\ year\ y.$

$\mathrm{YTM}_{\mathrm{i}}$: $Annual\ Yield\ to\ Maturity\ at\ issuance\ of\ debt\ instrument\ i.$

S_i^d: $Outstanding\ stock\ of\ debt\ instrument\ i\ in\ day\ d.$

D^y: $Number\ of\ days\ in\ the\ year\ y.$

I^Y: $Inflation\ rate\ for\ year\ y.$

F_i^d: $Daily\ floating\ interest\ rate\ for\ variable\ rate\ debt\ instrument.$

Adjusting Outstanding Amounts Post-Buybacks

The debt stock experiences intra-year variations owing to occurrences such as bond maturities and buybacks. In this context, each bond issuance, inclusive of re-openings, is considered a distinct unit until there is a discernible decrease in the outstanding amount of the bond line. When a reduction in any specific bond line is observed, its effect is systematically apportioned across both the original issuance and any subsequent re-openings in the day of the event. This allocation is executed in proportion to their respective outstanding amounts at that time.

$$S_{b,i}^{d} = S_{b,i}^{d-1} - \left(\frac{S_{b,i}^{d}}{\sum_i S_{b,i}^{d}}\right) \times R_b^d$$

Where:

$S_{b,i}^{d}$: *Outstanding stock of debt instrument i in the day d of the event for instrument i from bond line b.*

R_b^d: *Decline amount in the outstanding amount for the bond line b in the day of the event d.*

Consolidating EIR at the country, instrument, and OECD level

The instrument-level EIR is estimated using a stock-weighted average method. This approach involves multiplying the annual effective yield of each debt instrument by its daily average outstanding stock in the year. Subsequently, for each country and type of instrument, the yields are aggregated and then divided by the debt stock of each instrument sourced from the Borrowing Outlook Survey.

$$EIR_{t,c}^{y} = \frac{\sum_{i,d}\left(YTM_{i,t,c}^{y} \times S_{i,t,c}^{d,y}\right)}{\sum_{i,d} S_{i,t,c}^{d,y}}\ ;\ EIR_c^y = \frac{\sum_t EIR_{t,c}^{y} \times \phi_{t,c}^{y}}{\sum_t \phi_{t,c}^{y}}\ ;\ EIR_t^y = \frac{\sum_{t,c} EIR_{t,c}^{y} \times \phi_{t,c}^{y} \times X_c^y}{\sum_{t,c} \phi_{t,c}^{y} \times X_c^y}\ ;\ W_t^y = \frac{EIR_t^y \times \sum_c \phi_{t,c}^{y} \times X_c^y}{\sum_{t,c} EIR_{t,c}^{y} \times \phi_{t,c}^{y} \times X_c^y}$$

Where:

$EIR_{t,c}^{y}$: *Weighted average Effective Interest Rate for the instrument type t in year y and country c.*

EIR_c^y: *Weighted average Effective Interest Rate for the country c in year y.*

EIR_t^y: *Weighted average Effective Interest Rate for the instrument type t in year y for the OECD area.*

$\phi_{t,c}^{y}$: *Debt stock for the instrument t in country c in year y.*

X_c^y: *Foreign exchange rate between country c's domestic currency and USD on the last day of year y.*

W_t^y: *Portion of the interest rates attributed to the instrument type t*

Annex 1.D. EMDE marketable debt calculations

Primary sovereign bond market data and country groupings

Primary sovereign bond market data are based on original OECD calculations using data obtained from LSEG that provides international security-level data on new issues of sovereign bonds. The data set covers bonds issued by emerging market sovereigns in the period from 1 January 2007 to 31 December 2023 and includes both short-term and long-term debt. Short-term debt ("bills") is defined as any security with a maturity less than or equal to 365 days but no less than 30 days, as bill issuances with a maturity less than 30 days are considered to be done for cash management purposes and excluded from calculations. The data provides a detailed set of information for each bond issue, including the proceeds, maturity date, interest rate and currency structure.

The definition of emerging markets used in this report is consistent with the IMF's classification of Emerging Markets and Developing Economies used in its World Economic Outlook. The regional definitions are also those used by the IMF, while the income categories used (high income, low income, lower middle income, upper middle income) are defined by the World Bank according to GNI per capita levels.

A number of bonds have been subject to reopening. For these bonds, the initial data only provide the total amount (original issuance plus reopening). To retrieve the issuance amount for such reopened bonds, specific data on the outstanding amount on each reopening date for the concerned bonds have been downloaded separately from LSEG. As the reopening data only provide amounts outstanding, the outstanding amount on the previous date is subtracted from the outstanding amount on that given date, in order to obtain the issuance amount on each relevant date. These calculated issuance amounts are converted on the transaction date using USD foreign exchange data from LSEG. To ensure consistency and comparability, the same method is used for all bonds, including those which have not been subject to reopening.

Exchange offers and certain bonds in the dataset have been manually excluded when they did not have any identifier (ISIN, RIC or CUSIP) and when they have not been able to be manually confirmed by comparing with official government data.

Notes

[1] Fiscal deficits denote government fiscal funding needs, and NBR represents market borrowing beyond refinancing. Discrepancies between NBR and government fiscal deficits may arise when governments finance their fiscal needs through means other than issuing debt. Such alternative methods encompass the utilisation of existing cash reserves, asset sales (such as real estate and state-owned enterprises), or the acquisition of different liabilities, including accruing arrears or obtaining loans. Overborrowing of USD 1.6 trillion in 2020, driven by forecasting uncertainties from the pandemic, resulted in abnormal cash accumulation. However, in 2021 and occasionally in 2022, excess cash was used to smooth debt issuances in times of rising yields.

[2] As debt values are converted to USD, a stronger dollar magnifies the United States' debt size with the currency effect accounting for 40% of the growth in the country's share.

[3] Quantitative tightening is the process where central banks reduce the size of their balance sheets by selling off bonds or by not fully reinvesting the proceeds of maturing bonds, effectively withdrawing liquidity from the financial system and increasing the market holdings of bonds.

[4] According to the OECD 2023 Survey on Liquidity in Government Bond Secondary Markets the demand for linkers declined in New Zealand and the United Kingdom and rose in Chile, Hungary, Iceland, Mexico, Portugal, Spain and Türkiye.

[5] According to the OECD 2023 Survey on Primary Market Developments, these are Australia, Costa Rica, Hungary, Latvia, Lithuania, Mexico, Netherlands, New Zealand, Portugal, Slovenia, Sweden and Türkiye.

[6] This represents the average across the 38 OECD member countries. The OECD aggregate is predominantly shaped by major issuers, particularly G7 countries, potentially obscuring unique circumstances in the 38 member countries. The simple average treats all countries uniformly.

[7] This approximation likely underestimates the short-term impact of inflation on debt levels. Inflation also increases tax revenues in the short-term, thereby reducing net borrowing requirements. This partially explains improvements in net borrowing requirements which coincided with a rise in inflation in the period of 2021-23 (refer to Figure 1.1A).

[8] Forecasts for the 2022-24 period indicate entirely positive real yield curves exclusively in Canada, Denmark, Norway, and the United States.

[9] The pandemic's impact on EU public finances has intensified discussions on reforming EU fiscal rules. The European Commission, after a public consultation, published orientations for reforming these rules, emphasising the role of debt sustainability analysis (DSA) in assessing fiscal risks (Blanchard, Leandro and Zettelmeyer, 2021[68]; European Parliament, 2023[60]). The Commission's proposed DSA-based fiscal adjustment paths, covering at least four years, aim to ensure a downward public debt trajectory and compliance with the 3% of GDP fiscal deficit limit.

[10] Breakeven inflation is defined as the difference between the yield on a zero-coupon default-free nominal bond and on a zero-coupon default-free inflation-linked bond of the same maturity.

[11] The likelihood of this scenario decreases with declining inflation, as central banks may opt to reduce policy rates sooner.

12 The OECD currently forecasts a soft landing for its member countries (OECD, 2023[1]; OECD, 2024[16]).A soft landing in a monetary tightening cycle refers to the successful slowing of economic growth by central banks to curb inflation without triggering a recession.

13 Not all OECD countries are covered in this figure due to data availability in the OECD Economic Outlook (OECD, 2023[1]).

14 Accrual accounting, employed in the OECD National Accounts and by the majority of OECD countries, records interest expenses as they accumulate over time, irrespective of the actual timing of coupon and principal repayments. Consequently, the effective interest rate for a particular year is calculated as a weighted average of the yield to maturity, adjusted for any associated indices or rates for index-linked or floating rate debts, of all outstanding debt.

15 Inflation typically increases nominal tax bases, thereby boosting tax revenues (Garcia-Macia, 2023[67]). This increase often counterbalances the inflationary effects on the interest costs of inflation-linked bonds.

16 According to the OECD 2023 Survey on Primary Market Developments, 65% of OECD sovereign issuers with an inflation-linked programme reported the programme was responsible for an increase in their debt portfolio's maturity.

17 In fact, some linkers' programmes originated in the 1980s, serving as an important method for market funding during a period when central banks didn't have operational independence to conduct monetary policy.

18 This figure more directly reflects potential increases in interest payments, differing from the proportion of debt maturing or being refixed. Most of the debt due has already been refixed at higher rates, indicating the probability of lower future borrowing costs (assuming rates fall). Additionally, short-term instruments have been refinanced at these higher rates. Lastly, countries with significant debt refixing or refinancing in the next three years but low debt-to-GDP ratios face limited exposure to increased borrowing costs, like Poland with a 30% debt-to-GDP ratio and nearly half its debt maturing or due to be refixed by the end of 2026.

19 This calculation presupposes that the YTM of fixed-rate issues in 2024-26 will reflect their 2023 YTM.

20 Accounting practices for securities held for monetary policy purposes vary among central banks (OECD, 2023[26]). The US Federal Reserve and the BoJ account for these securities at historic cost accounting, delaying the impact of market valuation changes until the securities are sold. These banks only report unrealised valuation changes for transparency purposes. The ECB has a flexible accounting principle, allowing the country's central banks to choose between amortised cost and current market price valuation – most national central banks in the euro area opt for amortised cost. Other central banks, including those in Australia, Canada, New Zealand, Sweden, Switzerland, and the United Kingdom, apply mark-to-market accounting to their monetary policy securities. Central banks not using mark-to-market accounting for their holdings may still face losses when actively selling securities purchased at low rates during a period of comparably higher rates.

21 For instance, when incurring losses, the Fed accumulates them in the form of a "deferred asset". This asset's value is deducted when the Fed has positive net income. At one point, this asset value is cleared, and the Fed recommences remittances to the Treasury (Castro and Jordan-Wood, 2023[31]).

22 This selection excludes countries where the central bank's holdings in 2022 were less than 10% of the national debt and which did not respond to the relevant question in the OECD 2022 and 2023 Survey on

Liquidity in Government Bond Secondary Markets. The specific question asked was: "Please indicate the share of the central bank's holdings of national government debt in total, distinguishing between your central bank's holdings and those of foreign central banks as of 30 June 2023 (2022)".

[23] The central banks of Australia, Hungary and Israel are also adopting a passive QT approach (RBA, 2022[58]; Lybek, 2023[59]; OECD, 2023[34]; BIS, 2023[35]). While central banks in New Zealand and Sweden are actively selling bonds as part of their QT programmes. (RBNZ, 2022[56]; SRB, 2022[57]). The Bank of Korea did not engage in QT due to the small size of its now discontinued QE programme (BIS, 2023[35]).

[24] Where central banks are actively selling bonds as part of their QT programme, this directly increases the level of debt and duration for the market to absorb. Where QT is passive, central banks are no longer taking debt and duration out of the market via reinvestments, meaning the net level of debt and duration for the market to absorb will increase assuming the same issuance profile by sovereigns.

[25] The ATM of the government securities sold by the BoE under QT was nearly 20 years.

[26] Foreign exchange reserves are mainly allocated to government securities and overnight or term deposits at the relevant central bank.

[27] The term "price insensitive seller" reflects that the central bank sells government bonds not based on yield considerations, but to uphold its policy mandate of price and financial stability. However, the sale of these bonds is not entirely insensitive to the price offered. For example, the BoE conducts bond auctions with predetermined minimum bid prices and may choose to decrease the supply in these auctions if there is notably weak demand, with such reductions being deferred to future auctions, ensuring the BoE achieves its intended reduction in the bond stock (Bank of England, 2022[66]).

[28] According to the OECD 2023 Survey on Liquidity in Government Bond Secondary Markets, this includes Austria, Canada, Finland, Iceland, Ireland, Israel, Italy, Japan, Korea, Latvia, Lithuania, Portugal, Slovakia, Switzerland and the United Kingdom.

[29] Hedge funds' interaction with government bond markets varies significantly across countries (FSB, 2022[49]). For instance, in 2020, US hedge funds were heavily involved in the cash-futures basis trade, leveraging positions to profit from small price differences. However, market volatility led to mark-to-market losses and fire sales. Conversely, in the United Kingdom and euro area, hedge funds focused more on relative value trades like on-the-run/off-the-run arbitrage.

[30] According to findings from the OECD 2023 Survey on Liquidity in Government Bond Secondary Markets.

[31] The latest SBO edition examines the UK's mini-budget crisis (OECD, 2023[24]), and the Financial Stability Board (FSB) provides an in-depth analysis of the 2020 government bond fire sale (FSB, 2022[49]).

[32] The increased presence of the non-banking financial sector in the government bond market has prompted action from international organisations, financial regulators, and central banks. In 2023, the US updated its MMF regulations to improve liquidity and reporting management (US SEC, 2023[61]). The European Commission, likely to follow suit, has identified the need for further adjustments in its evaluation of the MMF Regulation (EC, 2023[62]). The UK is advancing its reform agenda, as evidenced by a recent public consultation on MMFs (FCA, 2022[63]). Concurrently, the FSB is conducting an extensive review of reforms in the global non-banking financial intermediation sector to ensure enhanced financial stability (FSB, 2023[64]; FSB, 2022[65]).

[33] According to the OECD 2023 Survey on Liquidity in Government Bond Secondary Markets, this group comprises Canada, Denmark, Ireland, Netherlands, Norway, and Portugal.

[34] The bid-to-cover ratio is calculated by dividing the total amount of bids received in a bond auction by the amount of bonds being offered.

[35] Sovereign issuers engage in borrowing not only through auctions but also via syndications to end investors and tender offers. The volumes transacted through these methods vary considerably between countries, most notably between smaller and larger issuers.

[36] In the United States, Principal Trading Firms (PTFs) are also active in inter-dealer markets. They trade with their own capital, primarily engaging in proprietary, electronic, and algorithmic trading. They act as intermediaries in markets dealing with government bonds, derivatives, and other securities, playing a crucial role in liquidity provision and price discovery.

[37] According to the OECD 2023 Survey on Liquidity in Government Bond Secondary Markets, the number of primary dealers ranges from 4 in Norway to 32 in Germany, averaging 12-13. Only 13 countries currently include non-bank entities as dealers.

[38] A US Fed's study showed that when dealer capacity utilisation is approximately 20%, there is negligible estimated effect on market illiquidity from further capacity increases, but as capacity utilization escalates from 40% towards 80%, the market's estimated illiquidity surges by about three standard deviations above the level anticipated based on volatility alone (Duffie et al., 2023[47]).

[39] According to the OECD 2023 Survey on Liquidity in Government Bond Secondary Markets, pprimary dealers (PD) are selected based on the following criteria: maintaining a competitive environment (in 22 countries), secondary market activity (22), distribution capacity of PDs (21), PD system stability (17), geographical distribution (13), size of the borrowing requirement (13), and warehousing capacity (8).

[40] A tap issuance or reopening is a method by which a sovereign issuer sells additional amounts of a previously issued bond, increasing its supply without creating a new maturity or coupon rate. By adding volume to an existing issue, especially off-the-run bonds, tap issuances enhance market liquidity, facilitating easier trading and price discovery for those securities.

[41] The US Treasury's planned buyback program, set to start in 2024, focuses on liquidity support and cash management, involving regular operations across nine security buckets with a quarterly maximum buyback amount of USD 30 billion for liquidity support and up to USD 120 billion for cash management in the first year, subject to market conditions and operational adjustments.

2 Corporate debt markets in a changing macrofinancial landscape

Corporate indebtedness has increased significantly in the last fifteen years. Globally, there were USD 34 trillion of corporate bonds outstanding at the end of 2023, an increase in real terms of USD 13 trillion since 2008. Alongside accommodative monetary policies, companies have been able to increase their borrowing and lock in favourable terms. In parallel, the characteristics of corporate bond markets have changed in at least four respects: sectoral composition, geographic composition, investor universe and credit quality.

The funding environment that enabled the vast expansion in borrowing has now come to an end, and refinancing needs are substantial. The investment grade segment is increasingly concentrated in lower-rated bonds, and identically rated bonds have very different characteristics today than they did fifteen years ago. The non-financial sector in particular is more leveraged than at any other point in recent history.

In this context, this chapter explores the implications of this new macrofinancial landscape on corporate bond markets globally.

2.1. Introduction

Corporate bond markets have grown significantly since the 2008 financial crisis. Companies have taken advantage of an environment of accommodative monetary policies by increasing their borrowing, locking in favourable interest rates and extending maturities. In parallel, the characteristics of corporate bond markets globally have changed in at least four different respects: sectoral composition, geographic composition, investor universe and credit quality. This chapter illustrates these developments and examines how they might interact with a changing macrofinancial context. It focuses on corporate bond markets and does not cover commercial papers or asset backed securities.

Key findings

- **Sharp increases in corporate bond issuance**. In real terms, the total outstanding amount of corporate bond debt has increased from USD 21.0 trillion in 2008 to USD 33.6 trillion in 2023. Over 60 per cent of this increase comes from non-financial corporations, which more than doubled their average annual issuance from the 2000-08 period to the 2009-23 period.
- **Changing geographic composition**. The geographic composition of corporate bond markets has changed significantly. Chinese issuers have gone from representing less than one per cent of the total outstanding amount in 2008 to almost one-fifth by the end of 2023.
- **Companies have locked in favourable conditions**. In a favourable funding environment, investment grade companies globally extended the average maturity of their debt from 5.6 years in 2000 to 7.9 years in 2023. In addition, the vast majority of all corporate bonds are issued with fixed interest rates, reducing immediate exposure to interest rate fluctuations.
- **A changing investor landscape**. Following regulatory efforts to diversify credit intermediation away from the banking sector, the investor landscape for corporate bonds has changed. Open-ended investment funds and ETFs have become significant players. The number of fixed income funds participating in corporate bond markets has more than tripled since 2000. These funds have also become increasingly exposed to corporate bonds, with over 30% globally having a net exposure to corporate bonds representing more than 75% of their total portfolio value.
- **Structural decreases in credit quality**. Corporate bond markets around the world have become riskier over time as value-weighted average credit ratings have decreased sharply. This is a combined effect of the expansion of the non-investment grade segment, which has grown faster than the broader market, and a decrease in credit quality among investment grade issuers.
- **Tightening financial conditions and market strain**. Despite increased borrowing and decreases in credit quality, corporate defaults have remained subdued as low interest rates have helped ensure the sustainability of high debts. However, USD 12.3 trillion of corporate bonds globally are maturing by the end of 2026. The sharp tightening in monetary policy since 2022 means much of this debt will need to be refinanced at significantly higher rates than at issuance.
- **Vulnerabilities at the investment grade threshold**. An increasing share of non-financial corporate bond markets globally sit just above the non-investment grade threshold. The share of BBB rated bonds in total investment grade issuance reached 53% in 2023, more than twice the share in 2000. Simultaneously, the characteristics of BBB rated bonds have changed. In 2023, 42% of all BBB rated bonds were issued by companies with debt-to-EBITDA ratios over 4, compared to 11% in 2008. Their position on the threshold of non-investment grade makes these securities vulnerable to fire sale dynamics, especially where investors have rating-based mandates.

2.2. A portrait of developments in global corporate bond markets

Corporate borrowing through bond markets has grown significantly in the last two decades alongside an environment of accommodative monetary policy since the 2008 financial crisis. Yields have been held down both by very low policy rates and by large-scale central bank purchases of both sovereign and corporate bonds. In parallel, the bond market landscape has evolved, with new characteristics of both issuers and investors. Using deal-level data, this section provides an overview of developments in corporate bond markets globally since 2000.

2.2.1. Issuer-side trends: corporations' use of bond markets

The total amount of corporate bonds outstanding has increased by two and a half times in real terms, from USD 13.6 trillion in 2000 to USD 33.6 trillion in 2023 (Figure 2.1, Panel A). The increase has been particularly pronounced in the non-financial sector since the 2008 financial crisis, as companies around the world have taken advantage of the lower borrowing costs brought about by accommodative monetary policies. Tighter banking regulations have also contributed to this growth. Average non-financial issuance has more than doubled in real terms, from USD 1.1 trillion annually between 2000 and 2008 to USD 2.3 trillion between 2009 and 2023 (Panel B). This trend holds even when excluding the record issuance levels during the COVID-19 pandemic in 2020 and 2021 (of USD 3.4 trillion and USD 2.8 trillion, respectively).

The increase is more moderate for financial companies, from USD 2.5 trillion between 2000 and 2008 to USD 2.8 trillion from 2009 and 2023. Consequently, over 60 per cent of the increase in corporate bond debt globally comes from increases in non-financial corporate debt. The share of non-financial company bonds in total outstanding corporate bond debt in 2023 was nine percentage points higher than in 2008. Expansionary monetary policy since 2008 has also affected the relative cost between debt and equity. Bond issuance as a multiple of total equity issuance has increased significantly over time, particularly for financial companies (Panel C).

Figure 2.1. An overview of global corporate bond markets

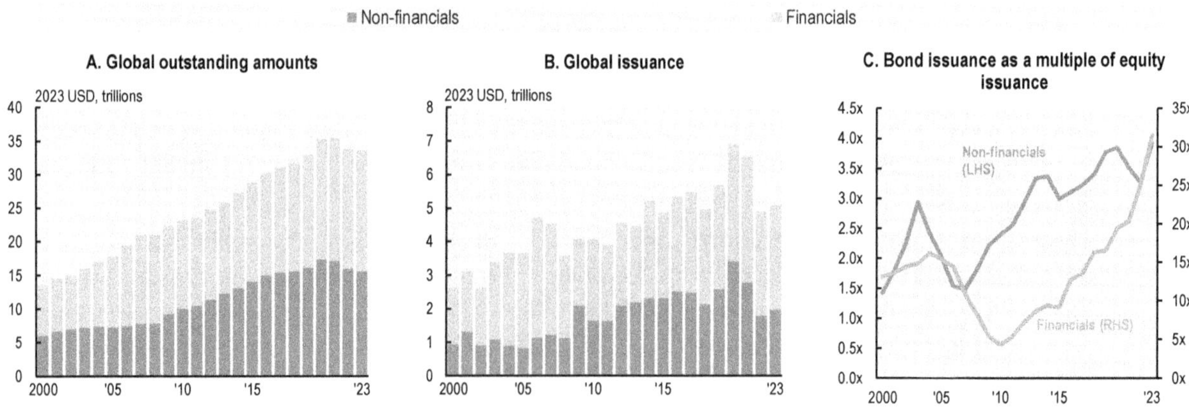

Note: Panel C shows three year rolling averages. Total equity issuance refers to the sum of initial public offerings (IPOs) and secondary public offerings (SPOs).
Source: OECD Capital Market Series Dataset, LSEG, see Annex 2.A for details.

While non-financial corporate bond debt has increased significantly across advanced economies since 2008 (in real terms, by 72% in the United States, 51% in Europe and 28% in Japan), the picture is less one-sided for financial corporate bonds (Figure 2.2, Panel A). In both the United States and Europe, the outstanding amount of bonds issued by financial companies has in fact decreased slightly in real terms since 2008 (by 5% and 6%, respectively), whereas it has increased significantly in Japan, although from much lower levels. In the People's Republic of China (China), there has been a manifold increase in the levels of both financial and non-financial corporate bonds outstanding since 2008.

This has led to a significant shift in the regional distribution of corporate bond markets. Chinese corporate bond debt has grown from negligible levels in 2008 to representing almost a fifth of the global total in 2023 (Panel B). By contrast, Europe's share has decreased from 42% to 28%. This is partly because the European corporate bond market is dominated by financial companies, notably banks, a market segment that has been growing much more slowly than non-financial companies. At the end of 2023, bonds issued by financial companies made up more than two-thirds of total European debt, compared to 54% globally and 36% in the United States.

Figure 2.2. Growth and regional distribution of outstanding corporate bonds

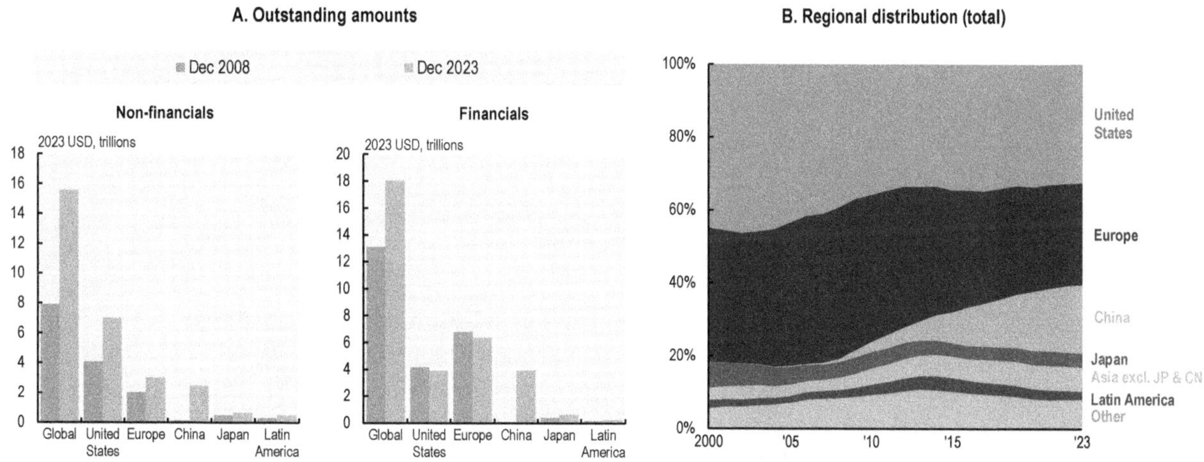

Source: OECD Capital Market Series Dataset, LSEG, see Annex 2.A for details.

In addition to increasing the amount of their borrowing, the low interest rate period also saw high-rated companies extend the maturity of their debt. Globally, the average value-weighted maturity for all investment grade corporate bonds has increased from 5.6 years in 2000 to 7.9 years in 2023. This trend holds true for both financial and non-financial companies, which have followed very similar trajectories, although non-financial companies have slightly longer average maturities. As shown in Figure 2.3, it also holds across countries. Average maturities have been extended in all regions shown below, with the notable exception of China, where the average maturity has decreased from 10.0 to 6.3 years, driven by a significant expansion of the market to include smaller issuers (see (OECD, 2022[1])). In the United States, investment grade maturities have more than doubled since 2000, and stood at above 10 years in 2023.

Figure 2.3. Value-weighted average maturities, investment grade companies

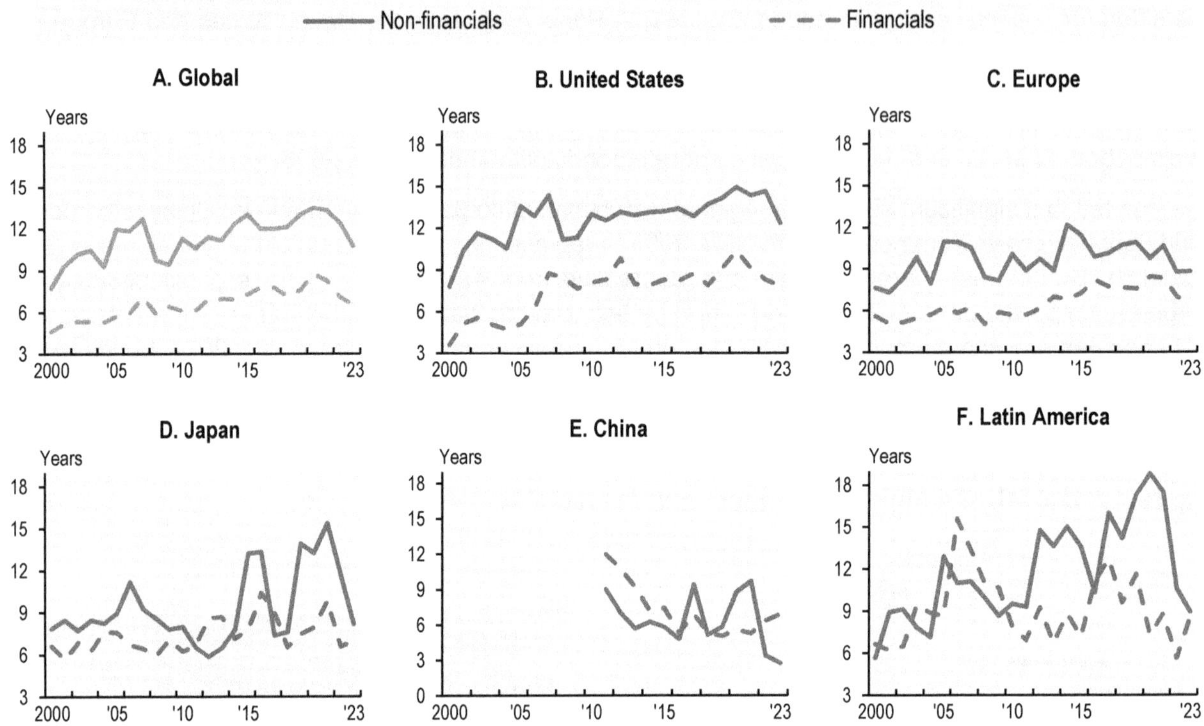

Note: The time series in Panel E starts in 2010 because there were very few rated issues by Chinese companies prior to that.
Source: OECD Capital Market Series Dataset, LSEG, see Annex 2.A for details.

The vast majority of corporate bonds are issued with fixed interest rate structures (Figure 2.4). For non-financial companies in advanced economies, 94% of the total issuance since 2008 was made up of fixed-rate (Panel A). The share was similar in emerging economies at 93% (Panel B). There are no significant differences between investment grade and non-investment grade issuance in either group of economies. The picture is different for financial companies though, where 72% of total issuance in advanced economies was fixed rate, compared to 92% in emerging markets. However, because financial companies have positive exposure to increases in interest rates through their lending activities, floating rate debt exposure poses less of a risk for this sector. Still, financial companies have increased their share of fixed-rate borrowing over time to lock in beneficial rates. Between 2000-2008, the fixed-rate share of total financial company issuance was only 50% in advanced economies and 58% in emerging economies. There is one notable exception to this trend: non-investment grade financial companies in advanced economies have decreased the fixed-rate share of issuance from 82% between 2000-2008 to 78% over the 2008-2023 period, reaching a historical low of 44% in 2022.

Figure 2.4. Share of fixed-rate issuance (by amount)

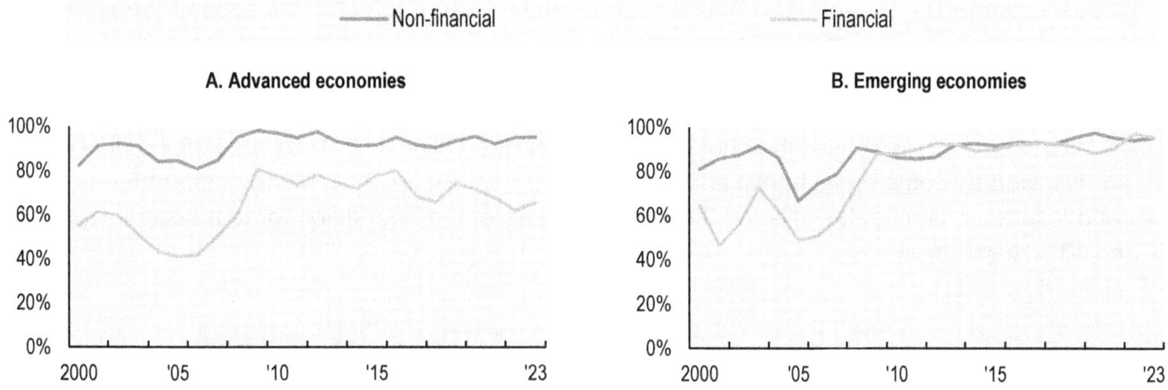

Source: OECD Capital Market Series Dataset, LSEG, see Annex 2.A for details.

The predominance of fixed-rates coupled with the extension of maturities has on aggregate lessened the near-term impact of higher interest rates and reduces the refinancing risks faced by the corporate sector in advanced economies. As illustrated in Figure 2.5, the share of debt coming due in the next three years stood at 32% at the end of 2023, down from 37% in 2008. However, given the growth in borrowing, in absolute terms the amounts to be repaid or refinanced in the next three years remain substantial at USD 8 trillion.

The situation in emerging economies is more challenging, with redemptions coming due in the next three years having grown significantly not just in absolute amounts but also as a share of total outstanding debt. At the end of 2023, they totalled USD 4.4 trillion, representing 51% of total outstanding amounts (Panel B). This is a marked increase from around 2008, until which point the share was trending downwards. This increase since is driven to very large extent by the growth of the Chinese market, where maturities have been shortening (see Panel E of Figure 2.3), with a consequent increase in the share of debt due within the next three years for both financial and non-financial companies. China's share of total outstanding corporate bonds amongst emerging markets has grown from 29% in 2010 to 74% in 2023, which significantly impacts the aggregate figure. When looking at emerging markets excluding China, the share coming due in the next three years is more stable over time, but still stood at 48% at the end of 2023.

Figure 2.5. Outstanding amounts of corporate bonds coming due in the next 3 years, all companies

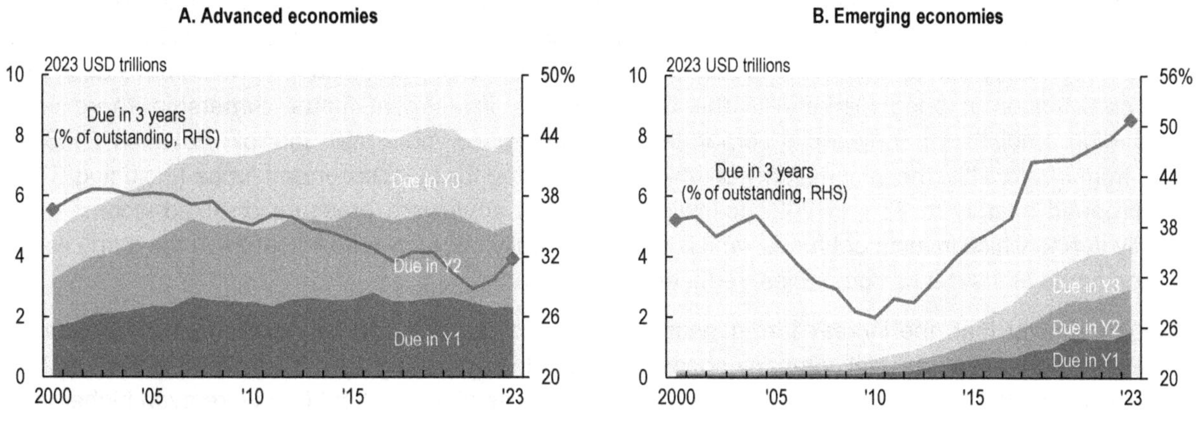

Source: OECD Capital Market Series Dataset, LSEG, see Annex 2.A for details.

2.2.2. Investor-side trends: a changing creditor landscape

The increased borrowing by both sovereigns (see Chapter 1) and corporations around the world since 2008 has primarily been absorbed by central banks and institutional investors. At the end of 2022, the seven investor categories listed below held a total of USD 74.6 trillion in debt securities (corporate and sovereign) compared to USD 61.4 trillion in 2007. The single largest investors in debt securities globally are central banks, which increased their holdings from USD 3.5 trillion in 2007 to USD 18.4 trillion in 2022. They are followed by commercial banks and investment funds (Figure 2.6). Money market funds, central banks and insurance companies allocate the largest shares of their portfolios to debt securities, at 46%, 33% and 43% respectively.

Figure 2.6. Debt security holdings of selected financial institutions, 2007 and 2022

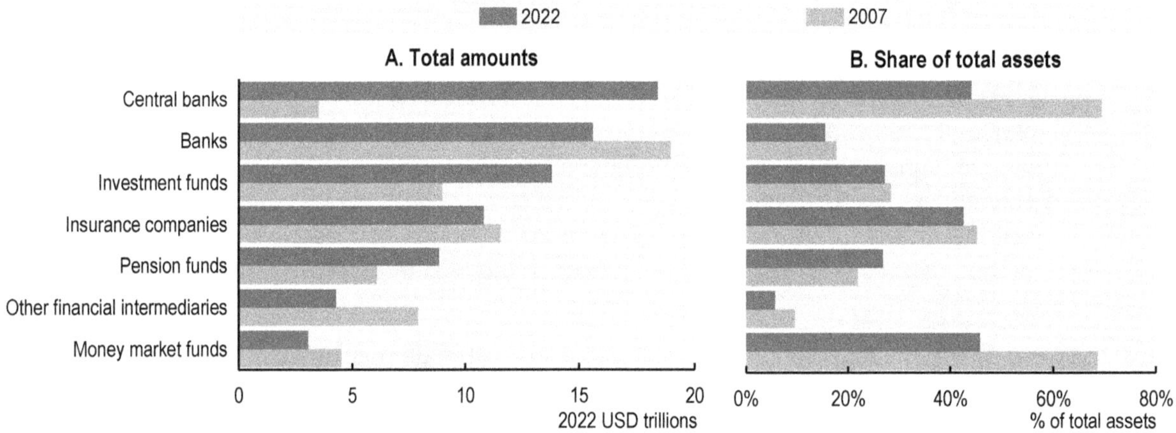

Note: Based on national sector balance sheet data for 42 economies. Other financial intermediaries include specialised branches of financial institutions (financial corporations engaged in the securitisation of assets, security and derivatives dealers, financial corporations engaged in lending, and other specialised financial corporations), financial auxiliaries and captive financial institutions and money lenders. The OECD Financial accounts non-consolidated data is supplemented initially with consolidated data and then further complemented with OECD Pension Statistics in cases where the financial accounts data are not available.
Source: OECD Financial Accounts, OECD Pension Statistics, OECD calculations.

For jurisdictions that provide flow of funds data on a whom-to-whom basis, it is possible to analyse how ownership structures have shifted for specific types of debt securities such as corporate bonds. Using such data, Figure 2.7 highlights a notable trend in the world's two largest corporate bond markets (the United States and the euro area) which is the growing prominence of investment funds as holders of corporate bonds. This increase is particularly notable for non-financial corporate bonds since the 2008 financial crisis following regulatory efforts to de-risk the banking sector and diversify credit supply, which have decreased bank participation in bond markets. In the United States, investment funds' ownership share of the outstanding amount of non-financial corporate bonds increased more than fourfold between 2008 and 2021, from 8% to 34%, the vast majority of which is accounted for by open-ended funds (including ETFs). This dropped sharply to 23% in 2022 following significant downward pressure on fixed-income prices globally during which investment funds, which are not typically buy-and-hold investors in the same way as pension funds or insurance companies, reduced their holdings.

Although smaller than the increase in investment funds holdings of non-financial corporate bonds, the increase is marked for financial company bonds too, more than doubling from 8% in 2008 to 19% in 2021, before falling to 15% in 2022 (Figure 2.7, Panel A). The shares at the end of 2022 were even higher in the euro area specifically at 35% of non-financial corporate bonds and 20% of financial corporate bonds (Panel B).

Available data for the US is broken down further by fund type, allowing for a more granular analysis and revealing an important development within the investment fund universe. Exchange-traded funds (ETFs) have grown from holding a near-zero (0.3%) share of outstanding non-financial corporate bonds in 2008 to 6% at the end of 2022, equivalent to more than a fifth of total investment fund holdings (Figure 2.7, Panel A).

Figure 2.7. Share of outstanding corporate bonds held by investment funds

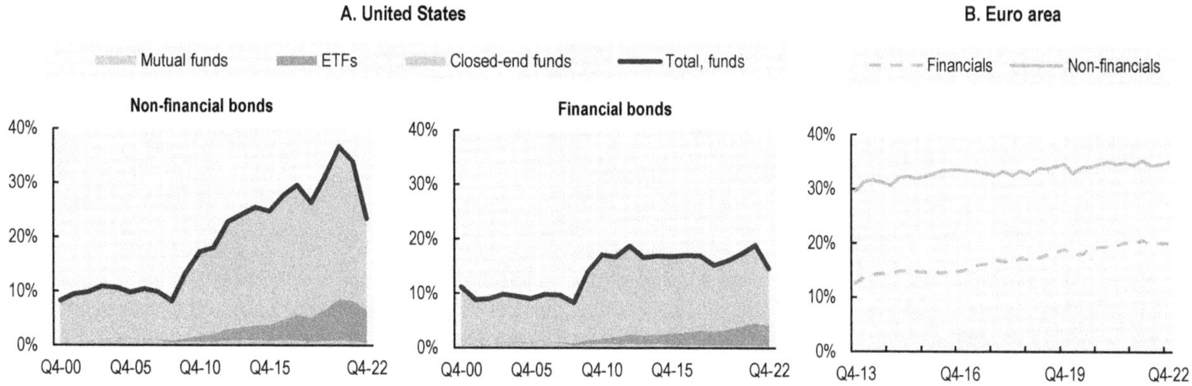

Note: Shares of total domestic holdings. Euro Area data refer to total non-money market fund investment holdings. Euro Area data availability starts in 2013.
Source: US Federal Reserve System, ECB, OECD calculations.

To further assess how investment funds' participation in corporate bond markets has developed, the analysis is extended using a detailed dataset containing all fixed income-focused open-ended funds (OEFs) and ETFs globally. A fund is defined as participating in the corporate bond market if its net exposure (long positions minus short positions) to corporate bonds is at least 1% of its total portfolio as of the latest available date. All the analysis in this section refers to this universe of funds.

The first thing to note is the sustained expansion of investment fund involvement in parallel with growing corporate bond issuance. For both open-ended funds and ETFs, the net number of new funds (new creations minus dead funds) has been positive in every year since 2000 (Figure 2.8, Panel A). A clear acceleration can be seen in the wake of the 2008 financial crisis, as credit intermediation moved out of the banking sector and new investors absorbed increases in corporate borrowing. Consequently, the cumulative number of fixed income funds participating in corporate bond markets more than tripled from 4 776 in 2000 to 15 144 in 2023 (Panel B).

The growth of ETFs seen in the US is also visible globally. Out of the roughly 15 000 funds in the dataset globally at the end of 2023, over six percent were ETFs, compared to less than half a percent in 2008. However, despite their rapid growth, ETFs remain much smaller than the broader open-ended investment fund universe. At the start of 2024, the aggregate size of all funds was USD 8.9 trillion, of which USD 939 billion (11%) was ETFs (Panel C). In terms of investment area, the United States is by far the largest market for ETFs, representing 31% of the analysed universe. This is over four times higher than in Europe, which is the second largest.

Figure 2.8. Fixed income funds participating in the corporate bond market

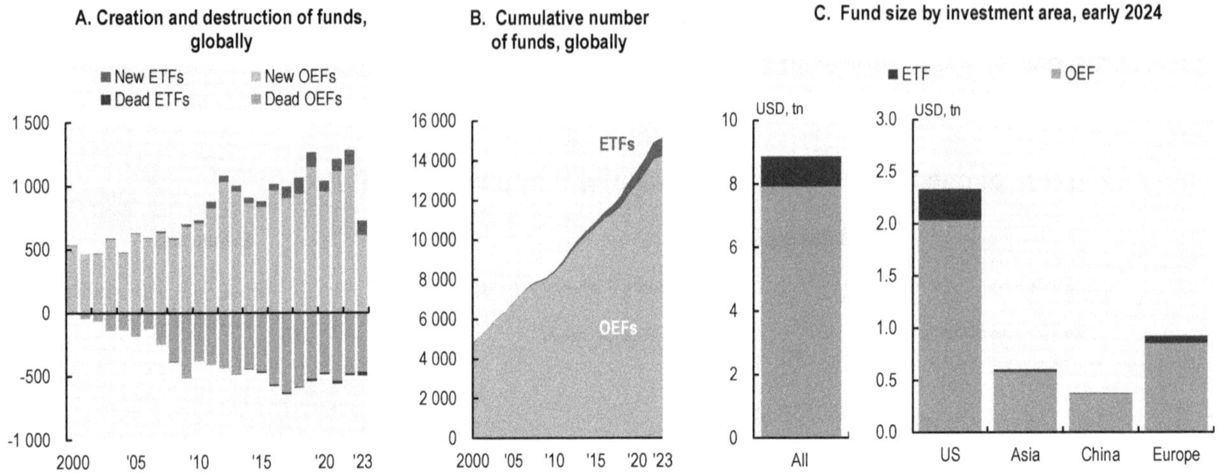

Note: Refers to fixed income funds with at least 1% net exposure (long exposure minus short exposure, measured as a share of the total portfolio) to corporate bonds (latest available observation). Excludes closed-end funds and money market funds. Dead funds can be either liquidated or merged into another fund. The cumulative data in Panel B sum up net funds (new minus dead) since the start of the data series (with the first inceptions in the early 1950s). Panel C is based on reported geographical focus area of funds, rather than domicile or listing. This means, for example, the US category will include non-US investors focusing on the US market. "All" includes all funds, including those for which a specific investment area is not indicated. Only funds for which portfolio data was reported in 2023 or later are included. The regional categories (Asia, Europe) include funds with country-specific focus (meaning e.g. China is fully included in the Asia category).
Source: Morningstar Direct, OECD calculations, see Annex 2.A for details.

It is not just the number of investment funds engaged in the corporate bond market that has increased. In addition, these funds have increased their exposure to corporate bonds (Figure 2.9). For open-ended funds, the average net exposure to corporate bonds has increased from 38% in 2005 to 51% in 2023. The average exposure of ETFs is even higher at 64% (Panel A). This has led to a shift in the composition of investment funds globally. At the end of 2023, half of all funds had more than 50% net exposure to corporate bonds, an increase of 13 percentage points compared to 2008 (Panel B). The increase is particularly striking for funds with over 75% net exposure, which now make up over 30% of all funds, up from 20% in 2008 (Panel C). The lowest exposure category (1-10%) represents just 10% of the number of funds.

These developments are indicative of a global shift towards higher-risk investments in an environment of lower yields on traditional safe haven assets in the period that followed the 2008 financial crisis. Panel C below shows a calculation of the actual corporate bond holdings (as opposed to total fund size as shown in Panel C of Figure 2.8) by investment funds, split by their net exposure to corporate bonds. In early 2024, fixed income open-ended funds and ETFs with more than 75% net exposure to corporate bonds held USD 1.4 trillion and USD 442 billion, respectively, of corporate bonds. In the case of ETFs, this represents almost three-quarters of their total corporate bond holdings.

Figure 2.9. Corporate bond exposure of investment funds globally

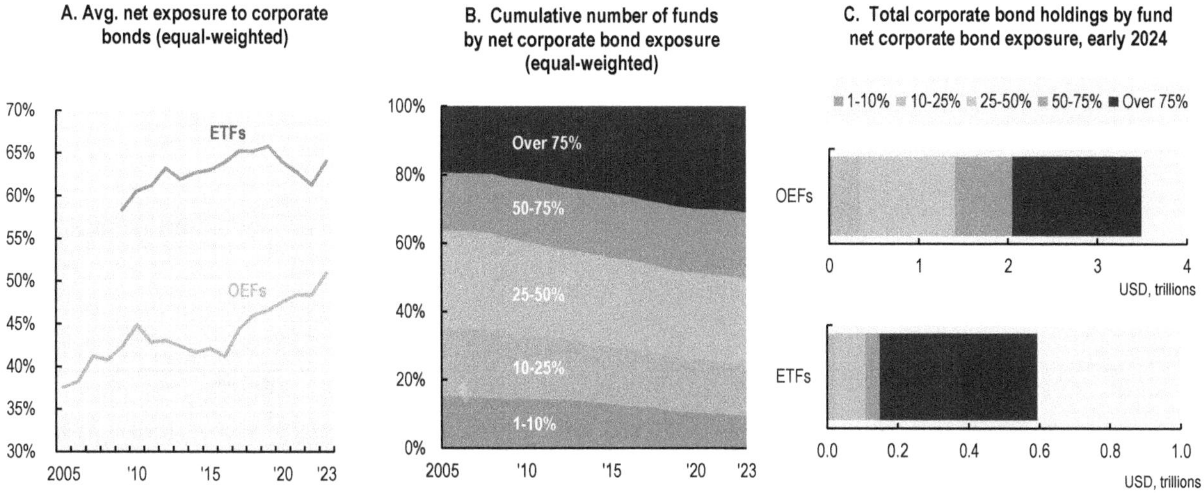

Note: Only fixed income funds with at least 1% net exposure to corporate bonds (measured as a share of the total portfolio) are considered. Because ETF observations are very limited before 2009, that is used as the starting period in Panel A. In Panel C, corporate bond holdings are calculated by multiplying the average net exposure to corporate bonds for each fund in 2023 with the total fund size (reported in 2023 or later).
Source: Morningstar Direct, OECD calculations, see Annex 2.A for details.

2.3. Build-up of risks and vulnerabilities

In parallel to increasing levels of corporate bond debt, there has been a marked decrease in credit quality. For more than a decade after the 2008 financial crisis, a lower-interest rate environment and ample availability of capital served to structurally lower yields around the world. Consequently, investors seeking to increase returns allocated larger shares of their capital to higher-risk investments, enabling lower credit quality companies to better access corporate bond markets and thereby expanding riskier market segments.

2.3.1. Decreases in credit quality and the growth of the non-investment grade market

Aggregate credit quality has seen a sustained decrease over time. Figure 2.10 shows long-term developments in corporate bond credit ratings using an index constructed by value-weighting the credit ratings of all rated bonds issued globally. While there is clear cyclicality over time in this index, there also appears to be a downward trend structurally for both non-financial and financial companies. For non-financial companies (Panel A), the index reached its lowest value of 12.5 (half a notch above BBB-, the lowest investment grade rating) in 2021, down two full notches compared to the average from 1980 to 2008. In 2022 the index value increased relatively sharply to 13.8, owing to a significant reduction (of 74% globally) in non-investment grade issuance in the face of increasing interest rates and tightening financial conditions. It remained at this level in 2023.

The decrease in credit quality in the aftermath of the 2008 financial crisis is even more striking for financial companies, for which bond ratings have historically been very high and less volatile than those of non-financial company bonds. In the period between 1980 and 2011, the index never fell below 16.9 (approximately equivalent to a rating of A+) for financial companies. However, by 2021 it had fallen to 14.7 (between A- and BBB+) following a decade of steep decreases in credit quality. Similar to non-financial corporate bonds, 2022 and 2023 saw sharp increases.

Figure 2.10. Global corporate bond rating index

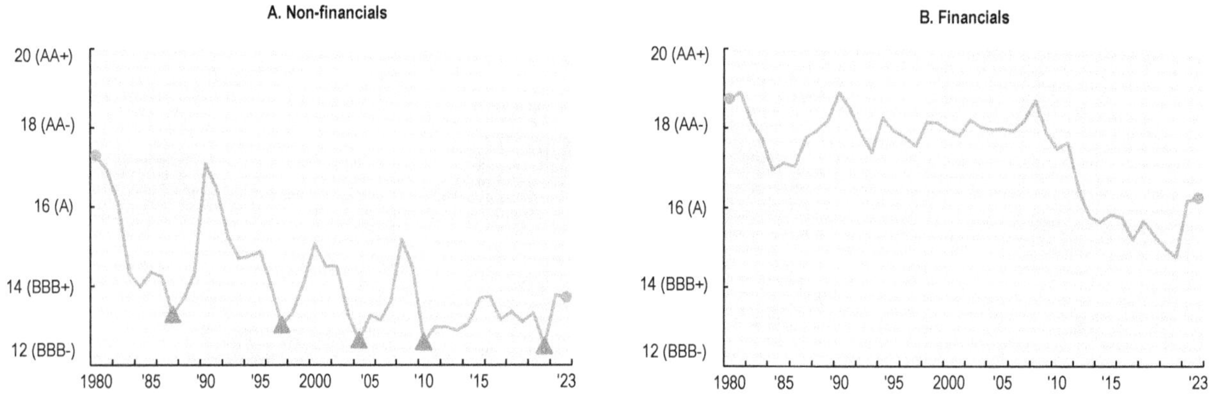

Note: A score of 1 is assigned to a bond if it has the lowest credit rating and 21 if it has the highest rating. The corporate bond rating index is then calculated by averaging individual bond scores, weighted by issue amounts. The calculations are based on 250 988 rated bonds issued by companies in 126 jurisdictions.
Source: OECD Capital Market Series Dataset, LSEG, see Annex 2.A for details.

This decrease in credit quality is partly a result of an expansion of the non-investment grade market. Figure 2.11 provides an overview of how this market segment has developed globally, highlighting three important trends.

Firstly, non-investment grade borrowing has grown significantly. Total outstanding amounts almost doubled in real terms between 2008-23, reaching USD 3.4 trillion. Secondly, unlike the broader market, the share of financial company bonds in total non-investment grade outstanding amounts has increased markedly since the 2008 financial crisis, more than doubling from 15% in 2008 to 38% in 2023 (Panel A). The increase can largely be attributed to the expansion of the European and Chinese non-investment grade financial company bond markets. Europe increased its share of the total global non-investment grade market from 14% to 30% between 2008-23 and increased the share of financial company bonds in its own non-investment grade market from 20% to 58% during the same period. Similarly, Chinese companies have gone from representing 2% of the global non-investment grade market in 2008 to 8% in 2023. During the same period, the share of financial companies in the total Chinese non-investment grade market increased from 17% to as much as 81%.[1] In terms of sub-industries, the global increase is driven primarily by increased issuance by companies active in *banking services* and *investment banking and investment services*.

Thirdly, the global non-investment grade segment has grown faster than the larger investment grade market in recent years. Looking at three-year rolling averages, the share of total issuance accounted for by non-investment grade has more than doubled from 6% in 2008 to 14% in 2023 (Panel B).

Figure 2.11. The global non-investment grade market

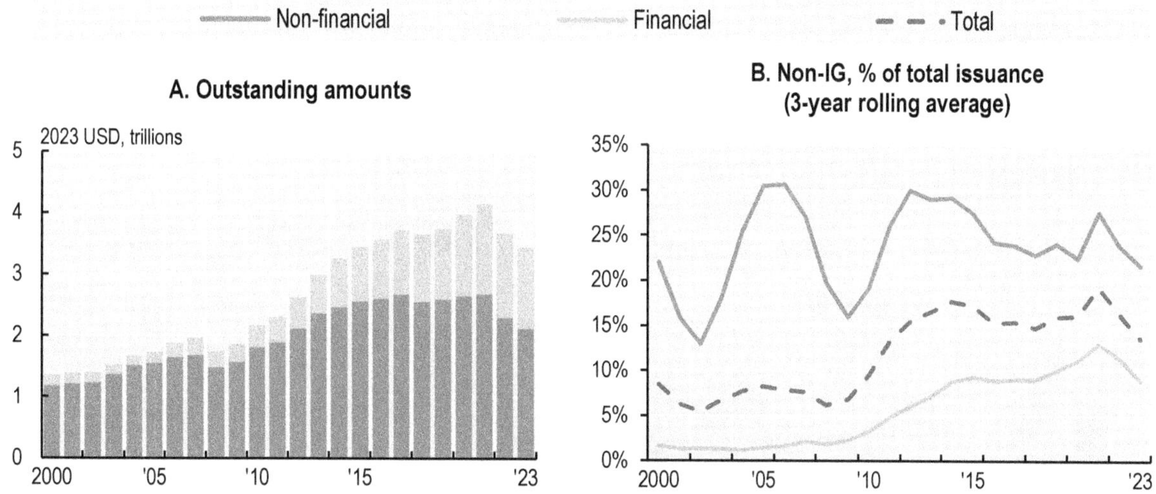

Source: OECD Capital Market Series Dataset, LSEG, see Annex 2.A for details.

Unlike the investment grade market, value-weighted average maturities have not increased for non-investment grade bonds. Globally, maturities have remained constant at around 8 years for the past fifteen years (Figure 2.12). Although the vast majority of outstanding non-investment grade bonds have fixed interest rate structures, near-term refinancing needs are significant. Globally, USD 1.1 trillion of non-investment grade bonds will need to be repaid or refinanced by the end of 2026, most likely under significantly tighter financial conditions than at issuance.

Figure 2.12. Maturities and redemptions, non-investment grade bonds globally

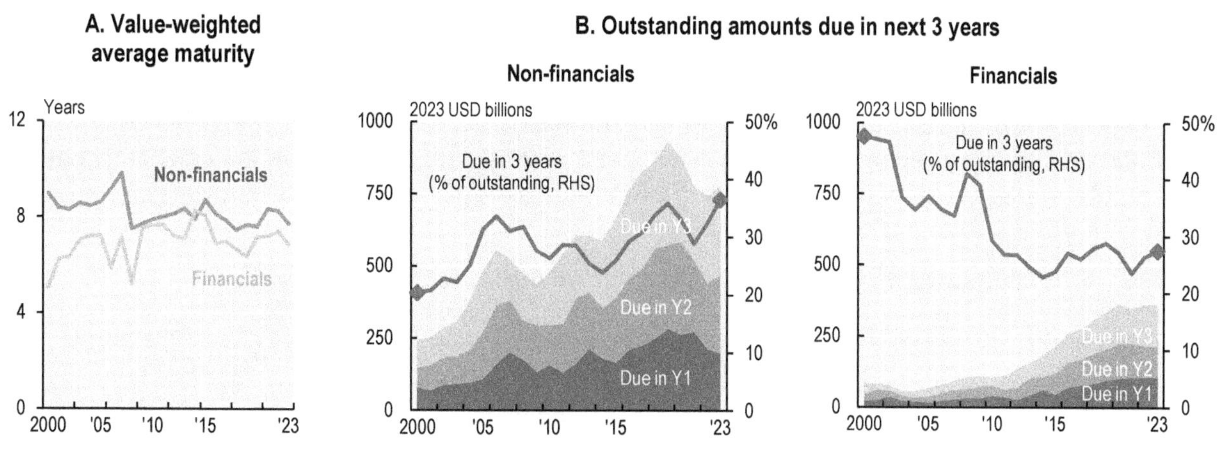

Source: OECD Capital Market Series Dataset, LSEG, see Annex 2.A for details.

The extent to which non-investment grade companies use bond markets differs between regions. US firms are dominant in the non-investment grade, non-financial bond market. Although the US share has decreased over time, it was still as high as 59% at the end of 2023 (Figure 2.13), significantly more than the US share of the global non-financial market of 45%. This is down from 78% of the entire non-financial, non-investment grade market in 2000. This relative decrease has been driven primarily by the expanded use of bond markets by European non-investment grade firms, whose share has increased from 8% in 2000 to 21% in 2023, similar to their share in the broader non-financial market (19%).

The picture differs for non-investment grade financial companies. Firstly, US-based firms are much less dominant in this segment, accounting for 24% of the global outstanding amount, similar to their share of global financial company bond debt (Panel B). European firms, conversely, represent as much as 46% of the market, significantly higher than their 35% share of the global financial corporate bond market. Compared to the non-financial non-investment grade market, US and European firms also make up a smaller portion of the global financial market total (70% at the end of 2023). The majority of the remainder is made up of Asian firms, mostly from China.

Figure 2.13. Regional distribution, outstanding amounts of non-investment grade bonds

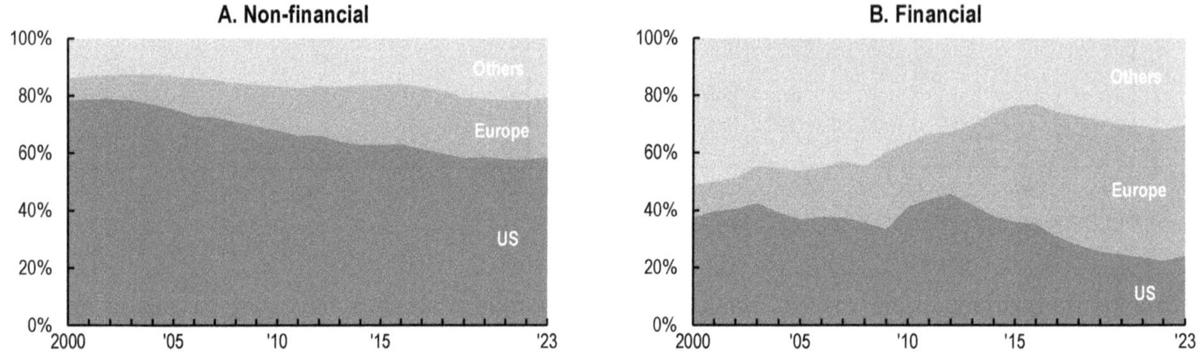

Source: OECD Capital Market Series Dataset, LSEG, see Annex 2.A for details.

2.3.2. Leverage in the non-financial corporate sector

As highlighted in Section 2.2.1, the non-financial corporate sector has sharply increased its share of total outstanding corporate bond debt. To further assess these developments, this section expands the analysis to all debt financing by non-financial corporations.

The results show that increasing credit risk is not limited to corporate bond markets, but part of a broader trend of a more leveraged corporate sector. Indeed, looking at all listed companies globally, the single most indebted group of companies is those with a debt-to-EBITDA ratio over 4 in both advanced (45% of total debt) and emerging economies (52%). By the end of 2022, the total debt on the balance sheets of these highly leveraged companies amounted to USD 12.8 trillion globally.

Figure 2.14. Total debt by leverage, listed non-financial companies

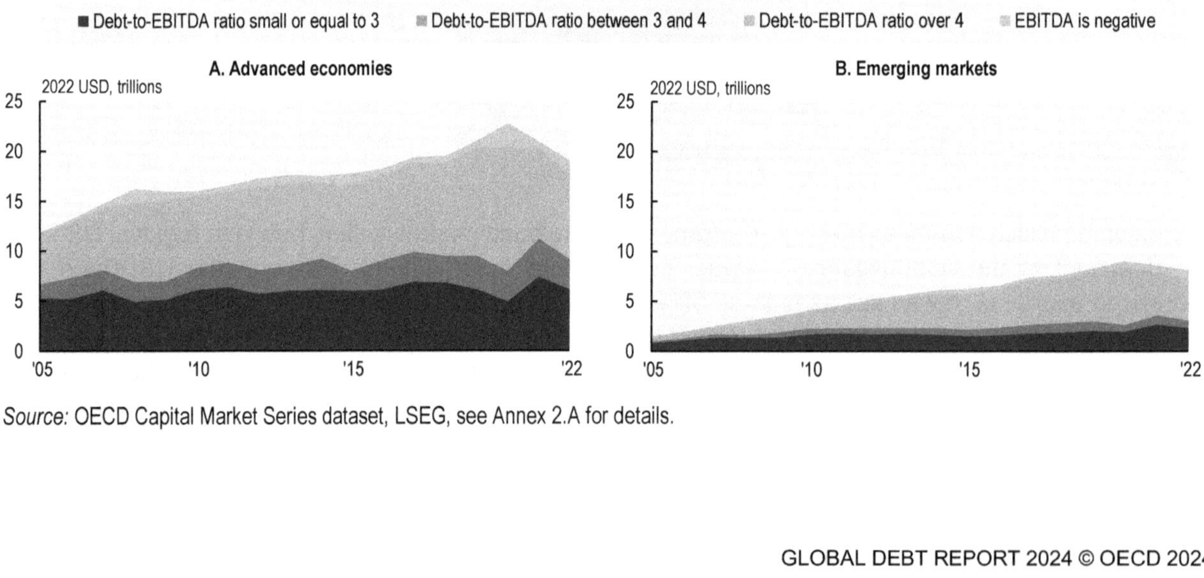

Source: OECD Capital Market Series dataset, LSEG, see Annex 2.A for details.

This increasing prevalence of highly leveraged companies holds across most regions, both measured as the share of companies and the amount of debt (Figure 2.15). At the end of 2022, approximately one-fourth of all listed Chinese companies were classified as highly indebted, using the definition of a debt-to-EBITDA ratio over 4, representing 57% of the total outstanding debt. Similarly, in Japan, 22% of listed companies, representing almost 55% of the total outstanding debt, fall into the highly leveraged category. In the United States, even though the share of highly leveraged companies has increased, the share of debt owed by these companies has remained roughly constant. Notably, when it comes to the share of debt owed by highly indebted companies, the 2022 levels are slightly lower than those in 2019 across most regions. This shift is largely tied to the post-pandemic profit spike in listed companies around the globe.

Figure 2.15. Share of highly indebted listed non-financial companies, by region

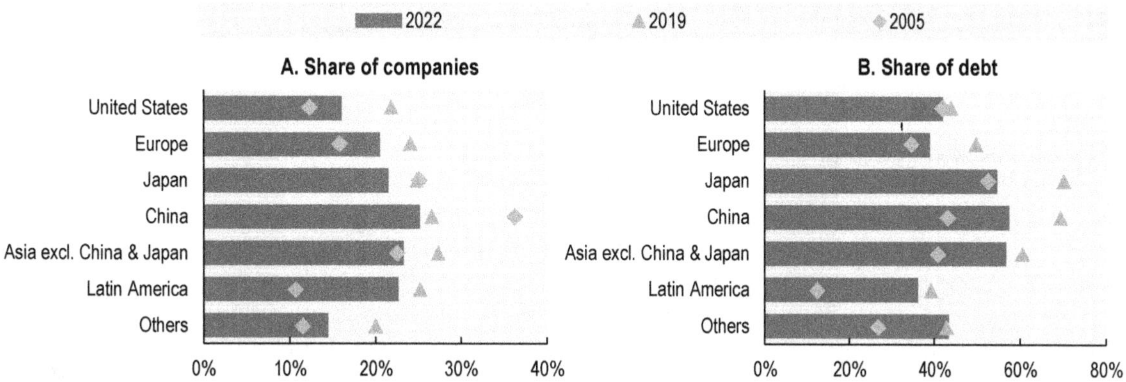

Note: Highly indebted companies are defined as those with a debt-to-EBITDA ratio over 4.
Source: OECD Capital Market Series dataset, LSEG, see Annex 2.A for details.

While there has been a general increase in corporate leverage, the levels differ significantly between industries, as shown in Figure 2.16. With the exception of the industrial sector, all industries have seen an increase in aggregate debt-to-EBITDA since 2005. The increase is most pronounced in the real estate sector, where the ratio has grown from an average of 4.2x to 13.5x. The surge in real estate company indebtedness – by far the most leveraged of the industries below – is mainly driven by Chinese companies, which have seen a significant drop in profits coupled with a rise in indebtedness in recent years. Box 2.1 looks at risks and vulnerabilities in the real estate sector in greater detail.

Figure 2.16. Debt-to-EBITDA ratio of listed non-financial companies, aggregate ratio by industry

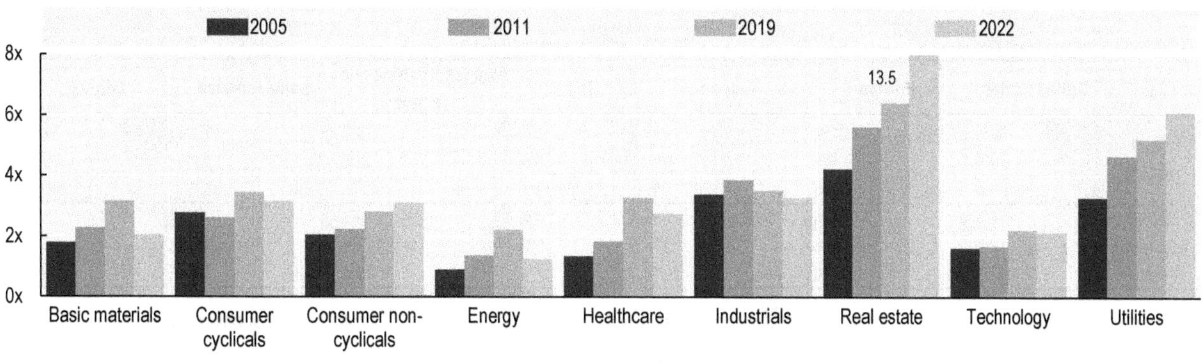

Source: OECD Capital Market Series dataset, LSEG, see Annex 2.A for details.

Box 2.1. Risks in the real estate sector

The real estate sector has made extensive use of corporate bond markets in recent years, even more so than other sectors. The share of non-financial bond issuance accounted for by the real estate sector has increased from 0.7% in 2000 to a historical peak of 3.1% in 2021, before dropping sharply to 2.0% in 2023 (Figure 2.17, Panel A). In 2023, the outstanding amount of bonds issued globally by the companies in the sector reached USD 881 billion. Similar to other corporate bonds, the vast majority of these are issued with a fixed interest rate. However, the real estate sector is highly leveraged, and a significant amount of debt will have to be refinanced or repaid in the near-term. This challenge is particularly notable in certain Asian economies. By the end of 2026, 70% of the total outstanding amount of real estate bonds is coming due in China, and 51% in Asian economies excluding China and Japan.

Figure 2.17. Trends in bond financing by real estate companies

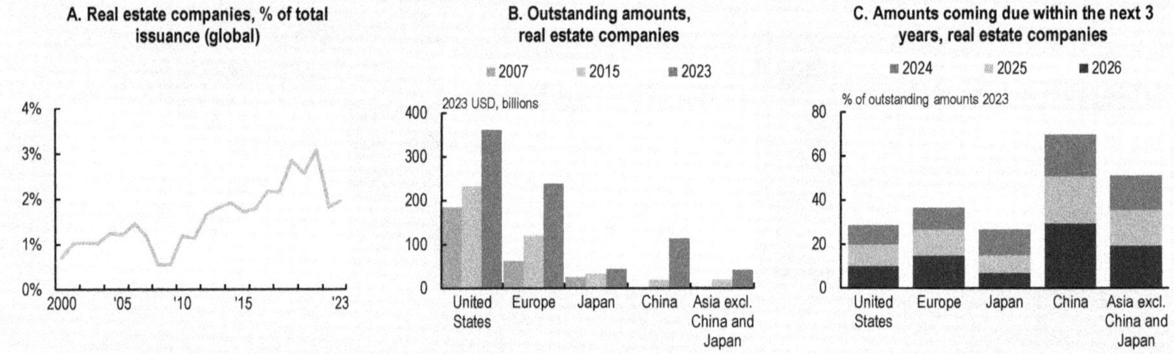

Source: OECD Capital Market Series dataset, LSEG, see Annex 2.A for details.

Leverage in the real estate sector has increased much more than in most other industries in recent years. Using an interest coverage ratio measure, Figure 2.18 compares the share of debt owed by high-risk companies in the real estate sector with those in other industries across countries. The share of at-risk companies has increased substantially in several regions, notably in China, where it was as high as 71% at the end of 2022, and the United States, where it was 69%. Deteriorating credit conditions in certain real estate segments in the US can also be seen in the uptick in the commercial mortgage-backed securities delinquency rate in the office and lodging sectors (Trepp, 2023[2]).

Figure 2.18. Share of debt owed by at risk companies across industries

	Year	United States	Europe	Japan	China	Asia (excl. China and Japan)	Latin America	Others
Real estate	2007	39%	32%	2%	8%	8%	19%	32%
	2019	30%	6%	1%	55%	18%	13%	29%
	2022	69%	45%	0%	71%	37%	32%	45%
Other economic sectors	2007	14%	4%	2%	4%	9%	6%	13%
	2019	12%	4%	3%	9%	17%	11%	16%
	2022	12%	7%	12%	18%	15%	14%	9%

Note: Refers to listed companies, excludes the financial sector. At-risk companies are defined as having an interest coverage ratio below 2.
Source: OECD Capital Market Series dataset, LSEG, see Annex 2.A for details.

More stringent banking regulation and investors' search for yield over the last decade have supported the growth of non-bank real estate financing and forms of collective investment vehicles in real estate finance (OECD, 2021[3]). Available data on institutional investors' (insurance companies, pension funds and investment funds) exposure to such investments, show heterogeneity across regions and by type of investor. On average, among the jurisdictions shown below investment funds have the highest exposure to real estate, at 15.6% of total assets. Pension funds and insurance companies' average exposures are lower at 5.0% and 4.2%, respectively. However, even these investors have significant exposure in certain jurisdictions, notably in Japan and some European economies.

Figure 2.19. Institutional investor exposure to real estate

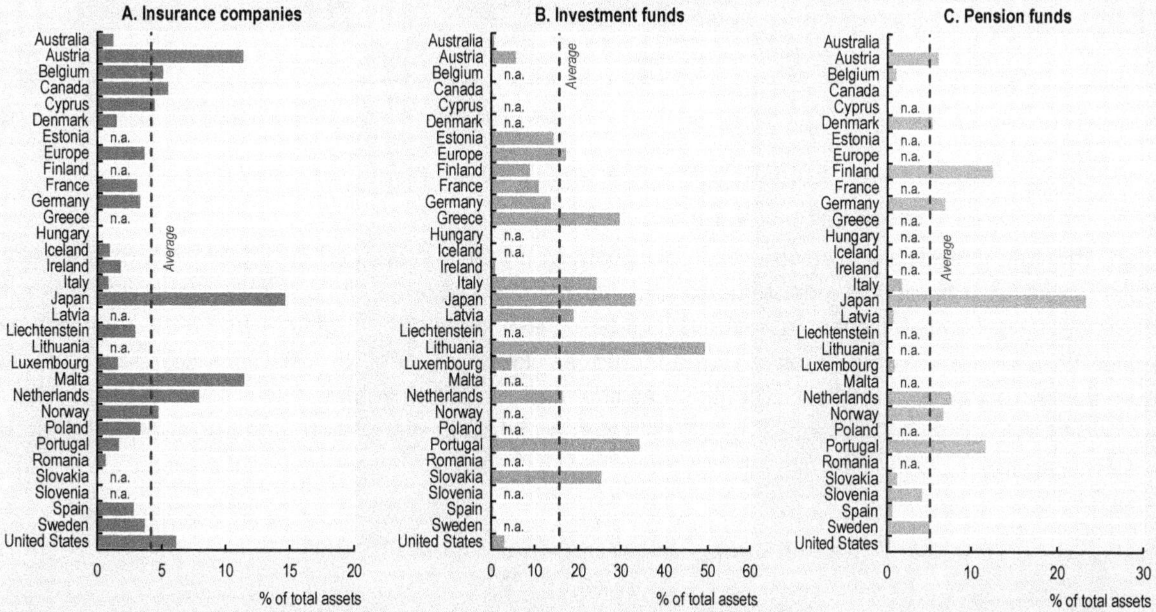

Note: Data refer to 2022-Q4. Real estate exposures are proxied by real estate property holdings (not for own use), commercial real estate mortgages, commercial mortgage-backed securities and real estate investment funds shares. Data are not available for the United Kingdom.

Source: Australian Bureau of Statistics, Bank of Japan, EIOPA Insurance and Pension statistics, European Central Bank, Federal Reserve, UK Office for National Statistics, Statistics Canada, OECD calculations.

Despite increases in leverage, the share of at-risk companies has not increased markedly over the past two decades when looking at debt servicing capacity. Figure 2.20 below looks at the share of companies with low capacity to service interest payments, defined as an interest coverage ratio (ICR) below 2, a threshold sometimes used to determine "at risk" companies (Palomino et al., 2019[4]). Across most regions, the share of companies with low interest coverage ratios in 2022 was approximately the same as in 2005. The primary reason for this has been accommodative monetary policy, which has kept interest expenses lower.

Figure 2.20. Share of listed non-financial companies with low interest coverage ratios

A. Share of companies

Year	United States	Europe	Japan	China	Asia excl. China&Japan	Latin America	Others
2005	10%	22%	10%	19%	20%	10%	10%
2019	9%	23%	9%	18%	29%	9%	9%
2022	9%	22%	9%	23%	26%	9%	9%

B. Share of debt

Year	United States	Europe	Japan	China	Asia excl. China&Japan	Latin America	Others
2005	9%	5%	3%	12%	9%	3%	12%
2019	12%	5%	3%	20%	17%	3%	16%
2022	13%	9%	11%	29%	19%	11%	13%

Note: The interest coverage ratio is the ratio of earnings before interest, taxes, depreciation and amortisation (EBITDA) to interest expenses. Low interest coverage ratios are defined as below 2.
Source: OECD Capital Market Series dataset, LSEG Datastream, see Annex 2.A for details.

Indeed, the low interest rate environment of recent years has produced a notable trend: a negative correlation between corporate indebtedness and interest costs. Both advanced economies and emerging markets have seen interest costs (measured as interest expenses over total financial debt) decrease over the last fifteen years, while leverage (measured as financial debt to total assets) has increased (Figure 2.21). This trend is unlikely to continue as financial conditions tighten. Given the high current levels of corporate indebtedness, increases in interest rates could push many more companies into the higher-risk ICR category.

Figure 2.21. Leverage and interest cost of listed non-financial companies

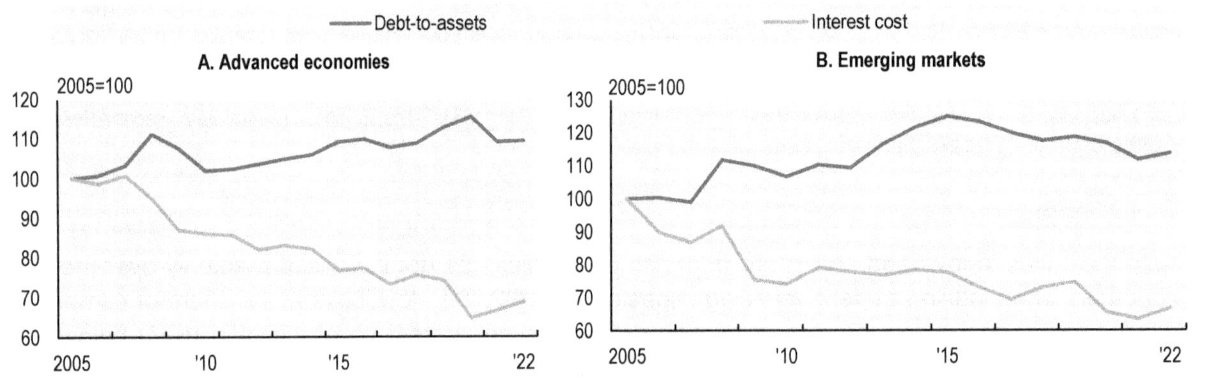

Note: Interest costs are measured as interest expenses over total financial debt.
Source: OECD Capital Market Series dataset, LSEG, see Annex 2.A for details.

2.3.3. Developments in corporate defaults

Despite a surge in corporate indebtedness and widespread decreases in corporate bond credit quality, corporate defaults have remained subdued in recent years compared to historical levels. Aside from an uptick in 2020 there has not been any significant spikes in non-investment grade defaults since the 2008 financial crisis (Figure 2.22, Panel A). Defaults increased somewhat in 2022 following more restrictive monetary policy and tighter financial conditions, although remained significantly lower than in 2020 (MIS, 2023[5]). Notably, owing to substantial government support schemes and the containment of a full-blown financial crisis, deteriorating credit quality (measured as the ratio between credit rating downgrades and upgrades) has not translated into increased defaults to the same extent as in the immediate aftermath of the 2008 financial crisis (Panel B). In both 2002 and 2009, the number of downgrades was more than 3.5 times the number of upgrades, with non-investment grade default rates reaching 16.1% in 2009. In contrast, while the downgrades to upgrades ratio reached as much as 6.7 in 2020, by far the highest in the below series, the non-investment grade default rate remained relatively low at 6.3%.

Figure 2.22. Corporate bond defaults and credit rating changes

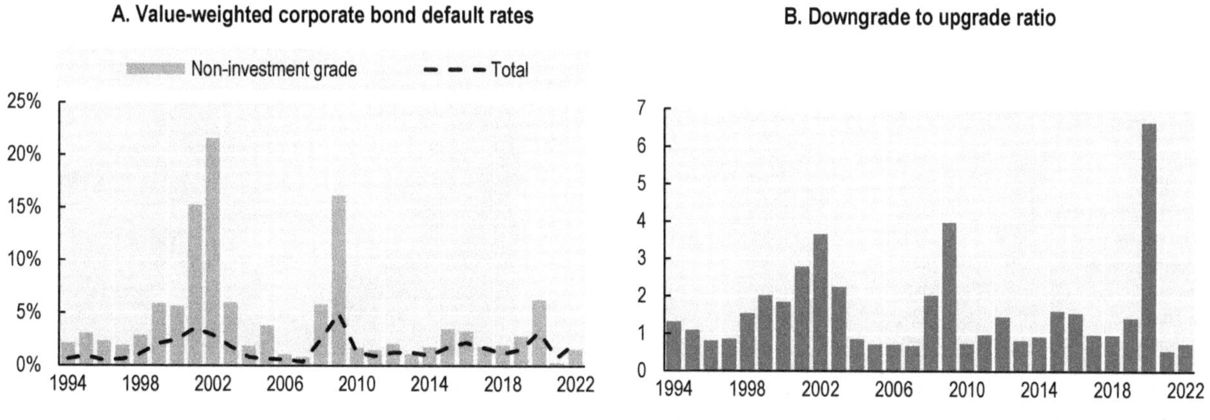

Source: MIS (2023[5]), for Panel A and S&P (2023[6]) for Panel B.

A central question is therefore whether further defaults should be expected as the sharp tightening of monetary policy gradually feeds through. As shown in Figure 2.4, the vast majority of corporate bonds are issued with fixed-rate structures. This means that many non-investment grade companies will be exposed to the increase in interest rates only with a lag. On the other hand, corporations have improved their liquidity buffers since the 2008 financial crisis, aided further by the support provided by governments and central banks at the start of the pandemic in 2020. Liquidity buffers strengthened significantly between 2008 and 2022, with median cash holdings measured as a share of total financial debt increasing from 32% in 2008 to 65% in 2022 (Figure 2.23, Panel A). The same trend can be seen at the industry level, with all industries improving their median cash position from 2008 to 2022 (Panel B).

Figure 2.23. Liquidity levels (cash to financial debt) of listed non-financial companies globally

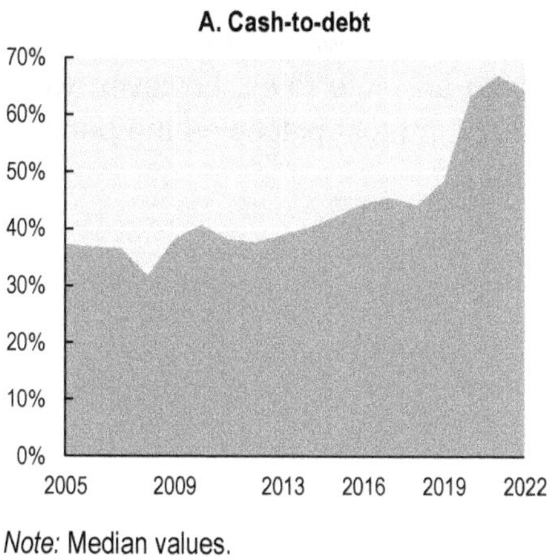

B. Cash-to-debt by industry

	2008	2022	Change
Overall	32%	65%	33.0%
Utilities	16%	21%	5.5%
Real estate	20%	25%	5.3%
Consumer non-cyclicals	24%	43%	19.3%
Energy	24%	47%	23.7%
Basic materials	23%	53%	29.9%
Consumer cyclicals	25%	49%	23.2%
Industrials	40%	71%	31.4%
Healthcare	59%	147%	88.8%
Technology	72%	158%	86.5%

Note: Median values.
Source: OECD Capital Market Series dataset, LSEG, see Annex 2.A for details.

To see whether aggregate figures mask variations between companies of different debt servicing capacity, the sample is split into high- and low-risk companies based on debt-to-EBITDA ratios. Over the 2008-22 period, both high- and low-risk companies improved their cash positions. As would be expected, liquidity buffers are significantly lower in high-risk companies (Figure 2.24). The utilities, energy, real estate and consumer non-cyclical industries had the lowest cash-to-debt ratio among high-risk companies. The difference in the cash position between low-risk and high-risk companies in 2022 was most significant in the healthcare, technology, industrials and real estate sectors, at over 100 percentage points each.

Figure 2.24. Liquidity levels of listed non-financial companies by risk and industry, end-2022

	A. High risk		B. Low risk	
	2008	2022	2008	2022
Overall	15%	22%	69%	137%
Utilities	10%	12%	31%	52%
Energy	14%	17%	42%	69%
Real estate	13%	18%	63%	129%
Consumer non-cyclicals	11%	18%	48%	92%
Basic materials	12%	21%	45%	84%
Consumer cyclicals	14%	21%	62%	112%
Healthcare	14%	24%	84%	218%
Industrials	22%	29%	86%	150%
Technology	28%	45%	151%	305%

Note: Liquidity is measured as the median ratio of cash to financial debt for each risk group. High- and low-risk companies are defined as those with debt-to-EBITDA ratios over 4 and below 3, respectively. Companies with negative EBITDA are excluded.
Source: OECD Capital Market Series dataset, LSEG, see Annex 2.A for details.

2.4. Navigating financial stability risks in a changing macrofinancial landscape

The extended period of benign financial conditions which has enabled the development in corporate bond markets covered here ended abruptly in 2022 as central banks in most major economies began rapidly tightening monetary policy in response to the highest annual inflation rate in the OECD as a whole since 1989. This section addresses how global corporate bond markets might respond to this changing macrofinancial landscape, highlighting possible financial stability implications.

2.4.1. Monetary policy tightening and central bank withdrawal from bond markets

In absolute terms, key policy rates are similar to the levels at the end of 2006 in the United Kingdom (5% then and 5.25% in February 2024) and the United States (5.25% then compared to a range between 5.25 – 5.50% in February 2024). The European Central Bank's (ECB) deposit facility was higher in February 2024 (4%), a historic high, than at the end of 2006 (2.5%). Rather than absolute rates, however, what characterises this tightening cycle, which began between 2021 and 2022 in most places, is the pace of tightening, which is the fastest in decades (Figure 2.25).

Figure 2.25. Tightening cycles by major central banks since 1990

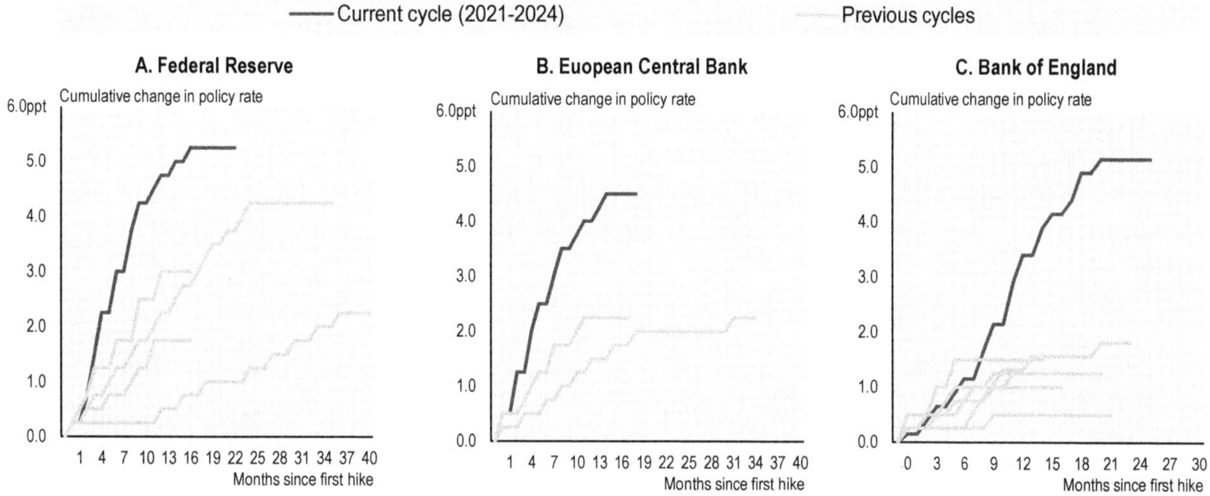

Note: A tightening cycle is defined as period of at least 14 months, starting from the first monetary policy tightening decision and ending at the first occurrence of either a rate cut or a 12-month consecutive period without any interest rate increases. The cycles are as follows: Federal Reserve: 1994-1995, 1999-2000, 2004-2007, 2015-2019, 2022-2024; ECB: 1999-2001, 2005-2008, 2022-2024; Bank of England: 1994-1995, 1996-1998, 1999-2000, 2003-2005, 2006-2007, 2017-2019, 2021-2024.
Source: LSEG, OECD calculations.

In other words, the conditions which enabled the expansion of higher-risk bond issuance are no longer present. Even in a scenario where inflation is brought down fully and remains at or near target, interest rates and corporate financing costs are likely to remain substantially higher than they have been in recent years, especially when considering the withdrawal of central bank liquidity support. Box 2.2 provides an overview of how listed companies' debt servicing capacity would be affected under different scenarios for future interest rates.

As interest rates were brought down to near or even below zero in many countries over recent years in efforts to stimulate the economy and bring inflation back up to target, many central banks expanded their monetary policy toolkits to include quantitative easing (QE), undertaking significant asset purchase programmes. Many of these were launched in the wake of the 2008 financial crisis, but they were expanded significantly in response to the COVID-19 pandemic. While asset purchases have primarily targeted government securities, major central banks also purchased significant amounts of corporate bonds, as shown in Figure 2.26 below.

As part of the shift in monetary policy, these programmes are now being unwound. Net purchases under the European Central Bank's (ECB) Pandemic Emergency Purchase Programme (PEPP) were discontinued in March 2022, with reinvestment of maturing holdings potentially ending in 2024, and net purchases under the Corporate Sector Purchase Programme (CSPP) ending in June 2022, with full reinvestment ending in February 2023 (ECB[7]) (ECB[8]). The Bank of Japan (BoJ) decided at the end of March 2022 that it would reduce its purchases of corporate bonds and commercial paper to the same pace as prior to the pandemic from April 2022, meaning the outstanding amounts held would gradually reduce to a total of JPY 5 trillion (JPY 3 trillion in corporate bonds and JPY 2 trillion in commercial paper) (Bank of Japan, 2022[9]). The BoJ has noted it will give "due consideration to corporate bond issuance conditions" as part of this adjustment (Bank of Japan, 2022[10]).

In February 2022 the Bank of England (BoE) decided to cease reinvesting its maturing corporate bond holdings and to begin a programme of active corporate bond sales (Bank of England, 2022[11]). This sales programme began in September 2022 and was concluded in June 2023, at which time the Bank had reduced its holdings to GBP 833 million, a reduction by 96% compared to nine months earlier. The remaining amount refers to very short maturity bonds, which will remain in the portfolio until fully matured in April 2024 (Bank of England, 2023[12]).[2] The US Federal Reserve, which first bought corporate bonds in response to the COVID-19 pandemic in 2020, began selling its holdings of ETFs and corporate bonds as early as June and July of 2021, respectively (Federal Reserve Bank of New York[13]). As shown below, the entire position had been completely unwound by the end of August 2021.

Figure 2.26. Corporate debt security holdings by major central banks

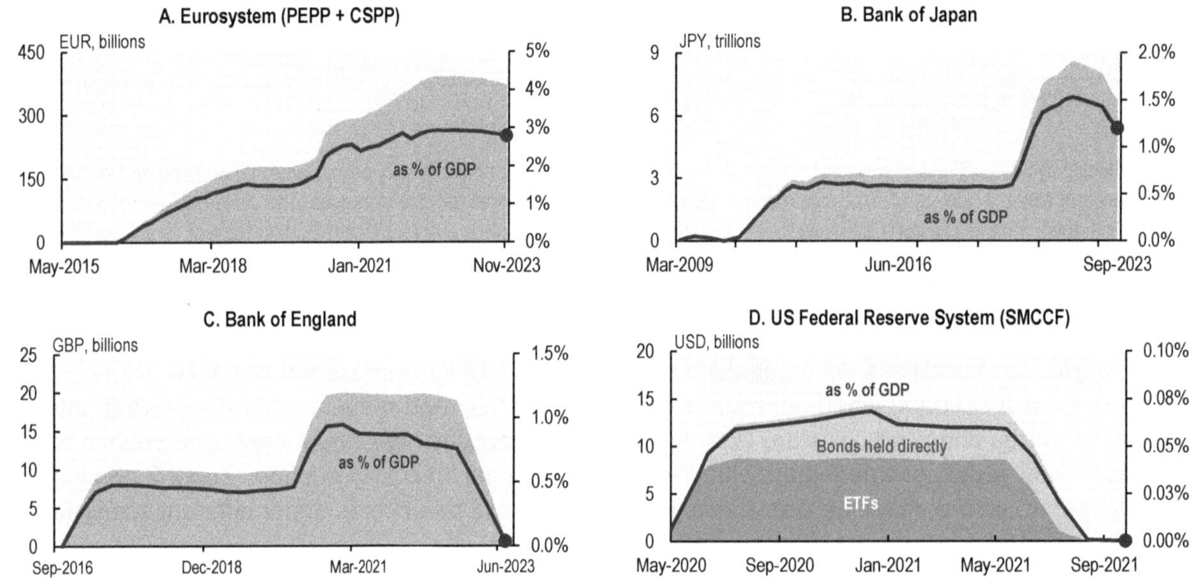

Note: Eurosystem holdings include both corporate bonds and commercial paper.
Source: ECB, Bank of Japan, Bank of England, Federal Reserve, Eurostat, National Accounts of Japan, UK Office for National Statistics, IMF.

The corporate bond holdings that have been unwound, i.e. those of the Federal Reserve and the BoE, were much smaller in scale, both in absolute amounts and as shares of gross domestic product (GDP) and total bond markets, than those of the ECB (Eurosystem) and the BoJ. The Federal Reserve's corporate bond holdings which were purchased via the Secondary Market Corporate Credit Facility (SMCCF) at its peak in December 2020 amounted to roughly 0.14% of the total US corporate bond market. The BoE's holdings were proportionately larger at 1.4%, but still significantly lower than those of the ECB and BoJ, which held 6.7% and 3.4% of their respective corporate bond markets at the end of 2023. The move to shrink their holdings by decreasing or ceasing net purchases and reinvestments has resulted in the most negative net purchases by the ECB and the BoJ since they began buying corporate bonds (Figure 2.27).

Figure 2.27. Central bank net purchases of corporate debt securities

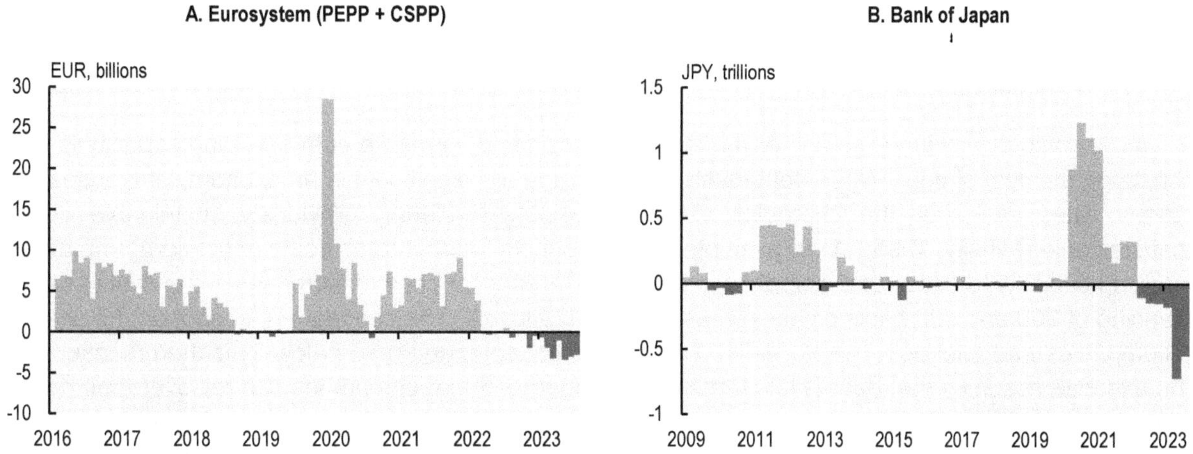

Note: Refers to both corporate bonds and commercial paper for the Eurosystem. Net purchases in PEPP are disclosed bi-monthly, monthly values are assumed by even distribution. Bank of Japan data refer to transactions in "industrial securities", which are bonds issued domestically by joint-stock corporations, corresponding to secured or unsecured bonds under the Financial Instruments and Exchange Act. Nominal values.
Source: ECB, Bank of Japan.

The reversal of QE (so-called quantitative tightening - QT) represents the withdrawal of a major holder in certain corporate bond markets. To sustain issuance, other investors need to absorb this additional net supply. As discussed under Section 2.2.1, USD 12.3 trillion worth of corporate bonds globally is coming due within the next three years, a significant share of which will need to be refinanced, testing the market's absorption capacity. However, with an increase in supply on the secondary market as central banks, simultaneously offload their existing holdings it may be difficult for the market to absorb such large quantities of new debt at a viable cost to issuers. Even though current central bank holdings are limited to investment grade bonds, this may also be a concern for the non-investment grade market, as the return of higher yields in the less risky investment grade market may shift traditionally more risk-averse investors' demand away from the non-investment grade market, where USD 1.1 trillion worth of bonds will need to be repaid or refinanced globally by the end of 2026.

Even so, QE directly involving corporate bonds has been relatively limited in size. The much greater market impact of QT will be on sovereign bonds, where central bank holdings are often several hundred times larger than their corporate bond holdings (see Chapter 1). Crucially, by design, central bank purchases of sovereign securities also affect markets for corporate debt. Indeed, a key purpose of quantitative easing is to put "downward pressure on longer-term interest rates and easing overall financial conditions" (US Federal Reserve System[14]). The US Federal Reserve's asset purchases contributed to lowering corporate bond yields (Gagnon et al. (2011[15]), Krishnamurthy and Vissing-Jorgensen (2011[16])). Similarly, in the EU, the ECB's (pre-pandemic) QE supported increased corporate bond issuance (Todorov (2020[17]). In addition, QE which focused solely on domestic sovereign securities by major central banks appears to have significant effects on international markets as well; QE by the US Federal Reserve has been found to have stimulated non-financial corporate bond issuance globally, particularly in emerging markets (Lo Duca, Nicoletti and Martinez (2014[18]).

Consequently, the withdrawal of this support is likely to have the inverse impact on corporate bond markets, adding to the tightening of financial conditions already stemming from higher policy rates. If, in addition to cessation of liquidity injections, central banks were to pursue widespread quantitative tightening on their holdings of sovereign securities (actively selling in the secondary market), it may set off a dynamic where greater supply of government bonds with higher yields could shift demand away from corporate bond markets. Given the significant amounts of corporate bonds maturing in the near term, this may limit capacity to undertake additional borrowing via the corporate bond market.

Box 2.2. Listed companies' debt servicing capacity under scenarios of increasing interest rates

The most obvious way in which tighter monetary policy affects corporate debt servicing capacity is by increasing the cost of debt. When debt levels and leverage are significant in an economy, increases in interest rates can alter the character of debt, possibly rendering previously sustainable debt unsustainable (Minsky, 1995[19]). To evaluate how increasing interest rates could affect corporate debt servicing capacity, a stress test is applied using two different scenarios of increases in the cost of debt financing of 200 and 400 basis points versus actual 2022 levels. The consequent impact on the share of companies and total debt at risk (defined as an interest coverage ratio below 2) is then measured. The exercise assumes that debt levels remain unchanged and that companies can roll over their debt at the higher cost. It also assumes that other balance sheet items remain unchanged. As shown in Panel A of Figure 2.28, if the cost of debt were to increase by 400 basis points, an additional 6-11% of companies would fall into the at-risk category across regions. In the United States, 45% of companies would be at-risk in the 400 basis point scenario. The effect is even more pronounced when looking at the share of debt, shown in Panel B. For instance, in China, 48% of debt would be owed by at risk companies following an increase in the cost of debt by 400 basis points, up from 29% at actual 2022 levels.

Figure 2.28. Impact on the share of listed companies and debt at risk under increasing debt financing cost scenarios, by region

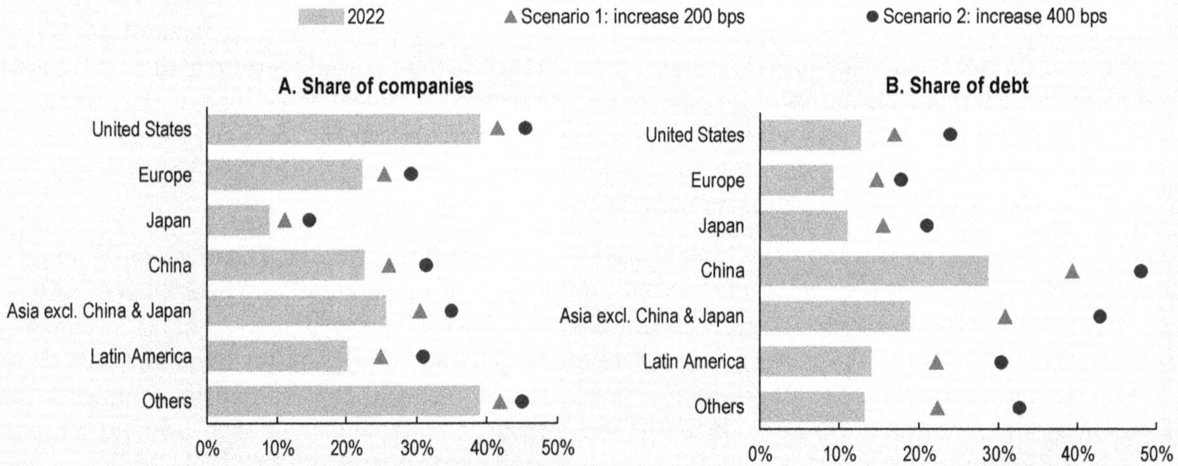

Note: Refers to listed non-financial companies. At-risk companies are defined as those with an interest coverage ratio below 2. The interest coverage ratio is the ratio of earnings before interest, taxes, depreciation and amortisation (EBITDA) to interest expenses.
Source: OECD Capital Market Series dataset, LSEG, see Annex 2.A for details.

The stress tests are also carried out at the industry level. As shown in Panel A of Figure 2.29, in the 400-basis point scenario an additional 4-19% of listed companies would fall into the at-risk category across industries. The effect is again more pronounced in terms of the share of debt. There are significant differences between industries. In the 400 basis point scenario, the share of debt owed by at-risk companies would remain relatively low at 15% in the energy industry, whereas it would reach as much as 78% in the real estate sector.

Figure 2.29. Impact on the share of companies and debt at risk under increasing debt financing cost scenarios, by industry

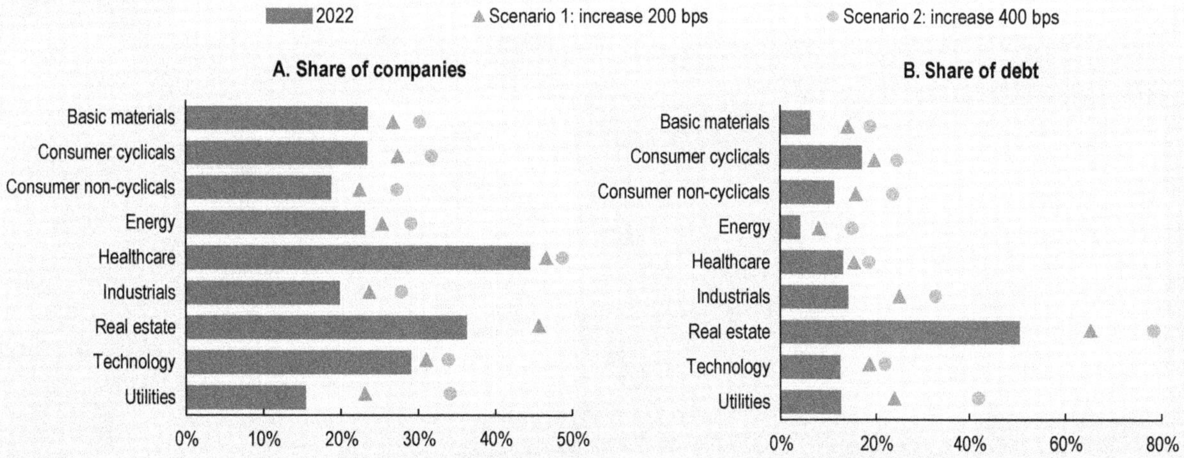

Note: Refers to listed companies. At-risk companies are defined as those with an interest coverage ratio below 2. The interest coverage ratio is the ratio of earnings before interest, taxes, depreciation and amortisation (EBITDA) to interest expenses.
Source: OECD Capital Market Series dataset, LSEG, see Annex 2.A for details.

2.4.2. The investment grade threshold and the role of credit rating agencies

Part of the general decrease in credit quality outlined in Section 2.3 comes from a change in composition within the investment grade category. The average investment grade bond today has a significantly lower rating than prior to 2008, and this is the case for both financial and non-financial companies. For non-financial companies, the share of BBB rated bonds – the lowest investment grade category – in total investment grade issuance has increased from 25% in 2000 to 53% in 2023. In addition, the share of issues rated BBB-, which in turn is the lowest sub-category rating within BBB, has increased as a share of total BBB issuance over time (Figure 2.30, Panel A). This means that a significant share of investment grade bonds now sits just above the non-investment grade threshold. At the end of 2023, the total outstanding amount of BBB rated bonds issued by non-financial companies stood at USD 4.3 trillion.

The ability of the non-investment grade market to absorb downgrades from the BBB rated category therefore merits consideration, in particular for non-financial companies. Many institutional investors are bound by regulations and/or investment mandates to restrict their holdings primarily to investment grade bonds, meaning the investor universe for non-investment grade bonds is significantly smaller than for investment grade. To measure the impact of possible downgrades, Panel B of Figure 2.30 shows the amount that different hypothetical transition rates from BBB to non-investment grade would correspond to, expressed as a share of the 2018-23 average annual non-financial, non-investment grade issuance. This serves as a proxy for the market's ability to absorb new non-investment grade debt. A downgrade of 7.5% of the stock of BBB rated bonds (equivalent to the rate in 2009) to a non-investment grade rating would represent 87% of the 5-year average annual non-investment grade issuance globally. Even a less marked transition rate of 5%, close to historical averages (S&P Global Ratings, 2023[20]), would result in an increase in non-investment grade bonds equivalent to 58% of the average issuance during the past 5 years. For a more significant transition rate of 10% (which would be higher than it was in the immediate aftermath the 2008 crisis), the figure would be 117%.

Figure 2.30. Issuance at the investment grade threshold and different downgrade scenarios

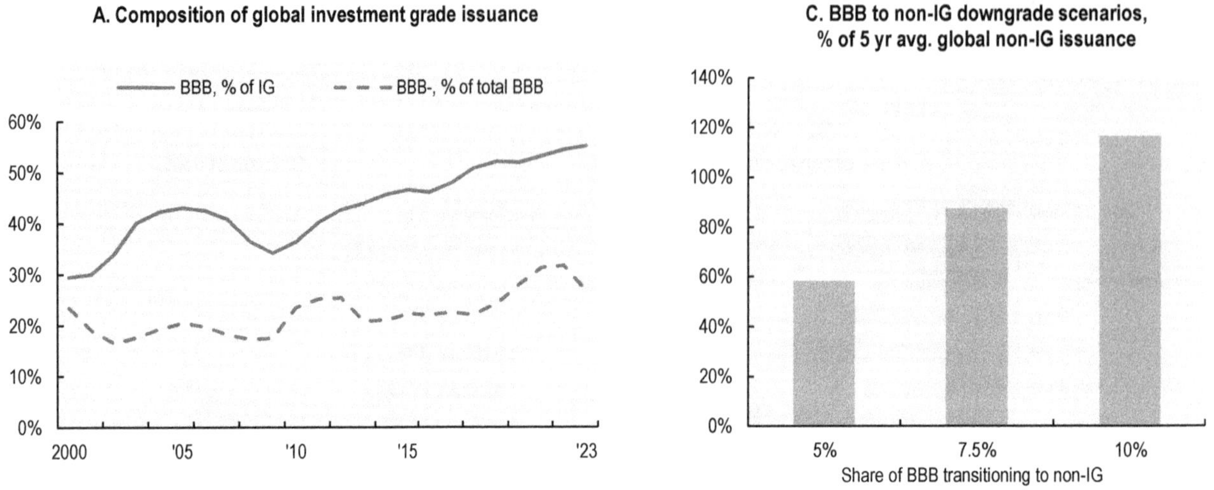

Note: Refers to non-financial companies. Panel A shows three-year rolling averages.
Source: OECD Capital Market Series Dataset, LSEG, see Annex 2.A for details.

Historically, one-step downgrades have been least common for bonds rated BBB- (Figure 2.31). This is not unexpected; given the significance of the investment grade threshold and the impact on the availability of capital and financing costs of moving either side of it, companies are likely to pay close attention to their credit quality metrics (such as leverage) when their debt is rated BBB- to avoid falling into non-investment grade territory. Similarly, companies that are just below the investment grade threshold make specific efforts to be upgraded, as is evident from the fact that BB+ rated bonds (the highest non-investment grade rating) have among the highest probability of being upgraded (Çelik, Demirtaş and Isaksson, 2020[21]). It is possible, however, that in addition to efforts by companies to maintain their creditworthiness, rating agencies, aware of the significance of an investment grade rating, exercise particular caution when it comes to downgrading bonds rated BBB-.

Figure 2.31. Long-term historical average downgrade probability by rating

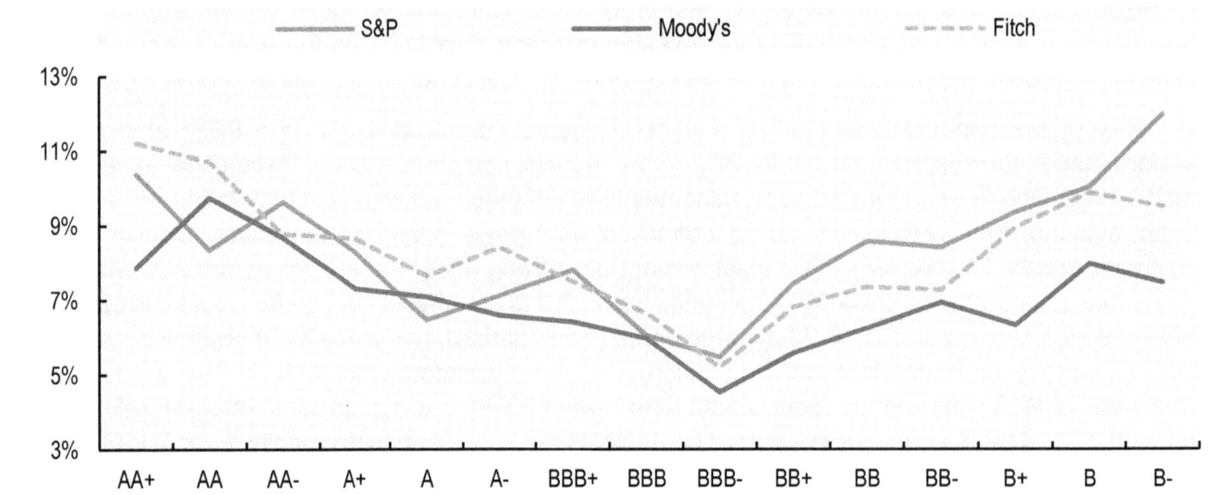

Note: Average one-year, one-step (e.g. A+ to A) transition rates for the follow periods: S&P 1981-2022, Moody's 1983-2022, Fitch 1990-2022. B- is the lowest rating since ratings below B- are grouped together in the transition reports. Triple A rated issuers are excluded due to sample size limitations.
Source: S&P 2022 Annual Global Corporate Default and Rating Transition Study; Moody's Annual default study 2022; Fitch 2022 Transition and Default Studies.

The concentration of investment grade issuance towards lower credit qualities coupled with sharp increases in borrowing begs the question of whether the historical trend shown in Figure 2.31 can hold in with tighter credit conditions. This is especially relevant when considering that the characteristics of BBB rated bonds have changed over time. As shown in Figure 2.32, the 3-year rolling average (median) leverage of a BBB rated issuance by a non-financial company was about 44% (35%) higher in 2023 than in 2008 in advanced economies and 162% (229%) in emerging economies (Panel A). Globally, the share of BBB rated bonds issued by non-financial companies with debt-to-EBITDA ratios over 4 was 42% in 2023, compared to 11% in 2008 (Panel B). In other words, the average BBB rated bond issuer today is significantly more leveraged than the average BBB rated bond issuer 15 years ago. Thanks to historically low interest rates in the post-2008 period, borrowers have been able to maintain similar repayment capacities with much higher leverage (see Figure 2.20).

However, rapid increases in interest rates will translate into higher debt servicing costs as companies need to refinance their debts, whereas leverage and debt levels do not automatically adjust, possibly lowering the debt servicing capacity of current investment grade-rated issuers to a level more typical of non-investment grade issuers. In addition, the withdrawal of central bank liquidity may have a particularly significant impact on issuers currently rated just above the investment grade threshold. Evidence suggests that these companies specifically have benefitted from subsidised financing costs on their bonds as a result of QE (Acharya et al., 2022[22]).

Figure 2.32. The changing characteristics of BBB rated issuers (non-financial companies)

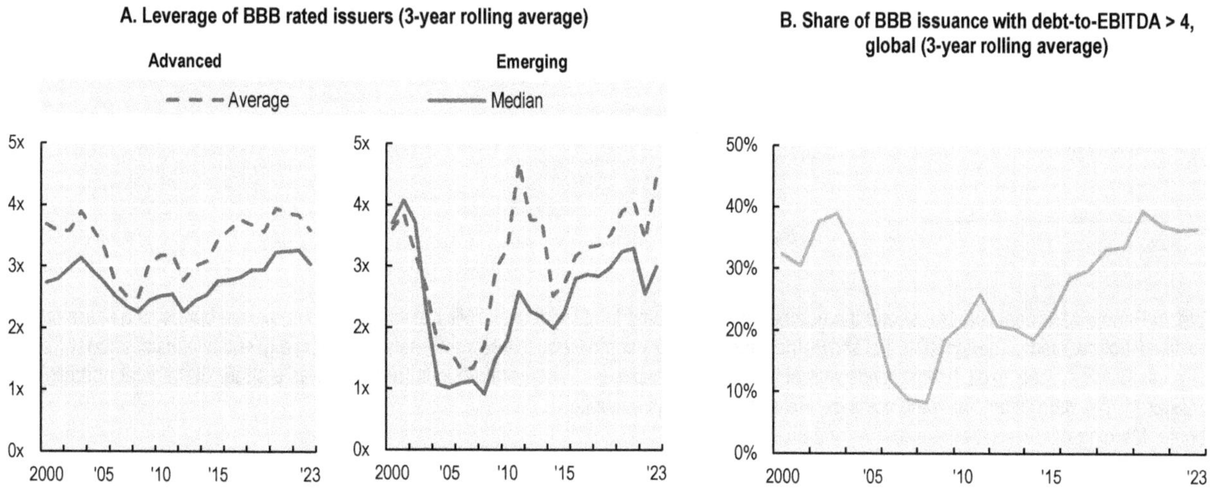

Note: Leverage is measured as debt-to-EBITDA, winsorized at 1%. Excludes issuers with negative EBITDA.
Source: OECD Capital Market Series Dataset, LSEG, see Annex 2.A for details.

2.4.3. Fund ownership and fire sale dynamics

The shift towards lower-rated issuance should be examined in connection with the increase in investment fund participation in corporate bond markets. Due to their structure which allows investors to redeem shares at short notice, open-ended investment funds typically manage their portfolios more actively than many other institutional investors. Other significant bond investors like pension funds and insurance companies tend to follow longer term buy-and-hold strategies. The increased prevalence of investment funds in corporate bond markets therefore affects market dynamics.

The increasing bond fund dominance is clear from Panel A of Figure 2.33, which provides an alternative way of looking at this. Firstly, it shows how fixed income funds have been steadily increasing as a share of all new funds (i.e. including e.g. equity and commodity funds) over time. On average, between 2000 and

2008 fixed income funds represented 14% of all new funds each year, compared to 18% from 2009 to 2023. Within this increasingly dominant universe of funds, the share of corporate bond-focused funds has also been increasing. Funds with more than 25% net exposure to corporate bonds, a stricter measure compared to that used in Section 2.2.2, grew from representing 26% of all new fixed income funds in 2010 to 45% in 2021, before falling back to 28% in 2023. Given that there is no equivalent drop in the share of fixed income funds in all new funds, this sharp decrease is likely to at least partly be an effect of increasingly attractive yields on sovereign securities and therefore a shift in composition of investment among fixed income funds.

In the standard universe of funds (minimum 1% net exposure to corporate bonds), the value-weighted average portfolio share of BBB rated securities (including non-corporate securities) is 18% for open-ended funds and as much as 26% for ETFs, of which BBB- represents 6 percentage points each (Panel B). This amounts to a total net exposure of USD 1.7 trillion to BBB rated securities, of which USD 519 billion refers to BBB- rated securities (Panel C).

Figure 2.33. Corporate bond funds' growth and exposure to BBB rated securities, globally

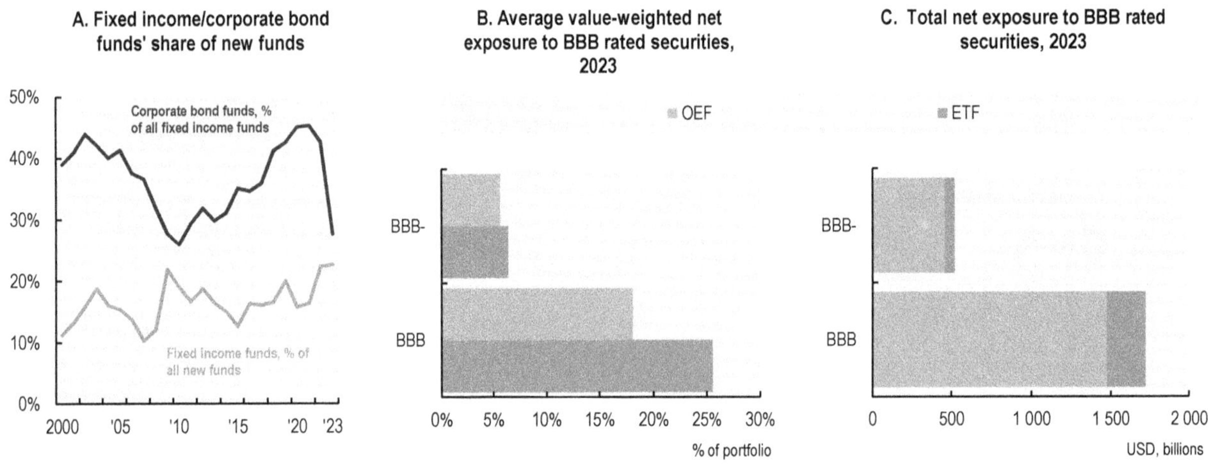

Note: In Panel A, the dark blue line shows the number of fixed income funds with over 25% net exposure to corporate bonds as a share of total new fixed income funds. The light blue line shows the share of fixed income funds in total new funds (including e.g. equity and commodity funds). In Panels B and C, only fixed income funds with at least 1% net exposure to corporate bonds (measured as a share of the total portfolio) are considered. The data refer to all rated holdings, including sovereign securities.
Source: Morningstar Direct, see Annex 2.A for details.

Significant exposure to corporate bonds by open-ended funds can have implications for broader market functioning. This stems from a liquidity mismatch between the funds and the underlying instruments. Similar to the liquidity transformation of a bank, this can be managed as long as flows are not too one-sided and large. However, in a scenario where there are significant redemptions in a short period, funds may have to sell substantial amounts of corporate bonds in a relatively illiquid secondary market which could trigger fire sale dynamics. Owing to the nature of the instrument and its main investors, corporate bond markets have never been particularly liquid, and there is evidence that liquidity has deteriorated since the 2008 financial crisis (Friewald, Jankowitsch and Subrahmanyam, 2012[23]). During the same period, fund exposure to corporate bonds has increased substantially.

Exposure to BBB rated securities is important to this discussion. Because of their position on the threshold between investment grade and non-investment grade, they are particularly sensitive to potential fire sale dynamics. This makes it critical to understand which funds are holding these securities. Of the USD 1.7 trillion total net exposure to BBB rated securities, 37% (USD 627 billion) corresponds to funds with more than 75% net exposure to corporate bonds (Figure 2.34). This concentration is particularly pronounced among ETFs, where 63% (USD 155 billion) of all BBB exposure sits in funds with over 75% corporate bond exposure (Panel B).

The dynamics for ETFs differ somewhat from that of other open-ended funds. Owing to the relative illiquidity, the difference between the share price and the underlying assets can fluctuate substantially for bond ETFs (more than for equity ETFs), which are in effect being actively managed through the security composition of the creation and redemption baskets. It has been argued that this flexibility allows bond ETFs to counteract fire sale dynamics, absorbing liquidity pressures in ETF shares rather than in the underlying bonds, thereby stabilising markets (Shim and Todorov, 2021[24]). In a high-outflow scenario, sponsors could change the composition of the redemption basket by including riskier and more illiquid bonds, thus leaving non-selling investors with higher-quality backing for their shares, mitigating sales pressures (Todorov, 2021[25]).

However, the potential effects of bond ETFs on financial stability are still a matter of debate. In contrast to the previous narrative, it has also been argued that while ETFs generally help improve corporate bond liquidity, they actually tend to worsen liquidity conditions in times of crises (Koont et al., 2022[26]). The ETF market proved resilient during the last significant stress episode in early 2020, but it is uncertain to what extent this was a result of the central banks' asset purchase programmes, as opposed to built-in shock absorbers in the ETFs themselves.

Figure 2.34. Global investment fund exposure to BBB rated securities for funds with different corporate bond exposure, early 2024

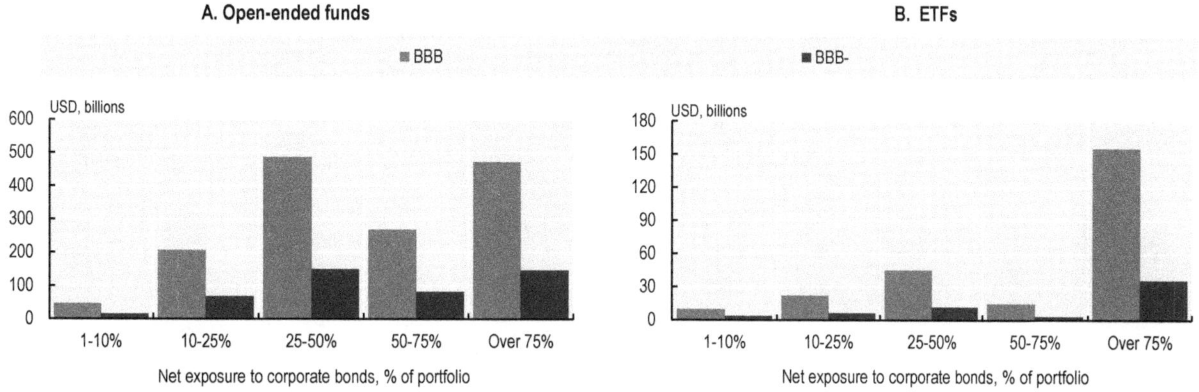

Note: Only fixed income funds with at least 1% net exposure to corporate bonds (measured as a share of the total portfolio) are considered. The data refer to all rated holdings, including sovereign securities.
Source: Morningstar Direct, see Annex 2.A for details.

The risk of fire sales is particularly relevant for the subset of funds whose investment mandate includes some form of rating-based restriction. To gauge the exposure of this market segment, a sample of 1 161 funds that are specifically categorised as investment grade funds is examined (Figure 2.35). The total size of these funds amounts to USD 3.2 trillion, representing 35% of the total size of funds with at least 1% net exposure to corporate bonds. Like other fixed income funds, these funds have also increased their exposure to corporate bonds in recent years (Panel A). Their value-weighted net exposure to BBB rated securities is 21% of the total portfolio. This amounts to USD 651 billion, of which USD 196 billion is rated BBB-, the lowest possible investment grade rating (Panel B). Should these bonds be downgraded to non-investment grade status, a significant share of these holdings would likely need to be sold. However, this particular subset remains a relatively small part of the global non-investment grade corporate bond market, which stood at USD 3.4 trillion at the end of 2023.

Figure 2.35. Investment grade funds' exposure to corporate bonds and BBB rated securities, globally

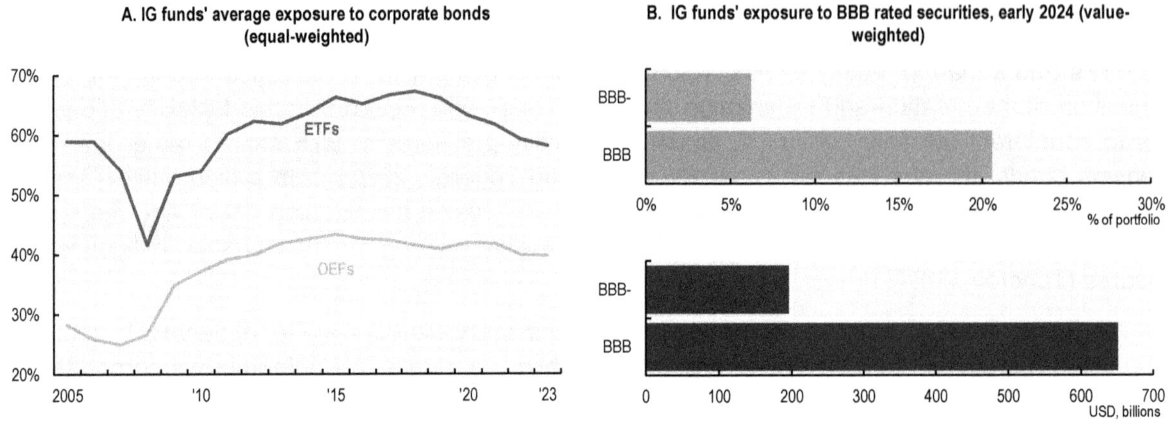

Note: Based on 1 161 different funds where the Morningstar Institutional Category includes an indication of "investment grade" or a specific investment grade rating, e.g. "BBB rated" and "A rated". Only fixed income funds with at least 1% net exposure to corporate bonds (measured as a share of the total portfolio) are considered. The data refer to all rated holdings, including sovereign securities.
Source: Morningstar Direct, see Annex 2.A for details.

References

Acharya, V. et al. (2022), "Exorbitant privilege? Quantitative easing and the bond market subsidy of prospective fallen angels", *BIS Working Papers*, Vol. 1002, https://www.bis.org/publ/work1002.pdf. [22]

Bank of England (2023), *Asset Purchase Facility: Bank of England concludes corporate bond sales programme – Market Notice 6 June 2023*, https://www.bankofengland.co.uk/markets/market-notices/2023/june/apf-boe-concludes-corporate-bond-sales-programme-6-june-2023. [12]

Bank of England (2022), *Monetary Policy Summary and minutes of the Monetary Policy Committee meeting ending on 2 February 2022*, https://www.bankofengland.co.uk/-/media/boe/files/monetary-policy-summary-and-minutes/2022/february-2022.pdf. [11]

Bank of Japan (2022), *Statement on Monetary Policy*, https://www.boj.or.jp/en/mopo/mpmdeci/mpr_2022/k220318a.pdf. [9]

Bank of Japan (2022), *Statement on Monetary Policy*, https://www.boj.or.jp/en/mopo/mpmdeci/mpr_2022/k221220a.pdf. [10]

Çelik, S., G. Demirtaş and M. Isaksson (2020), *Corporate Bond Market Trends, Emerging Risks and Monetary Policy*, OECD Capital Market Series, https://www.oecd.org/corporate/ca/Corporate-Bond-Market-Trends-Emerging-Risks-Monetary-Policy.pdf. [21]

ECB (2024), *Pandemic emergency purchase programme (PEPP)*, https://www.ecb.europa.eu/mopo/implement/pepp/html/index.en.html (accessed on January 2024). [7]

ECB (n.d.), *Asset purchase programmes*, https://www.ecb.europa.eu/mopo/implement/app/html/index.en.html (accessed on January 2024). [8]

Federal Reserve Bank of New York (n.d.), *Secondary Market Corporate Credit Facility*, https://www.newyorkfed.org/markets/secondary-market-corporate-credit-facility (accessed on January 2024). [13]

Friewald, N., R. Jankowitsch and M. Subrahmanyam (2012), "Illiquidity or credit deterioration: A study of liquidity in the U.S. corporate bond market during financial crises", *Journal of Financial Economics*, Vol. 105/1, pp. 18– 36, https://doi.org/10.1016/j.jfineco.2012.02.001. [23]

Gagnon, J. et al. (2011), "The Financial Market Effects of the Federal Reserve's Large-Scale Asset Purchases", *International Journal of Central Banking*, Vol. 7/1, https://www.ijcb.org/journal/ijcb11q1a1.pdf. [15]

Koont, N. et al. (2022), "Steering a Ship in Illiquid Waters: Active Management of Passive Funds", *National Bureau of Economic Research Working Papers*, https://www.nber.org/system/files/working_papers/w30039/w30039.pdf. [26]

Krishnamurthy, A. and A. Vissing-Jorgensen (2011), "The Effects of Quantitative Easing on Interest Rates: Channels and Implications for Policy", *National Bureau of Economic Research Working Papers*, https://doi.org/10.3386/w17555. [16]

Lo Duca, M., G. Nicoletti and A. Martinez (2014), “Global Corporate Bond Issuance: What Role for US Quantitative Easing?”, *ECB Working Papers*, Vol. No. 1649, https://doi.org/10.2139/ssrn.2397787. [18]

Minsky, H. (1995), “Financial Factors in the Economics of Capitalism”, *Journal of Financial Services Research*, pp. 197-208, https://doi.org/10.1007/BF01051746. [19]

MIS (2023), *Annual default study: Corporate default rate will rise in 2023 and peak in early 2024*, https://www.moodys.com/research/Default-Trends-Global-Annual-default-study-Corporate-default-rate-will--PBC_1357792. [5]

OECD (2022), *Corporate Finance in Asia and the COVID-19 Crisis*, OECD Publishing, https://doi.org/10.1787/87861cf0-en. [1]

OECD (2021), *The rise of non-bank financial intermediation in real estate finance: Post COVID-19 trends, vulnerabilities and policy implications*, OECD Publishing, https://www.oecd.org/daf/fin/financial-markets/The-rise-of-non-bank-financial-intermediation-in-real-estate-finance.pdf. [3]

Palomino, F. et al. (2019), *The information in interest coverage ratios of the US nonfinancial corporate sector*, https://www.federalreserve.gov/econres/notes/feds-notes/information-in-interest-coverage-ratios-of-the-us-nonfinancial-corporate-sector-20190110.html (accessed on December 2023). [4]

S&P (2023), *Default, Transition, and Recovery: 2022 Annual Global Corporate Default And Rating Transition Study*, https://www.spglobal.com/ratings/en/research/articles/230425-default-transition-and-recovery-2022-annual-global-corporate-default-and-rating-transition-study-12702145 (accessed on January 2023). [6]

S&P Global Ratings (2023), *Default, Transition, and Recovery: 2022 Annual Global Corporate Default And Rating Transition Study*, https://www.spglobal.com/ratings/en/research/articles/230425-default-transition-and-recovery-2022-annual-global-corporate-default-and-rating-transition-study-12702145. [20]

Shim, J. and K. Todorov (2021), “ETFs, illiquid assets, and fire sales”, *BIS Working Papers*, https://www.bis.org/publ/work975.pdf. [24]

Todorov, K. (2021), *The anatomy of bond ETF arbitrage*, https://www.bis.org/publ/qtrpdf/r_qt2103d.pdf. [25]

Todorov, K. (2020), “Quantify the quantitative easing: Impact on bonds and corporate debt issuance”, *Journal of Financial Economics*, Vol. 135/2, pp. 340-358, https://doi.org/10.1016/j.jfineco.2019.08.003. [17]

Trepp (2023), *Trepp CMBS Delinquency Report*, CMBS Research, https://www.trepp.com/hubfs/Trepp%20Delinquency_Report%20June%202023.pdf?hsCtaTracking=5d28d466-3d72-4d81-bb6d-c700ff3c607b%7Cc4b810e3-d869-4647-a4d8-1aa55e62943c. [2]

US Federal Reserve System (n.d.), *The Federal Reserve’s response to the financial crisis and actions to foster maximum employment and price stability*, https://www.federalreserve.gov/monetarypolicy/bst_crisisresponse.htm (accessed on January 2024). [14]

Annex 2.A. Methodology for data collection and classification

A. Corporate bond data

Data presented on corporate bond issuances are based on OECD calculations using data obtained from LSEG that provides international deal-level data on new issues of corporate bonds that are underwritten by an investment bank. The database provides a detailed set of information for each corporate bond issue, including the identity, nationality and sector of the issuer; the type, interest rate structure, maturity date and rating category of the bond, the amount of and use of proceeds obtained from the issue.

Convertible bonds, deals that were registered but not consummated, preferred shares, sukuk bonds, bonds with an original maturity less than or equal to 1 year or an issue size less than USD 1 million are excluded from the dataset. The industry classification is carried out based on The Reference Data Business Classification (TRBC) from LSEG. Yearly issuance amounts initially collected in USD were adjusted by 2023 US CPI.

Given that a significant portion of bonds are issued internationally, it is not possible to assign such issues to a certain country of issue. For this reason, the country breakdown is carried out based on the country of domicile of the issuer. The advanced/emerging market classification is based on the IMF's country classification.

Rating data

Rating information is based on OECD calculations using data obtained from LSEG that provides rating information from three leading rating agencies: S&P, Fitch and Moody's. For each bond that has rating information in the dataset, a value of 1 is assigned to the lowest credit quality rating (C) and 21 to the highest credit quality rating (AAA for S&P and Fitch and Aaa for Moody's). There are eleven non-investment grade categories: five from C (C to CCC+); and six from B (B- to BB+). There are ten investment grade categories: three from B (BBB- to BBB+); and seven from A (A- to AAA).

If ratings from multiple rating agencies are available for a given issue, their average is used. Some issues in the dataset, on the other hand, do not have rating information available. For such issues, the average rating of all bonds issued by the same issuer in the same year (t) is assigned. If the issuer has no rated bonds in year t, year t-1 and year t-2 are also considered, respectively. This procedure increases the number of rated bonds in the dataset and hence improves how representative the rating-based analysis is. When differentiating between investment and non-investment grade bonds, the final rating is rounded to the closest integer and issuances with a rounded rating less than or equal to 11 are classified as non-investment grade.

Early redemption data

When calculating the outstanding amount of corporate bonds in a given year, issues that are no longer outstanding due to being redeemed earlier than their maturity should also be deducted. The early redemption data are obtained from LSEG WS and cover bonds that have been redeemed early due to being repaid via final default distribution, called, liquidated, put or repurchased. The early redemption data are merged with the primary corporate bond market data via International Securities Identification Numbers (ISINs).

B. Investment fund data

Investment fund analyses are based on OECD calculations using fund-level data obtained from Morningstar Direct. The baseline dataset is split into nine broad categories (Morningstar Global Broad Category Group) based on the primary asset class orientation of the fund: Allocation, Alternative, Commodities, Convertibles, Equity, Fixed Income, Miscellaneous, Money Market and Property. In total, the dataset includes over 281 000 open-ended funds and ETFs, of which 48 805 are fixed income funds. Fund size is reported in current USD. Only observations for which fund size is disclosed in 2023 or later are included in the analysis.

To identify funds that participate in the corporate bond market, a subset of the fixed income funds with at least 1 per cent net exposure (long exposure minus short exposure, as a share of the total portfolio) to corporate bonds as of the latest available observation (typically early 2024) is created. For this subset, a separate time series dataset is created, including information about each fund's net exposure to corporate bonds over time (from 2005) as well as its holding weighted distribution by credit rating level (from 2017). The rating-based data refer to the portfolio as a whole and is not limited to corporate securities. Ratings must originate from credit rating agencies recognised by regulatory agencies.

Fund exposures to corporate bonds and to BBB rated securities are observed on a monthly basis. However, not every fund has exposure data available in every month. Therefore, an average annual exposure (based on available month-end observations), calculated for each fund, is used. To calculate fund exposure in absolute terms, the total fund size is multiplied by this exposure.

For analysis that is split by region, the fund's investment area is used. This denotes the geographic area that the fund focuses its investments in and may be different from the fund's domicile or region of sale.

Investment grade funds

Investment grade-focused fixed income funds are identified using the Morningstar Institutional Category. The following categories are included: A-Rated, BBB-Rated, Intermediate Investment Grade (4-6), Long Investment Grade (>6), Short/Intermediate Investment Grade (2.5-4), Short-Term Investment Grade and Ultrashort Investment Grade. This subset includes a total of 1 161 funds.

C. Balance sheet information for listed non-financial firms

The information presented in Section 2.3.2 and Box 2.2 of this chapter is based on OECD calculations using LSEG Datastream. The unbalanced Panel dataset contains financial statement information for listed non-financial companies between 2005 and 2022. The universe covers 57 053 companies registered in 138 countries.

Financial information cleaning

The raw financial dataset contains several firm-year observations when a company reports for different purposes. To construct a Panel with a unique firm-year observation, the following steps are applied:

- Financial companies are excluded
- Firms listed on an over-the-counter (OTC) market are excluded
- Security types classified as "units" and "trust" are excluded
- Firms identified as delisted are excluded
- For firms with multiple observations but different countries of domicile, their true country of domicile is manually checked to remove duplicates

- Financial statements covering a 12-month period are used
- Companies with at least one observation showing negative assets or negative fixed assets are excluded
- Financial information is adjusted by annual US Consumer Price Index (CPI) changes and information is reported in 2022 USD

Industry classification

LSEG Datastream uses LSEG's The Reference Data Business Classification (TRBC). The economic sectors used in the analysis are the following:

TRBC Economic Sector	
Basic materials	Healthcare
Consumer cyclicals	Industrials
Consumer non-cyclicals	Real estate
Energy	Technology
Financials	Utilities

D. Stress test

The stress test aims to assess the impact of increased financing costs on the ability of companies to service their interest expenses using their earnings before interest, taxes, depreciation and amortisation (EBITDA). To perform the test, 2022 financial statement data from 30 969 non-financial companies are used.

The stress test assumes that only the cost of financing changes and that all other balance sheet and income statement items remain unchanged.

The baseline financing cost is based on 2022 data and is calculated by taking the ratio of interest expenses to financial debt.

Two alternative scenarios are assessed:

1. Scenario 1: An increase in financing costs of 200 basis points compared to the baseline scenario.
2. Scenario 2: An increase in financing costs of 400 basis points compared to the base-line scenario.

For each scenario, the new projected interest expenses are calculated by multiplying the existing level of financial debt with the projected cost of financing. The interest coverage ratio is then calculated by dividing the earnings before interest, taxes, depreciation and amortisation by the new projected interest expenses. Companies with an interest coverage ratio below 2 are defined as at-risk.

Notes

[1] The industry identifier used in this analysis (TRBC Economic Sector) classifies companies active in real estate operations as financial firms. These make up a large share of the Chinese non-investment grade financial company issuance from 2010 to 2014.

[2] While the intention is to hold these bonds until maturity, the Bank of England will consider participation in open market tender offers on a case-by-case basis.

3 Sustainable bonds: State of the market and policy considerations

At the end of 2023, the outstanding amount of sustainable bonds issued by the corporate and official sectors totaled USD 2.3 trillion and USD 2.0 trillion, respectively. Green bonds dominate issuance in both sectors. The key difference between the sectors is that sustainability-linked bonds (SLBs) played a lesser role in the official sector, with only USD 9 billion issued in 2023. Additionally, sustainable bonds constituted a modest portion of funding for central governments, representing merely 0.4% of all sovereign bond issuances in 2023.

There is no statistically significant evidence that companies systematically benefit from a premium for issuing a sustainable bond. This is a sign that market practices and regulations may need to change for sustainable bonds to fulfil their potential. For example, sustainable bond contracts typically allow issuers to refinance existing projects with the proceeds, rather than invest in new projects. At the same time, the share of sustainable bonds being assured by second party opinion providers has grown from less than half in 2019 to nearly three-quarters in 2023.

3.1. Introduction

This chapter focuses on the key characteristics and trends in the markets of sustainable bonds. This introduction presents a definition of sustainable bonds, and the box below summarises the key findings in the chapter. The second section presents the trends in the issuance of sustainable bonds, their outstanding value, their investor base, assets under management in sustainable investment funds, and the use of standards and taxonomies. The third section covers key issues for policy makers, including the main goals of the largest investors in sustainable bonds, whether there is a premium for sustainable bonds, the roles of relevant service providers, key characteristics of sustainable bond contracts, and the development and liquidity of sustainable bond markets. The final section raises policy questions based on the data and analysis presented in the previous sections.

Sustainable bonds can be classified into two major categories (ICMA, 2022[1]). "Use of proceeds bonds" are bonds whose proceeds should be used to either partially or fully finance or re-finance new or existing eligible green, social or sustainable projects. In the case of "use of proceeds bonds" issued by financial institutions, the proceeds are typically allocated to finance or refinance the provision of loans for the development of eligible projects. "Sustainability-linked bonds" (SLBs) are bonds for which the issuer's financing costs or other characteristics of the bond (e.g., its maturity) can vary depending on whether the issuer meets specific sustainability performance targets within a timeline, but whose proceeds do not need to be invested in projects with an expected positive environmental or social impact.

The "use of proceeds bonds" include green, social and sustainability bonds (GSS bonds). As their name suggests, the proceeds of *green bonds* must be applied to finance projects with expected environmental benefits, which may include, for instance, projects in renewable energy, clean transportation, biodiversity conservation, and wastewater management (ICMA, 2021[2]). In this classification, "blue bonds" and "climate bonds", which focus on environmental issues related to the sea and climate change, respectively, would be classified as "green bonds". The resources raised through *social bonds* must be invested in projects that aim to address or mitigate a specific social issue or seek to achieve positive social outcomes, including affordable housing, food security and the empowerment of minorities (ICMA, 2023[3]). *Sustainability bonds* are bonds where the proceeds should be used to finance a combination of both green and social eligible projects.

The following sections of this chapter analyse the key characteristics of both categories of sustainable bonds and their implications for companies, investors, and the entities comprising the official sector (the latter category includes national and subnational governments and their agencies, as well as multilateral institutions). However, one basic characteristic of sustainable bonds should be clear from the start. Sustainable bonds present the same rights and risks to their holders as with any other conventional bond, but they also create a commitment. In the case of the GSS bonds, the issuer ordinarily commits to having developed or to plan to invest in eligible sustainable projects with a value that is equal to or higher than the outstanding value of the GSS bonds it has issued. In the case of SLBs, the issuer commits to reaching sustainability performance targets, such as reducing its greenhouse gas (GHG) emissions. The potential for these commitments to effectively change the investment decisions of companies and the official sector, as well as whether investors assign any value to such commitments, are central to the chapter.

Key findings

- **At the end of 2023, the outstanding amount of sustainable bonds issued by the corporate and the official sectors totalled, respectively, USD 2.3 trillion and USD 2.0 trillion**. The total amount issued through sustainable bonds in the corporate and official sectors was six and seven times larger in 2019-23 than in 2014-18, respectively.
- **Green bonds represented 74% of the total issued in corporate sustainable bonds in 2023**, and SLBs were the second most relevant type of sustainable bonds with 10%. The issuance of sustainable bonds by non-financial companies (USD 230 billion) represented 12% of all bonds issued by the non-financial corporate sector, while the issuance by financial companies (USD 253 billion) represented 8% of the issuance of all bonds issued by the financial sector.
- **The official sector has also been issuing a significant amount in sustainable bonds (USD 394 billion in 2023), but two significant differences are noticeable** compared to the corporate sector. First, SLBs are much less relevant than GSS bonds for the official sector, with only USD 9 billion in issuance in 2023. Second, sustainable bonds remain a relatively limited source of funding for central governments, representing only 0.4% of the total issuance of all sovereign bonds in 2023.
- **The standards developed by the International Capital Market Association (ICMA) were used to classify bonds as sustainable in issuances representing 93% of the total sustainable bond issuance in 2023**. Issuers may typically refer to third-party taxonomies for sustainable activities or to their own classification for eligible projects. The most-often used taxonomies in 2023 were the ones from the Climate Bonds Initiative (66%), the European Union (14%), and the People's Republic of China's central bank and securities regulator (12%).
- **There is no statistically significant evidence that companies systematically benefit from a premium for issuing a sustainable bond**. Based on a limited sample of matched bonds, this also seems to hold true for the official sector.
- **The share of sustainable bonds being assured by second party opinion providers has grown from less than half in 2019 to three-quarters in 2023**. These service providers verify whether the bond contract is aligned with a specific sustainable bond standard.
- **Two-thirds of the prospectuses mention that the refinancing of existing eligible projects with the proceeds is allowed**, and no prospectus in the same sample explicitly mentions that the proceeds would not be used for refinancing in a sample of GSS bonds. Additionally, no GSS bond prospectus in the sample refers to a contractual penalty in case the issuer does not use all proceeds to finance or refinance eligible projects.
- **There is limited evidence that sovereign issuance of green bonds has supported the development of the corporate green bond market**. Still, sovereign issuers may have other reasons to issue sustainable bonds, including the diversification of their investor base.

3.2. Trends

3.2.1. Issuance and outstanding amount

Over the past five years, sustainable bonds have experienced a noteworthy growth as a source of capital market financing for both the corporate and official sectors. The total amount issued through corporate sustainable bonds was six times larger in 2019-23 than in 2014-18. Similarly, the amount issued by the official sector in the last five years was seven times larger compared to 2014-18. Moreover, in 2021 a record amount of USD 713 billion was issued by corporates, of which 57% was issued by non-financial companies (Figure 3.1, Panel A). Concerning the sustainable bonds issued by the official sector, they displayed record amounts in 2020 and 2021, with a total amount issued of USD 461 billion and USD 580 billion, respectively (Figure 3.1, Panel B). In 2020, multilateral institutions issued almost USD 230 billion in sustainable bonds. In 2023, corporate sustainable bond issuance decreased by 32% compared to 2021, while the official sector also saw the same decrease in its issuance of sustainable bonds (see sustainable bonds issuance over the total amount of bonds issued in Figure 3.8 and Figure 3.12).[1]

Figure 3.1. Global sustainable bond issuance by issuer type

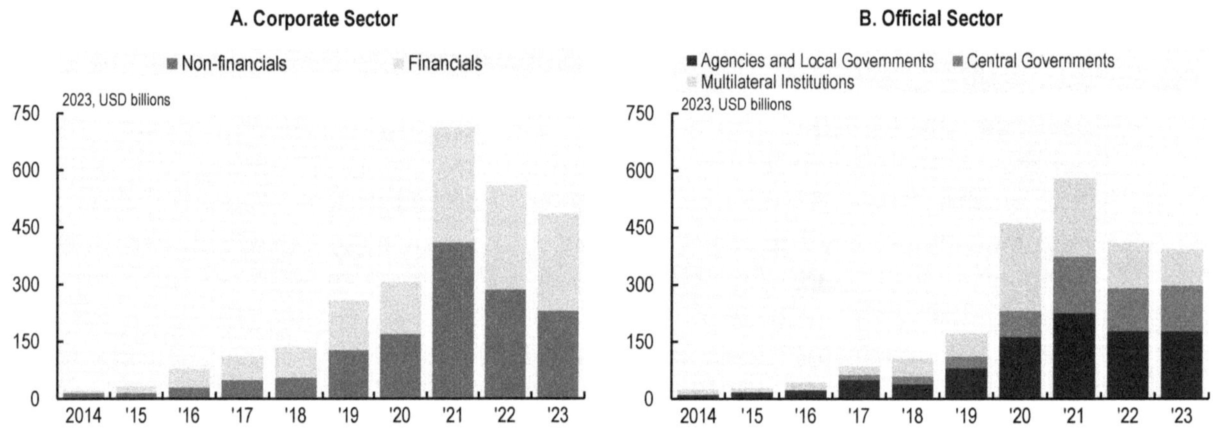

Note: In Panel B, *agencies and local governments* include national government agencies (e.g., KFW), local governments (e.g., Prefecture of Shiga), and national development banks (e.g., Brazilian Development Bank). The category *Multilateral Institutions* includes organisations formed by three or more jurisdictions (e.g., International Finance Corporation), and the European Union.
Source: OECD Corporate Sustainability dataset, LSEG.

In 2023, the outstanding amount of sustainable bonds issued by the corporate sector totalled USD 2.3 trillion against USD 1.99 trillion by the official sector. The outstanding amount of sustainable bonds issued by the non-financial corporate sector accounted for USD 1 230 billion, representing 8% of the outstanding amount of the bonds issued in this sector. Similarly, financial companies' outstanding amount of corporate bonds totalled USD 1 068 billion, which is 6% of the outstanding amount of all corporate bonds issued by financial companies (Figure 3.2, Panel A). Moreover, the outstanding amount of sustainable bonds stood at USD 853 billion for "agencies and local governments" and at USD 686 billion for "multilateral institutions", and for central governments this amount was comparably lower at USD 450 billion in 2023.

Figure 3.2. Outstanding sustainable bonds by issuer type

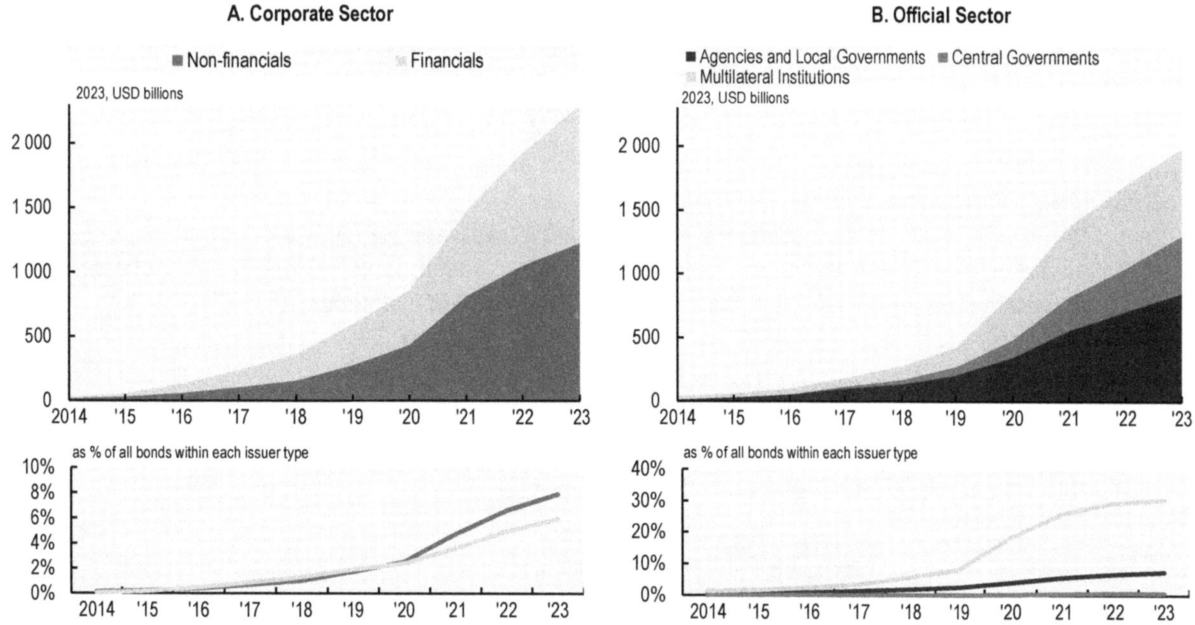

Source: OECD Corporate Sustainability dataset, LSEG.

Europe has been the most active region in the sustainable bonds market in both the corporate and official sectors. From 2014 to 2023, 45% of the global amount issued through corporate non-financial sustainable bonds was raised by European companies. The People's Republic of China (China) and the United States follow with 17% and 14% respectively (Figure 3.3, Panel A). Similarly, the issuance of sustainable bonds by financial corporates has been most relevant in Europe (54%), China (15%), Asia excl. China and Japan (10%) and the United States (7%). Central governments' issuance of sustainable bonds has been done mainly by European jurisdictions, accounting for 67% of the global issuance of sustainable bonds from 2014 to 2023, followed by Latin American central governments with 16% of the global amount. Agencies and local governments' sustainable bond issuance has also been dominated by European issuers (65% of the global amount), followed by agencies and local governments from Asia excl. China and Japan (13%) (Figure 3.3, Panel B).

Figure 3.3. Global sustainable bond issuance by region, 2014-23

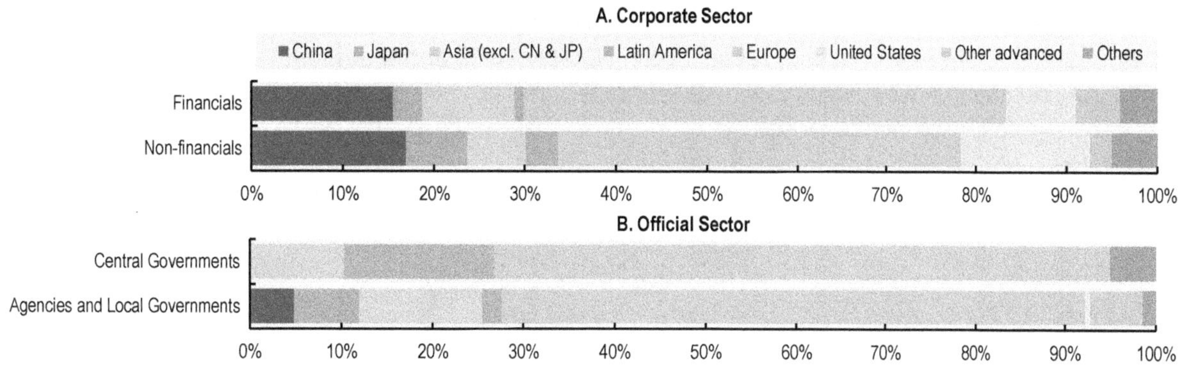

Source: OECD Corporate Sustainability dataset, LSEG.

Prior to 2020, most of the issued corporate sustainable bonds were green, averaging 92% of all the amount issued via sustainable bonds each year (Figure 3.4, Panel A). In 2020, sustainability as well as social corporate bonds represented more than 10% each of the amount issued through sustainable corporate bonds. In 2022 and 2023, SLBs, sustainability and social bonds averaged 12%, 10% and 7% of the total amount of issued corporate sustainable bonds, respectively.

The issuance of green bonds is less prevalent in the official sector, representing 45% of the amount issued in the last three years on average. Social (29%) and sustainability (26%) bonds have been commonly used by governments and multilateral institutions over the last three years (Figure 3.4, Panel B). SLBs were issued for the first time by central governments and multilateral institutions in 2022, making up only 1% of the share of sustainable bonds issued in the last two years in the official sector.

Figure 3.4. Global sustainable bond issuance by type

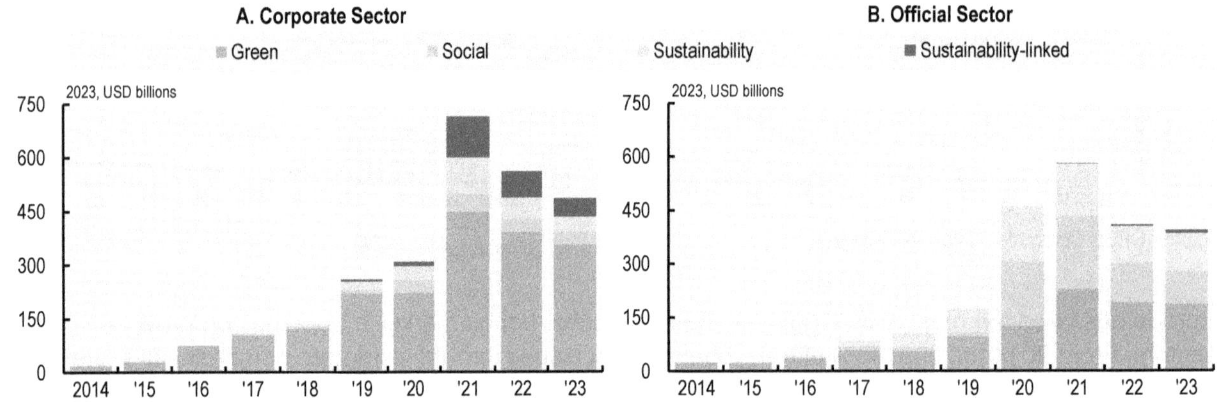

Source: OECD Corporate Sustainability dataset, LSEG.

When analysing the issuer's promised use of the proceeds as established in the GSS bond documentation, "renewable energy projects", "energy efficiency" and "green construction/buildings" rank first among GSS bonds issued by financial and non-financial corporates. "Eligible green projects", which effectively present an open scope for investments, ranks fifth among GSS bonds issued by non-financial corporates. In Table 3.1, the categories of "use of proceeds" in GSS bonds are ranked by their importance for each of the issuer types.

Agencies, local governments and multilateral institutions' top priority when issuing GSS bonds has been "social expenditures". Additionally, "biodiversity conservation", "social expenditures" and "clean transport" rank among the top three priorities in the central governments' issuance of GSS bonds, with 19%, 12% and 11% of the total amount raised, respectively. Notably, 10% of the amount raised via GSS bonds by multilateral institutions was issued with a general-purpose use of the proceeds and, thus, not a sustainability-related specific purpose.

Table 3.1. GSS bonds' use of proceeds, 2014-23

Top 1 Top 2 Top 3 Top 4 Top 5	Corporate Sector: Non-financials	Corporate Sector: Financials	Official Sector: Agencies and Local Governments	Official Sector: Central Governments	Official Sector: Multilateral Institutions
Agriculture	0%	0%	0%	1%	1%
Biodiversity Conservation	3%	4%	3%	19%	5%
Clean Transport	10%	11%	11%	11%	5%
Climate Change Adaptation	6%	6%	4%	10%	8%
Energy Efficiency	18%	15%	10%	11%	8%
Green Construction/Buildings	10%	17%	5%	7%	5%
Infrastructure	8%	4%	14%	3%	10%
Renewable Energy Projects	21%	15%	8%	7%	7%
Social Expenditures	3%	9%	28%	12%	25%
Sustainable Development Projects	1%	1%	2%	1%	7%
Waste Management	1%	2%	1%	4%	1%
Water or Wastewater management	4%	6%	4%	6%	4%
Eligible Green Projects	10%	7%	5%	6%	5%
General Purpose	5%	3%	4%	3%	10%

Source: OECD Corporate Sustainability dataset, LSEG.

Unlike GSS bonds, SLBs include specific sustainability performance targets to be met within a defined timeline. To this end, Key Performance Indicators (KPIs) are selected by the SLB issuer to achieve the sustainability objective at the entity level. As shown in Table 3.2, most of the KPIs in SLBs relate to climate transition, such as "scope 1 and scope 2 GHG emissions", accounting for 28% of the SLBs issued by corporates. Other prominent KPIs related to the climate transition in corporate SLBs are, for example, "carbon and emissions intensity", and "renewable energy". Although less frequently, non-climate transition key performance indicators were also mentioned for some corporate SLBs. These include, for instance, an "increase in women board members" (1.6%), an "increase in patient access to health treatments" (1.4%), and "racial and ethnic diversity" (0.9%). The KPIs of SLBs issued by the official sector are also included in Table 3.2, but only very few have so far been issued, which limits the comparability between the numbers of the corporate and official sectors.

Table 3.2. Key Performance Indicators (KPIs) in SLBs, 2019-23

Top 1 Top 2 Top 3 Top 4 Top 5	Corporate Sector	Official Sector
Carbon and Emissions Intensity	24%	24%
Energy Consumption and Efficiency	6%	10%
Increase in Women Board Members	2%	25%
Renewable Energy	9%	13%
Scope 1 and Scope 2 GHG Emissions	28%	8%
Scope 1, Scope 2 and Scope 3 GHG Emissions	3%	0%
Scope 3 GHG Emissions	7%	0%
Sustainable Forest Management	0%	6%
Other	21%	13%

Source: OECD Corporate Sustainability dataset, LSEG.

Almost 80% of sustainable corporate bonds from 2014 to 2023 have been issued with a medium-term maturity – ranging from 2 to 10 years. Short-term corporate sustainable bonds (with a maturity of less than two years) have represented only a fractional share over the years, accounting for only 3% of total corporate sustainable bonds. The official sector has issued sustainable bonds with longer maturities than the ones issued by the corporate sector. Indeed, while in 2023 long-term bonds accounted for 19% of the total amount issued by the corporate sector, long-term bonds by the official sector amounted to 37% (Figure 3.5).

Figure 3.5. Short, medium, and long-term sustainable bonds

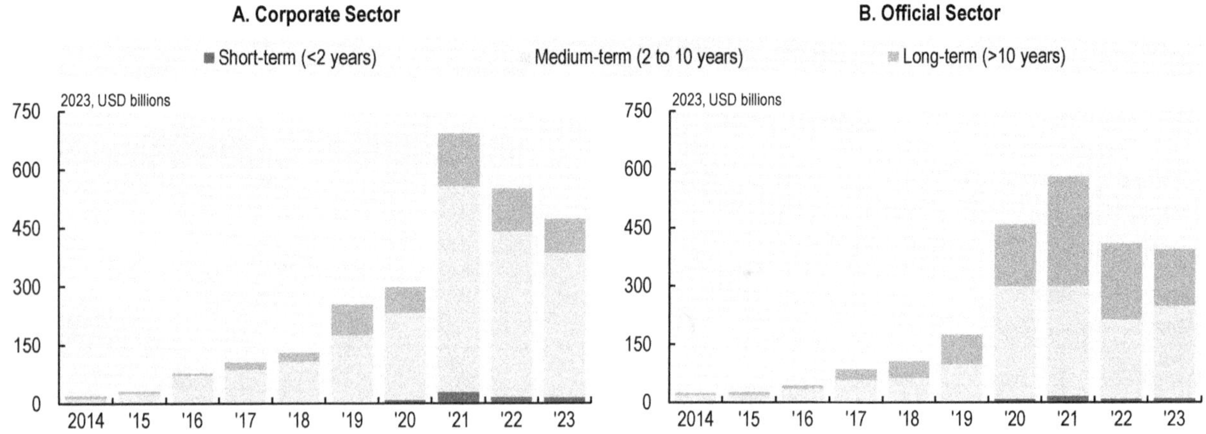

Source: OECD Corporate Sustainability dataset, LSEG.

Sustainable bonds issued by corporates and by governments and multilateral institutions display less stable value-weighted maturities when compared to all conventional and sustainable bonds during the past decade. On average, sustainable bonds issued by non-financial corporates present a value-weighted maturity of 11.9 years against a maturity of 9.4 years for all bonds issued by non-financial corporates (Figure 3.6, Panel A). In contrast, sustainable bonds issued by financial corporates display on average a slightly shorter value-weighted maturity of 6.1 years against 6.9 years for all bonds issued by financial corporates.

Multilateral institutions show similar maturities both for sustainable (7.9 years) and all bonds (8 years), although agencies and local governments' value-weighted maturity averages 8.3 years for sustainable and 9.6 years for all bonds (Figure 3.6, Panel B). In the case of the central governments, since 2017 the value-weighted maturity of the issued sustainable bonds has been almost twice as long as the one of all issued bonds, averaging 16.8 years against 9.1 years, respectively, within the same period.

Figure 3.6. Value-weighted average maturity

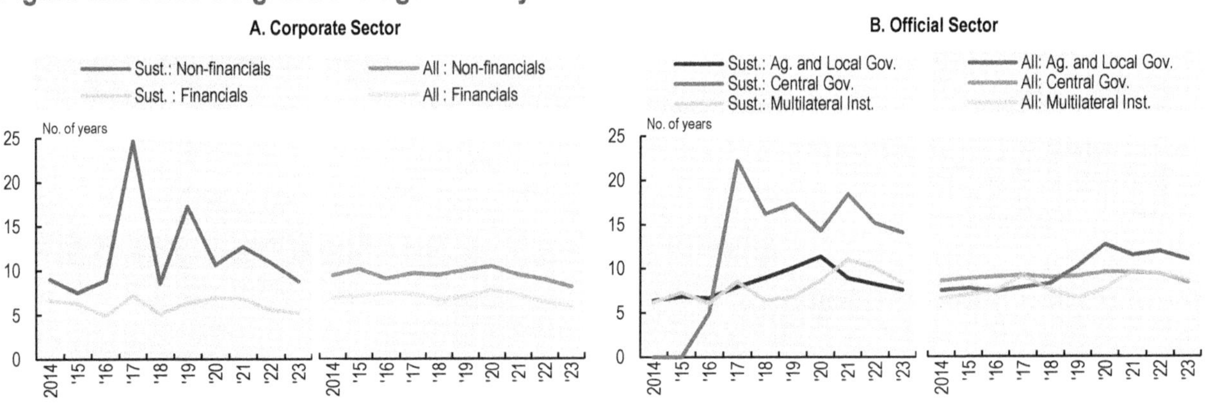

Note: Bonds with maturities less than 1-year maturity are excluded.
Source: OECD Corporate Sustainability dataset, OECD Capital Market Series dataset, LSEG.

A large share of SLBs include a call option that gives the issuer an option to redeem the bond before the end of its maturity. Over the 2014-23 period, while 45% of the amount issued via GSS bonds by the corporate sector included a call option, 80% of the SLBs issued by corporates included such an option (Figure 3.7, Panel A). A similar trend is also visible for the official sector. While 59% of the amount issued by official sector entities in SLBs included a call option, only 4% included such an option via GSS bonds. The existence of a call option in SLBs may raise a concern that issuers could seek to reduce the amount of any penalty that could arise from not meeting the sustainability performance targets by exercising the call option. The establishment of a penalty if targets are not met at the time of the exercise of the call option can potentially moderate that concern. Ul Haq and Doumbia (2022[4]) analysed 40 SLBs with a call option (up to December 2021) and found that 42.5% mentioned a penalty if the targets are not met at the time of the call.

Figure 3.7. Callable GSS bonds vs SLBs, 2014-23

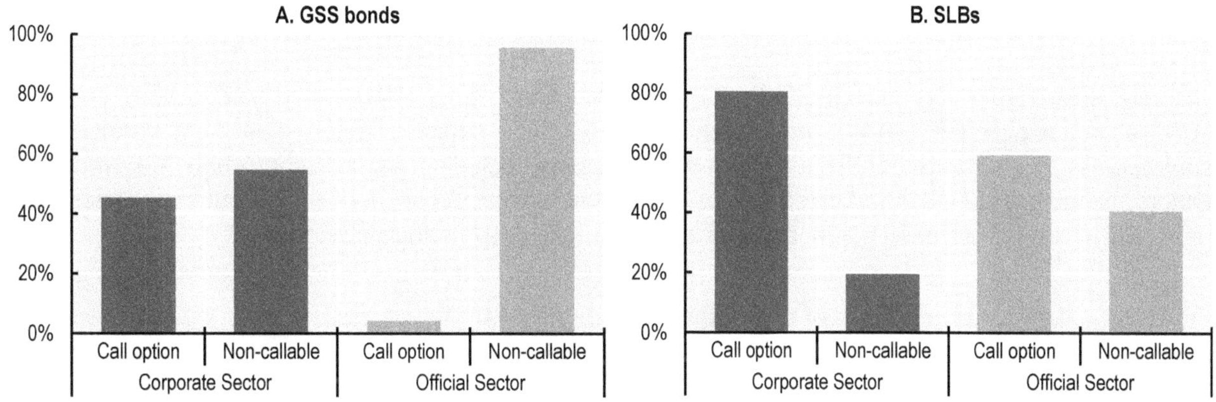

Source: OECD Corporate Sustainability dataset, LSEG.

3.2.2. Issuer characteristics

Corporate sector

In 2014, sustainable bonds accounted for only 0.6% of the total amount issued by all non-financial companies, yet in 2023 this ratio reached 11.7%, after having peaked at 16% in 2022 (Figure 3.8, Panel A). This rising trend has also been visible for corporate bonds issued by financial companies, whose equivalent ratio surged from 0.2% in 2014 to 8.1% in 2023. In 2023, every category of sustainable bonds experienced a drop in issuance with the exception of social bonds issued by financial companies, which presented a 23% increase from the year before (Figure 3.8, Panel B). Moreover, despite a decrease of 27% in SLBs issued by non-financial companies in 2023 in comparison to the previous year, their share still accounted for 20% of the amount issued by non-financials in 2023.

Figure 3.8. Sustainable bond issuance by corporates

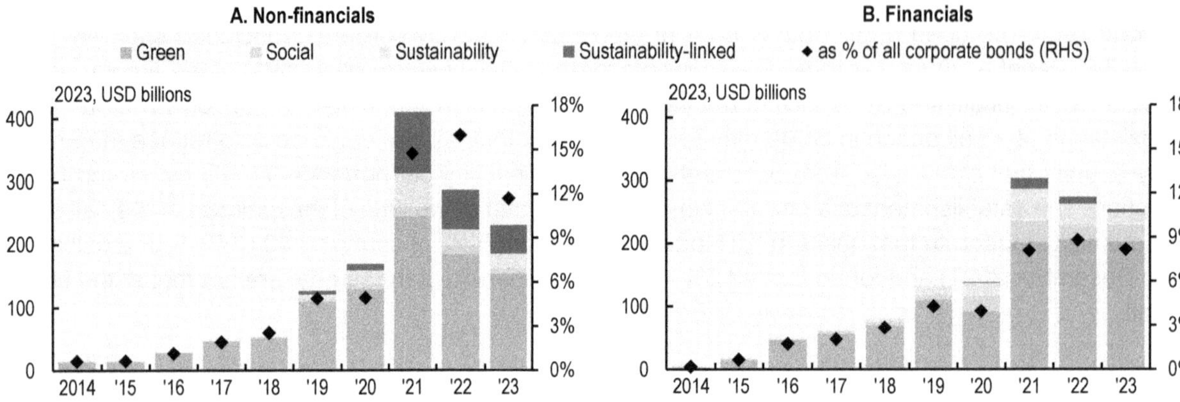

Note: The black dots correspond to the share of sustainable corporate bonds over all corporate bonds.
Source: OECD Corporate Sustainability dataset, OECD Capital Market Series dataset, LSEG.

Globally, sustainable non-financial (financial) corporate bonds accounted for 10% (7%) of all corporate bond issuance over the 2019-23 period. Sustainable bonds depict a larger relative importance when compared to all corporate bond issuance in some regions, including Japan, Latin America, Europe, and Others. Notably, in China, the United States and Other advanced economies, sustainable bonds have represented 7% or less of all non-financials and 4% or less of all financials (Figure 3.9).

Figure 3.9. Relative importance of sustainable bonds against all corporate bonds, by region, 2019-23

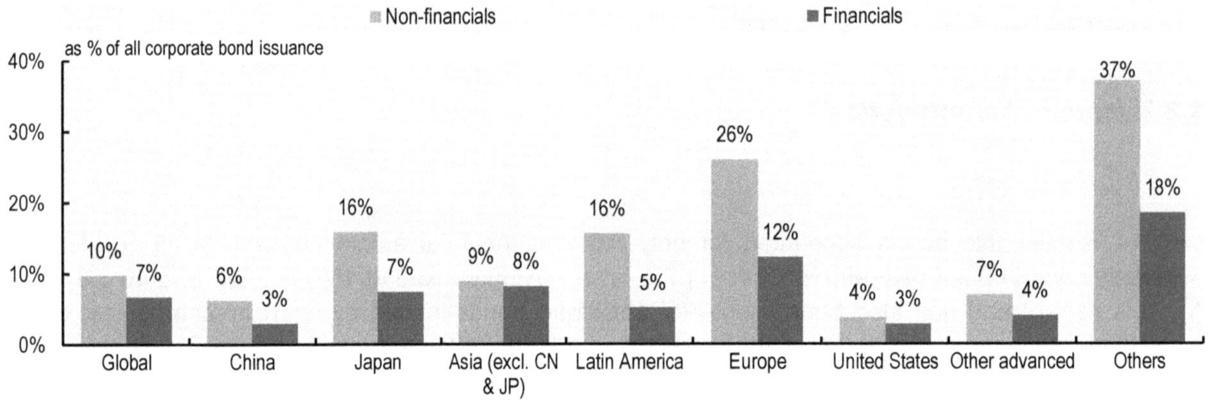

Source: OECD Corporate Sustainability dataset, OECD Capital Market Series dataset, LSEG.

In 2022-23, unlisted companies (i.e., companies that do not list their equity) issued about half of the sustainable bonds in both the non-financial and financial corporate sector, following the same pattern in the issuance of conventional bonds. In the non-financial corporate sector, unlisted companies issued 53% of all sustainable corporate bonds, followed by large listed companies that issued 26% of the amount, and smaller listed companies with 14% (Figure 3.10, Panel A). Similarly, unlisted financial companies issued 48% of the sustainable corporate bonds, and 27% was issued by large companies (Figure 3.10, Panel B). Interestingly, sustainable bonds have been issued to a larger extent by unlisted subsidiaries with a listed parent than other unlisted companies when compared to the issuance of all corporate bonds. For instance, while 14% of the amount of non-financial corporate bonds was issued by an unlisted subsidiary with a listed parent, 20% of the amount issued through non-financial sustainable corporate bonds was issued by the same type of issuer.

Figure 3.10. Corporate issuance by listed and unlisted issuers during 2022-23

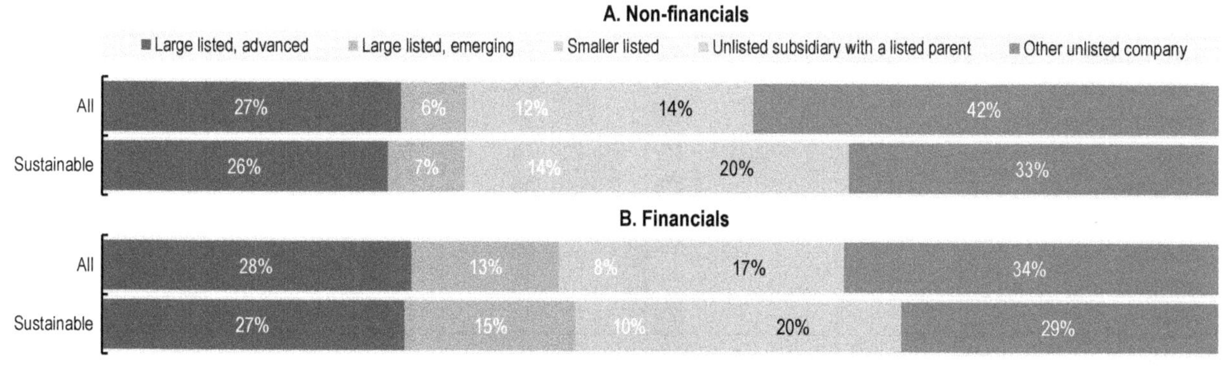

Note: The inclusion of a company in the MSCI World Index or in the MSCI Emerging Markets Index as of September 2023 is considered as a proxy for a listed company being large. Unlisted companies (i.e. companies that do not list their equity) were classified as either a subsidiary with a listed parent company or "other unlisted companies".
Source: OECD Corporate Sustainability dataset, OECD Capital Market Series dataset, LSEG, MSCI.

Although financial companies represent nearly half of the global issuance amount in corporate sustainable bonds over 2019-23, there are substantial regional differences (Figure 3.11, Panel A). Financial companies have been more important issuers in Asia excl. China and Japan (60%), as well as in Other advanced economies (63%), than in Latin America (14%), Japan (28%) or in the United States (34%). Panel B of Figure 3.11 shows the industry distribution of the issuers of sustainable bonds while excluding financial companies, which provide loans to companies in different industries.

Figure 3.11. Industry distribution of sustainable bonds, 2019-23

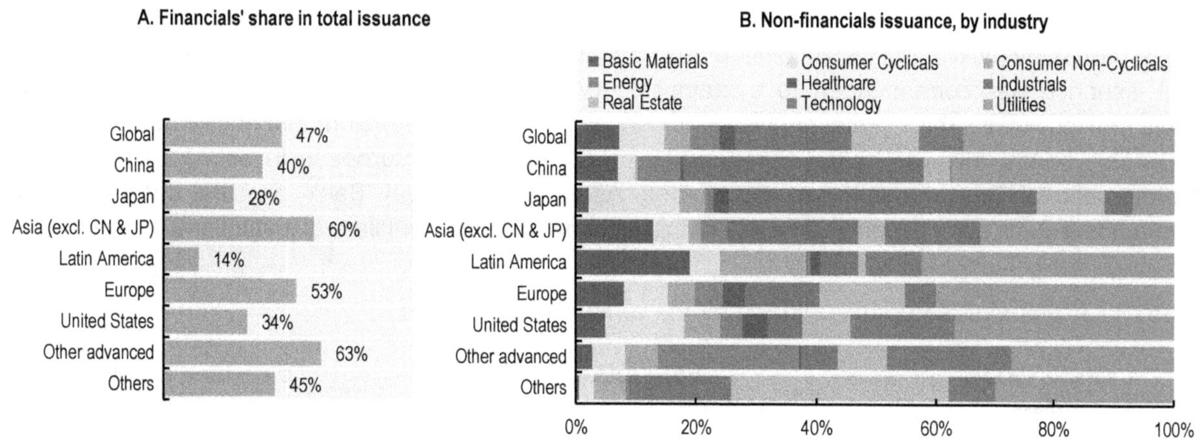

Source: OECD Corporate Sustainability dataset, LSEG.

In 2019-23, companies from the utilities industry have been the most important issuers of corporate sustainable bonds in nearly all regions except in China, Japan and Others (Figure 3.11), where industrials – in China and Japan – are the most active sector in the issuance of sustainable bonds and real estate – in Others – accounting for 40%, 52% and 36% of the amount issued (excluding financials), respectively. The same holds when comparing their relative importance against all corporate bonds. Indeed, sustainable bonds represented 23% of the total amount issued via corporate bonds issued by companies from the utilities industry in 2023, which is more than two times the ratio of 9% for all non-financial corporates in the same year. Renewable energy companies' issuance may explain, at least partially, the importance of the utilities industry in the sustainable bonds market (Table 3.3Table 3.3).

Table 3.3. Relative importance of sustainable bonds against all corporate bonds, by industry

	2019	2020	2021	2022	2023
Basic materials	4%	5%	18%	15%	14%
Consumer cyclicals	1%	2%	9%	11%	14%
Consumer non-cyclicals	2%	1%	11%	13%	6%
Energy	1%	1%	8%	12%	11%
Financials	5%	5%	9%	10%	8%
Healthcare	1%	2%	11%	6%	3%
Industrials	3%	4%	8%	10%	8%
Technology	2%	3%	8%	10%	9%
Utilities	17%	15%	37%	33%	23%

Note: "Real estate" has been merged with "Financials" for all years.
Source: OECD Corporate Sustainability dataset, OECD Capital Market Series dataset, LSEG.

Official sector

Agencies and local governments, central governments and multilateral institutions have increasingly made use of sustainable bonds, particularly since 2020. Nevertheless, in relative terms, the issuance of sustainable bonds is still of minor importance for central governments but has become quite significant for multilateral institutions (Figure 3.12). Central governments have been the least frequent issuers of sustainable bonds when compared to the issuance of all bonds. In 2023, only 0.4% of the amount issued corresponded to sustainable bonds. Agencies and local governments have been more regular users of sustainable bonds, as they averaged 10% of all issued bonds since 2020.

Recently, multilateral institutions have stood out as the issuer group that relies most heavily on sustainable bonds for their capital market funding when compared to both other official sector entities and the private sector. While up to 2017 sustainable bonds accounted for a maximum of 7% of the total amount issued through bonds by multilateral institutions, in 2020 they represented 54%. Since 2020, at least 32% of the bond issuance has corresponded to sustainable bonds (Figure 3.12, Panel C). Notably, among all multilateral institutions the International Bank for Reconstruction and Development has issued 37% of the sustainable bonds, followed by the European Union (22%) and the European Investment Bank (12%). The International Development Association, the Asian Development Bank and the Inter-American Development Bank each accounted for 4% of the amount issued by multilateral institutions.

Figure 3.12. Sustainable bond issuance by the official sector

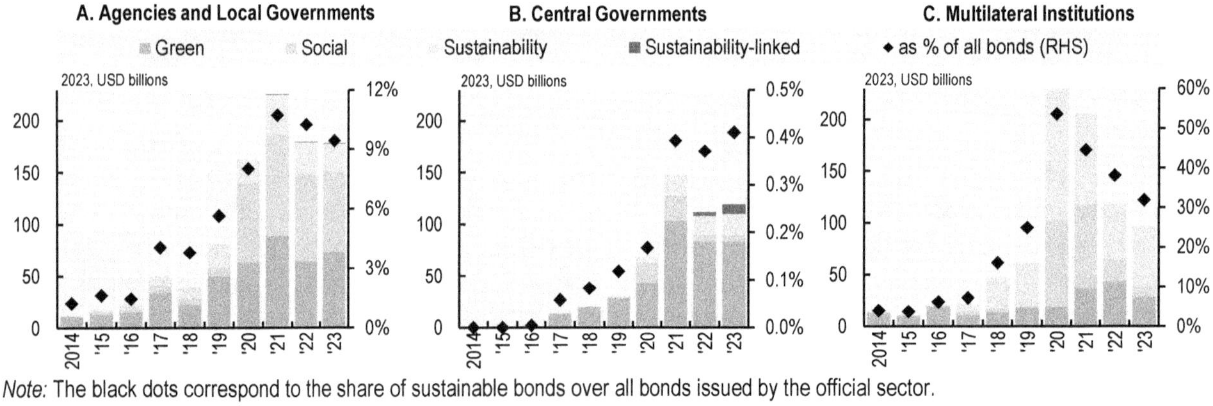

Note: The black dots correspond to the share of sustainable bonds over all bonds issued by the official sector.
Source: OECD Corporate Sustainability dataset, LSEG.

3.2.3. Investors

This section analyses a dataset that gathers information from publicly available sources on bond investments to compare the investor base of sustainable bonds with those of conventional bonds. Although this dataset covers all bonds, it does not cover all investors. In other words, it is biased towards large and especially institutional investors, who typically have to disclose their portfolios to meet regulatory requirements. Overall, it covers around one-fifth of the investor base for these assets. Due to this constraint, this section focuses mostly on examining patterns between sustainable and conventional bonds instead of making claims on the whole investor base for sustainable bonds. Box 3.1, at the end of this section, explores the primary market data for selected sovereigns, which covers the totality of their respective issuances for the selected bonds.

Figure 3.13 Panel A shows the composition of the publicly available investor base for all types of bonds and distinct types of sustainable bonds. It first reveals that asset managers, which manage assets on behalf of asset owners by mainly investing in marketable securities, are the main holders of sustainable bonds. This reflects not only the importance of these types of investors but also the fact that a larger share of asset managers discloses their portfolios and, thus, are over-represented in this sample. Secondly, the figure shows that there are a lot of similarities in the publicly available investor base across sustainable bond instrument types. For corporate GSS bonds and SLBs, the share of the publicly available investor base is composed mostly of asset managers (from 70% for green bonds to 73% for sustainability bonds) and banks (from 11% for sustainability bonds to 19% for green bonds). Likewise, for the official sector's sustainable bonds, asset managers represent the largest share of the publicly available investor base (from 59% for green bonds to 73% for social) followed by banks (from 17% for SLBs to 25% for green bonds).

The main difference between the publicly available holders of sustainable and all bonds is in the share held by banks and governments, which include, in the latter case, central banks. Notably, banks account for 10 and 20 percentage points more of the share of the publicly available investor base for sustainable bonds compared to all bonds issued by corporations and governments, respectively (Figure 3.13, Panels B and C). Another large difference presented in Figure 3.13 (Panels B and C) is the share held by governments of bonds issued by the official sector, which is roughly 49 percentage points smaller for sustainable bonds. It is worth noting that the disparity in the investor base can be attributable to variations in the underlying issuers of different bond types. For example, within the realm of sovereigns, the three largest issuers of conventional bonds – the United States, Japan, and China – have not to date issued sustainable bonds, and these differences in the publicly available investor base could, in theory, be attributed to the difference in the issuers. Nevertheless, upon examining a matched sample of the top 20 issuers of sustainable bonds, comprising nine sovereigns and eleven corporations, the noted disparity remains evident, reinforcing that these differences may not be driven by the issuer but rather by investors' preference.[2]

Figure 3.13. Publicly available investor base for sustainable bonds

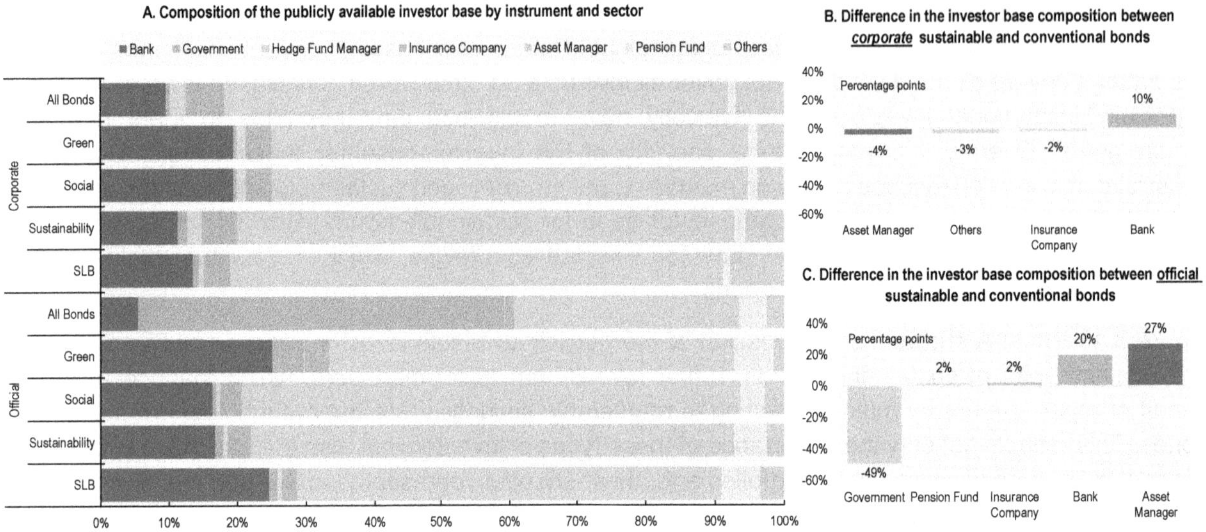

Note: Values as of January 2024.
Source: Bloomberg and OECD calculations.

Box 3.1. The investor allocation of sovereign GSS and conventional bonds at issuance for selected countries

Given the fact that sovereigns disclose information about the investors of their syndications, analysing sovereign primary markets makes it possible to obtain information on allocation of issuance amount by investor type. This box contrasts primary markets of all the GSS bonds issued by syndication in France, Germany and Italy, with those of conventional ones selected to match them by maturity, type, and issuance date. GSS bonds analysed were issued from 2017 to 2023 (see Annex 3.A for details).

Figure 3.14 compares the investor base by region and type of investor, revealing that, on average, GSS and conventional bonds have a similar regional investor base (Panel A). For both bonds, around 20% of their primary market buyers are domestic, roughly 70% are non-domestic from Europe, and 10% reside in other regions. French domestic investors have acquired relatively more GSS bonds than investors in French bonds from other countries. This is the opposite of Italy: non-domestic investors from Europe buy relatively more Italian GSS bonds than Italian conventional ones.

The share of GSS bonds from France, Germany and Italy purchased by pension funds and insurance companies is approximately double their share of matched conventional bonds, whereas the share acquired by hedge funds and public entities is roughly half that of their conventional bond counterparts (Figure 3.14, Panel B). This finding for pension funds and insurance companies diverges from the one in Figure 3.13, which did not show significant differences for pension funds and insurance companies.

Figure 3.14. Investor base of GSS and conventional bonds by region and investor type

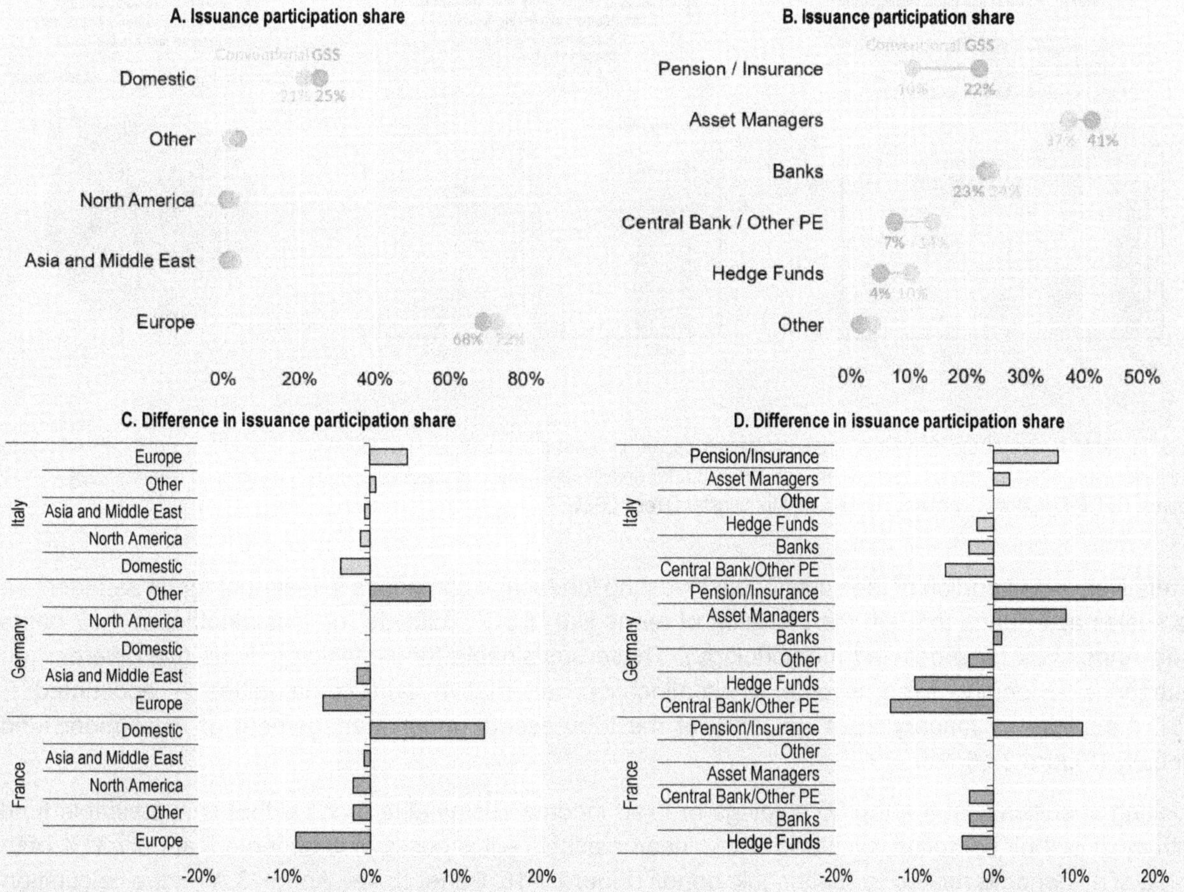

Note: Each GSS is paired with a conventional bond from the same country with the most similar maturity among those allocated by syndication since the issuance of the first national GSS bond. Italian bonds are Buono del Tesoro Poliennale (BTPs), French bonds are Obligation Assimilable au Trésor (OATs). Weighted averages by country and issue size are used. Other PE refers to other public entities.
Source: (Agence France Trésor, 2023[5]), (Bundesrepublik Deutschland, 2023[6]), (Italian Treasury Department, 2023[7]), OECD calculations.

3.2.4. Sustainable investment funds

Following Section 3.2.3 about the investors in sustainable bonds, this section provides insights into the role of sustainable bonds in the composition and strategy of ESG-labelled and climate-labelled funds, with a particular focus on open-ended funds and ETFs.

Even though the understanding of what constitutes sustainable investment can differ between countries and change over time, the total volume of assets overseen by professional investors who incorporate ESG and climate risk factors into their portfolio selection and management has seen considerable growth (OECD, 2022[8]). Nevertheless, as shown in Panel A of Figure 3.15 below, the assets under management of open-ended funds and ETFs (collectively called "investment funds" in this chapter) labelled as "sustainable" still represent only a small fraction of total assets under management in the investment funds industry.

Figure 3.15. Assets under management in traditional funds vs. sustainable-labelled funds

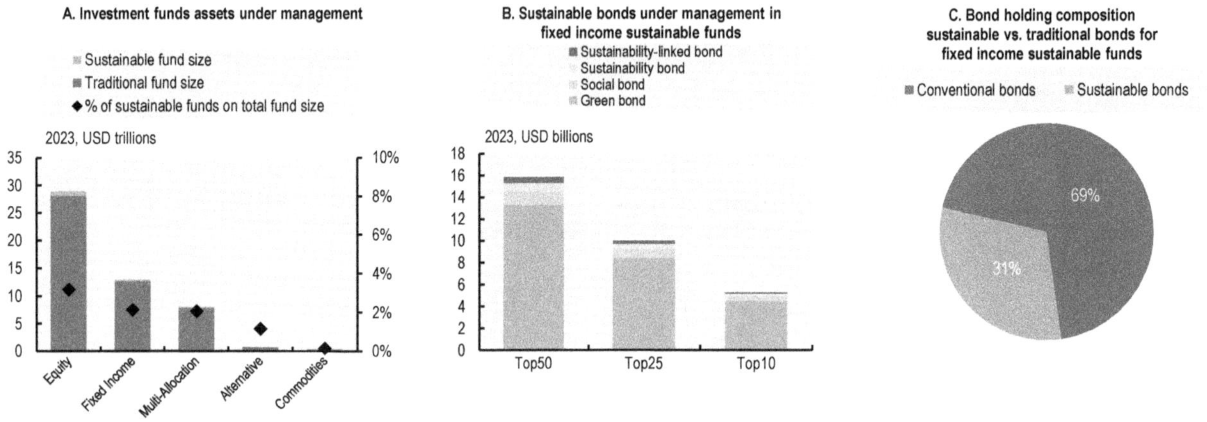

Note: In Panel A, five of the nine Morningstar categories based on asset classes under management are reported: Equity, Fixed Income, Multi-allocation, Alternative and Commodities. See Annex 3.A for detailed description of these categories. Values as of January 2024.
Source: OECD Corporate Sustainability dataset, Morningstar Direct, LSEG.

A relatively small portion of the sustainable investing landscape comprises investment funds self-identified as sustainable funds through the inclusion of terms like "ESG", "climate" or "sustainable" in their names (see Annex 3.A for a detailed methodology). These sustainable funds, which include five different fund categories – equity, fixed income, multi-allocation, alternative and commodities – accounted for USD 1.4 trillion in January 2024, or 2.8% of the total assets under management of investment funds globally (Figure 3.15, Panel A).

Looking specifically at the top 50 holdings of fixed income sustainable funds – that is sustainable funds with most of their portfolios invested in fixed income assets – it is possible to observe that only 31% of the value of all bonds is related to sustainable bonds (Figure 3.15, Panel C; see Annex 3.A for the calculation). Most of these sustainable bonds are GSS bonds (particularly green bonds, accounting for 84% of the total), with few investments in SLBs to date (Figure 3.15, Panel B).

There are at least two ways to explain the relatively low share of sustainable bonds in the portfolios of sustainable fixed income funds. First, it could be the case that asset managers, adequately fulfilling their mandate to consider the risks of their portfolio, financial returns and the impact of their investments on society and the environment, preferred to buy conventional bonds issued by entities with good sustainability-related practices instead of sustainable bonds. This would mean, in some cases, for instance, that asset managers diligently reviewed the prospectus of a sustainable bond but were not convinced about the potential sustainability-related impact of the issuance in the decision-making process of the issuer. The second explanation for the low share of sustainable bonds in the portfolios of sustainable fixed income funds would be a more negative one. It may be the case that asset managers can label their fixed income funds as "sustainable" without necessarily needing to consider the environmental and social impact of their investments. If the second explanation holds true, the low share of sustainable bonds in their assets under management would be evidence of the so-called "greenwashing" in the investment funds industry.

Arguably the most important incentive for asset managers to "green wash" their funds would be if they can charge higher fees simply for including the label "sustainable" or "ESG" in the fund names. According to OECD analysis on funds' fixed management fees for fixed income investment funds, it is possible to observe that sustainable funds charge average annual fees higher than traditional funds for both passive and active funds (Figure 3.16, Panel A).

Figure 3.16. Management fixed fees: sustainable vs. traditional fixed income funds

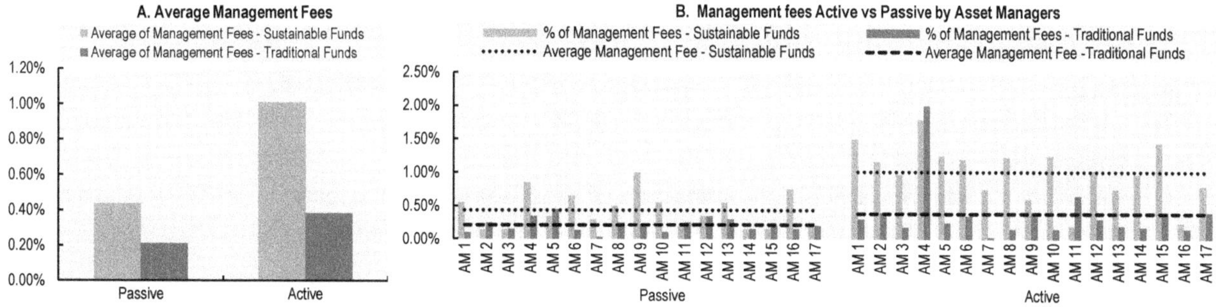

Note: Panel B only displays funds from managers of at least one active and one passive fund in both sustainable and traditional funds categories. Values as of January 2024.
Source: OECD Corporate Sustainability dataset, Morningstar Direct.

To have a more granular view, Panel B in Figure 3.16 analyses the fixed fees charged by the 17 largest asset managers who manage at least one active and one passive fund for both sustainable and traditional fund types. Focusing only on these asset managers may reduce any bias that may be present in Panel A of the same figure, such as the existence of more assets under management in regions where management fees may be higher. The analysis in Panel B, however, confirms that asset managers charge on average higher fixed fees for sustainable funds, both for active and passive funds. For active funds the average management fixed fees for sustainable funds are 1.00% while they are 0.38% for traditional ones. For passive funds the average management fixed fees for sustainable funds are 0.44%%, or more than the double of the management fees for traditional funds (0.21%).

3.2.5. Standards and taxonomies

As presented in Section 3.2, sustainable bonds are a recent innovation in debt markets. It is only natural, therefore, that very few jurisdictions have a regulatory or self-regulatory framework for sustainable bonds (e.g., as China and Japan do). There are two complementary and often-used international standards to classify a bond as sustainable, which are developed by two private sector-led institutions: the International Capital Market Association (ICMA) and the Climate Bonds Initiative (CBI) (see Figure 3.17). ICMA's Executive Committee is composed of 24 organisations comprising an equal distribution between investors, issuers, and underwriters (ICMA, 2020[9]). CBI's Board is comprised of associations representing institutional investors and environmental non-government organisations (CBI, 2023[10]).

ICMA published the first edition of its "Green Bond Principles" in 2014, and, in more recent years, its "Social Bond Principles", "Sustainability Bond Guidelines" and "Sustainability-Linked Bond Principles" ("ICMA Use-of-proceeds Principles" to refer to the first three and "ICMA Principles" to all of them) (ICMA, 2023[11]). The ICMA Sustainability-Linked Bond Principles have five core components:

1. the issuer must select KPIs that are relevant to the issuer's core sustainability policies, measurable or quantifiable, externally verifiable, and able to be benchmarked;
2. the targeted KPIs should be ambitious and determined on a predefined timeline set before or concurrently with the issuance of the bond;
3. the bond contract should establish that its financial and/or structural characteristics will vary depending on whether the targeted KPIs have been met (e.g., a variation of the coupon);
4. the issuer should report, at least annually, on the performance of the selected KPIs and on any information enabling investors to monitor the level of ambition of the targeted KPIs; and
5. the issuer should disclose an assurance attestation of the selected KPIs' performance.

The ICMA Use-of-proceeds Principles have four core components:

1. the proceeds of the bond must be used for eligible projects, which should be appropriately described in the legal documentation of the bond;
2. the issuer must communicate how it assesses whether a project is eligible;
3. the net proceeds of the issuance should be tracked to attest they have been used to invest in the eligible projects; and
4. the issuer should report annually on the use of proceeds until full allocation, as well as provide a brief description of the projects developed and their expected impact.

Notably, ICMA Use-of-proceeds Principles allow issuers to use proceeds for refinancing eligible projects but, if this is the case, it is recommended that issuers provide an estimate of the share of financing versus re-financing. The ICMA Principles recommend issuers to appoint an external review provider to assess the alignment of the sustainable bond with the relevant core components before issuing the sustainable bond (known as a "second party opinion") and to verify the allocation of the funds after the issuance, but issuers may claim the alignment even without these assessments.

CBI published the first edition of its Climate Bonds Standard (CBS) in 2012 and, in newer versions of the standard, it covers both green "use-of-proceeds" bonds and SLBs with climate-related KPIs (CBI, 2023[12]). The CBS current edition builds on the ICMA Principles and, notably, the CBS recommends how the pre- and post-issuance assurance of the sustainable bond would take place. The CBI also approves firms that can provide assurance that the sustainable bond is compliant with the CBS. Likewise, the CBI certifies bonds as compliant with the CBS after receiving an application that includes the assurance of such compliance by an approved assurance provider.

Importantly, ICMA Principles – and other standards that follow closely their framework – provide only a suggested and non-exhaustive list of broadly defined eligible green and social project categories. Issuers may typically refer to third-party taxonomies for sustainable activities or to their own classification of which projects would be eligible. The taxonomies classify economic activities in a similar way that nomenclatures for national economic statistics and international trade do (e.g., the International Standard Industrial Classification), but taxonomies also aim at defining whether these activities are sustainable (and, in some cases, setting different levels of sustainability). For activities that may not be considered inherently sustainable, the taxonomy would normally set a level of environmental or social performance above which the activity would be reckoned as sustainable (e.g., the construction of a building certified as green according to a specific benchmark).

Figure 3.17. Sustainable bonds issuance following different standards and taxonomies

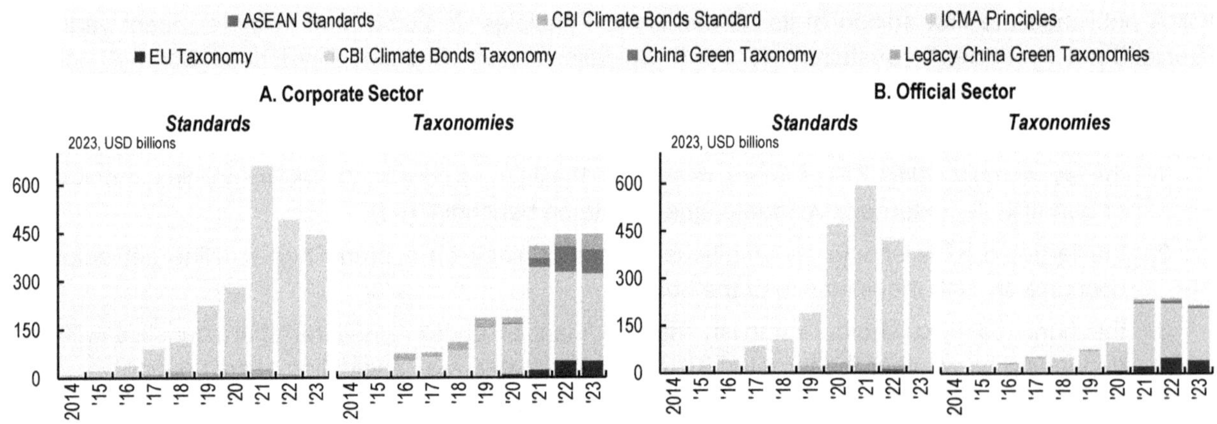

Note: The values displayed correspond to the total amount issued following different standards and taxonomies. The values indicate the standards or taxonomies a sustainable bond is conforming to or aligned with (as reported by the issuers). A single sustainable bond can exhibit compliance/alignment with one or more standards or taxonomies.

Source: OECD Corporate Sustainability dataset, LSEG.

There are many national and international taxonomies for sustainable activities as a result of both government and market-led initiatives, including, for instance, the "Green Bond Endorsed Project Catalogue – 2021" ("China Green Taxonomy" in the figure above) set by China's central bank and securities regulator (The People's Bank of China, 2021[13]) and the "Climate Bonds Taxonomy" developed by the CBI (CBI, 2021[14]). Notably, the taxonomies typically apply both to the corporate and official sectors, regardless of the differences in their activities. While the CBI Climate Bonds Taxonomy has been the prevalent taxonomy (see Figure 3.17 above), the most well-known taxonomy for sustainable activities is probably the one set by the European Union (Regulation EU 2020/852). It focuses on six environmental objectives: climate change mitigation; climate change adaption; sustainable use and protection of water and marine resources; transition to a circular economy; pollution prevention and control; and protection and restoration of biodiversity and ecosystems. For an economic activity to be considered environmentally sustainable, it should substantially contribute to at least one of the mentioned environmental objectives and do no significant harm to the other objectives, as well as to comply with minimum safeguards related to social and governance-related issues (e.g., ensuring the alignment with the OECD Guidelines for Multinational Enterprises on Responsible Business Conduct). The European Union is also one of the founding members of the "International Platform on Sustainable Finance" (IPSF, 2023[15]), which, among other goals, aims to improve the interoperability and comparability of the EU taxonomy and the ones established by other jurisdictions.

The greater use of new taxonomies for sustainable activities set by regional and national institutions may raise three concerns. First, comparability between sustainable bonds may be reduced if they follow taxonomies that are meaningfully different. Second, taxonomies focused on the needs of the corporate sector may not be easily used by official sector entities. Third, organised industry interests may be successful in securing the inclusion of their business activities in a national or regional taxonomy in a way that may not fully take account of scientific evidence and broader policy objectives. Initiatives to improve the interoperability and comparability of regional or national taxonomies, such as the one led by the International Platform on Sustainable Finance, should therefore be welcomed.

3.3. Key issues

3.3.1. Incentives for investors

Investors may have three main reasons for acquiring a sustainable bond instead of a conventional bond with similar characteristics. First, individual investors and clients of institutional investors may be concerned about the social and environmental impact of their investments, or face pressure from other relevant stakeholders to demonstrate such concern. Second, investors with well-diversified portfolios may consider how the externalities of the companies they invest in might affect their long-term financial return. Third, there may be a public policy that incentivises investments in sustainable bonds.

Sustainability-conscious investors and stakeholders

Individual investors can buy a bond through a brokerage firm. Arguably in most cases, they will have neither the sophistication nor the time to assess the bond's legal documentation and the issuer's business in detail. In the same way that one of these investors may consult the credit rating of the issuance to assess the credit risk profile of the bond, a sustainability-conscious investor might prefer to invest in a bond labelled as "sustainable" trusting that it will have a better social and environmental impact than a conventional bond.

Individual investors may often prefer to invest in capital markets through a professional investor, such as an asset manager or a pension fund. In this case, the individual investor will ordinarily choose among several investment vehicles that allow managers different levels of discretion on how to select assets to invest in. The mandates in these vehicles can restrict, for instance, the asset classes managers can acquire and, more recently, some of them promise to consider environmental and social matters in the investment-making process. As seen in Section 3.2.4, investment funds self-labelled as “sustainable” accounted for USD 1.3 trillion in January 2024, or 2.8% of the total assets under management of investment funds globally.

The precise obligations of asset managers and other professional investors when selecting bonds to invest in will largely depend on their contracts with their investors. In some cases, managers may need to simply follow an index composed of sustainable bonds and, therefore, they would not be able to buy conventional bonds. In most other cases, however, a mandate to consider both financial returns and the sustainability-related impact of investments may not mean that asset managers can only acquire sustainable bonds for their fixed-income portfolio. For instance, investing in the conventional bonds issued by a company with a positive social and environmental impact may be well-aligned with the sustainability-related goals of the asset managers. Nevertheless, it is undeniable that the label “sustainable” may be attractive for some asset managers with sustainability-related goals merely from a compliance perspective.

In a less direct way, insurance companies, banks and central governments may decide to invest in sustainable bonds to improve their reputation as “sustainable” or as a response to external pressure. For instance, insurance companies may invest part of their reserves in sustainable bonds in order to be able to advertise that it is a “sustainability-conscious” institution and, therefore, possibly attract more clients, even if the insurer does not offer any product labelled as “sustainable”. Also as an example, banks may suffer pressure from civil society organisations if their credit portfolio is concentrated in high-polluting companies, which can arguably harm their reputation with some environment-conscious clients and employees. Without discussing the substance of its content, the title of the following report serves as an example of mentioned pressure from civil society: “Lethal Investments: The Health Consequences of Cash Flows into Coal – how major global banks are financing some of the deadliest coal plants in the US” (Sierra Club, 2023[16]).

Governments and central banks may also face pressure from civil society organisations to consider sustainability-related matters in their asset allocation decisions because citizens are *de facto* the final beneficiaries of government’s holdings. Central banks, who are typically the main holders of securities in the official sector, acquire (especially sovereign) bonds for two main reasons: (i) due to central banks’ asset purchase programmes (i.e., quantitative easing); (ii) to establish foreign-currency reserves. In that regard, there is evidence that governments’ holdings of conventional and sustainable bonds differ in a relevant way (see Figure 3.13). Additionally, a minority of central banks have sustainability objectives in their mandates (Dikau and Ulrich, 2021[17]), which includes the ECB (European Central Bank, 2022[18]). Considerations to establish a sustainability objective for a central bank may include not only the environmental and social impact of its portfolio, but also the central bank’s example for institutional investors of good sustainability-related policies and practices.[3]

Considering the publicly available information, most central banks in G7 countries have not typically bought sustainable bonds as part of their asset purchase programmes (OECD analysis using central banks’ information on their websites). As central banks’ bond holdings are substantial (around USD 14 trillion in the G7 central banks as of 2023), the absence of some major central banks in the sustainable bonds market greatly affects its investor base compared to conventional bonds. Among G7 countries, the only central bank that holds a noticeable amount of sustainable bonds in its portfolio is the Eurosystem, which between 2018 and 2022 purchased an increasing amount of corporate and government sustainable bonds (Elderson and Schnabel, 2023[19]). Nevertheless, most central banks have discontinued their asset purchase programmes and are unwinding their balance sheets since the beginning of the monetary policy tightening cycle that started in 2021-22.

Portfolio management

Even for investors that are not concerned with the social and environmental impact of their investee companies, a decision to invest in sustainable bonds may still maximise their financial return for a given level of risk. This would be true in two circumstances. First, where the investor wants the company to adopt a new business strategy that takes into better account long-term environmental and social trends such as climate change, and, therefore, a strategy that would maximise the company's value. Second, where the investor wishes the company to reduce its negative externalities (or increase its positive ones) despite a possible reduction of the company's value, but with the view that the benefit for the investor's other investee companies would more than compensate the loss in value for the first company. An example of the second circumstance would be the reduction in GHG emissions by an investee major energy company that would facilitate the transition to a low carbon economy, which would be financially positive for investee companies in the tourism sector with assets in tropical regions.

In either of the abovementioned circumstances, the most important point within the scope of this chapter is to highlight that, at least potentially, the commitments in a sustainable bond contract can alter the decision-making process of a company in a more efficient way than, for instance, buying equity shares in the same company. For example, a SLB with ambitious targets for a company to reduce GHG emissions and a meaningful potential coupon increase in case the target is not met could be more effective in changing corporate behaviour than a minority equity stake where the investor would not be in a position to alter the company's strategy.

Public policies

Some jurisdictions offer favourable regulation and financial incentives to encourage investments in sustainable bonds, including tax credit bonds, direct subsidy bonds, and tax-exempt bonds (CBI, 2022[20]). Tax credit bonds offer investors the opportunity to receive tax credits in lieu of traditional interest payments. Direct subsidy bonds are another option that provides government cash rebates to offset net interest payments. Tax-exempt bonds, for instance in US municipal bonds and Brazilian wind projects, allow investors to avoid income tax on interest.

Some central banks are also supporting sustainable investments to meet climate targets, often through favourable policies for sustainable bonds (European Central Bank, 2022[18]). These measures may include lower capital requirements or preferential treatment in risk-weighting assessments, making such bonds potentially more attractive to financial institutions.

Banks hold bonds, among other reasons, to meet liquid asset requirements and manage their short-term liquidity. For these two objectives, banks use bonds as collateral for repurchase agreement (repo) transactions with other private institutions, the central bank or the country's debt management office. Therefore, the eligibility of an asset for meeting liquid asset requirements and to be used for repo transactions is a major incentive for banks to hold a security. An analysis of the repo eligibility of sustainable bonds issued by both governments and corporates reveals that sustainable bonds are mostly eligible in Europe, which helps explain why European banks held 84% of all banks' holdings in sustainable bonds that were publicly available in July 2023 (LSEG, OECD calculations). More specifically, of the 41 sovereign sustainable bonds that are repo eligible with central banks, 38 are eligible in European countries (32 eligible with the ECB, 4 in the United Kingdom and 2 in Hungary);[4] of the 823 corporate sustainable bonds that are repo eligible with central banks, 750 are eligible with the ECB;[5] and of the 501 agency and supranational sustainable bonds that are repo eligible with central banks, 463 are eligible in European countries (457 with the ECB, 4 in Sweden and 2 in Switzerland).[6]

Stewardship codes

The recently revised *G20/OECD Principles of Corporate Governance* recognise stewardship codes as a mechanism that may complement regulatory requirements to encourage institutional investors' engagement with their investee companies (Principle III.A). As a matter of fact, stewardship codes are increasingly integrating sustainability considerations into the engagement and voting policies of institutional investors.

Japan's Stewardship Code provides that institutional investors are responsible for enhancing their investee companies' corporate value and sustainable growth, taking into consideration ESG factors (Financial Services Agency, 2020[21]). Similarly, the Brazilian Stewardship Code states in its third principle that institutional investors should integrate ESG factors in their investment processes and scrutinise their impact on the sustainable development of the securities' issuers (Associação de Investidores no Mercado de Capitais, 2016[22]).

Stewardship consists of pursuing a long-term increase in investors' returns together with environmental and societal benefits, according to the UK Stewardship Code. In addition, the UK code also recognises the significant increase in investments other than listed equity. In this respect, they include reporting expectations for fixed income investments such as the review of prospectus and transaction documents (Financial Reporting Council, 2020[23]).

Stewardship codes do not typically, however, have specific recommendations related to investments in sustainable bonds. For instance, the major existing stewardship codes do not highlight the importance of investors' analysis on whether SLBs' performance targets are ambitious. SLBs are a promising tool for aligning investors' sustainability-related preferences with investee companies' impact on the environment and society. However, an SLB with an unambitious target functions *de facto* is a conventional bond because it does not change the decision-making process of the issuer's leadership.

3.3.2. Incentives for issuers

The growth of the sustainable bonds market might reflect investors' increasing focus on sustainable and responsible business issues, as an incentive to invest in these assets. However, at the same time, it is not clear if these assets provide economic incentives to issuers by trading at a premium, which is defined, for sustainable bonds, as 'greenium'. In the following part of this section, an overview of existing literature about this concept and the results of an OECD analysis are shown.

The term 'greenium' or 'green premium' refers to the yield difference between a conventional bond and a green bond with similar characteristics (Bolton et al., 2022[24]). Essentially, a 'greenium' infers that the yield an investor accepts to invest in a 'green' asset is less than the yield the same investor would be willing to accept to invest in an equivalent conventional asset, meaning that the issuer of the bond can obtain financing at lower cost when issuing a green security. This differentiation manifests itself in the primary market as a higher price for the green bond compared to a conventional bond at issuance. The existence of a 'greenium' in secondary markets would imply that a green bond is being traded at a superior price – or a lower yield – compared to a conventional bond with similar traits. This indicates that an environmentally conscious investor is willing to receive a reduced yield in return for the chance to contribute to a greener alternative.

Literature on greenium in bond markets

In past studies, several methodologies and key variables have been used for possible identification of a greenium, with different and not always consistent results. The conclusions indicate varied outcomes concerning the presence of a green premium in the primary market, while showing a more consistent agreement in studies focused on the secondary market (MacAskill et al., 2021[25]).

A first strand of literature found mixed evidence about the existence of the greenium. Hinsche (2021[26]) conducted its studies employing differing methods and samples to check the existence of the greenium, discovering a negative premium confined to Next Generation EU (NGEU) bonds. Zerbib (2019[27]) evaluated the influence of pro-environmental preferences on bond prices using a matching method, before employing a two-step regression process to compare yield spreads of green and conventional bonds within the secondary market. Across a sample ranging from July 2013 to December 2017, a negative marginal premium of 2 basis points was found, primarily for financial companies and low-rated bonds. Bolton et al. (2022[24]) reveal several key findings. Initially, they observe that the greenium, if present, is not immediately apparent within the data. Even with a robust attempt to identify it within a sample of 63 bond pairs issued by the same entity in the same currency and with similar maturity (within a year), their search proved unfruitful. In their second point, upon comparing "twin bonds" (those of identical maturity) issued by EU countries, they discern a statistically significant, albeit minor, greenium – within the range of single-digit basis points (Bolton et al., 2022[24]). Evidence from the US municipal green bond market suggests the green premium is only a more recent development. A review of a large dataset of US municipal bonds indicated that, overall, the yield curve of green bonds systematically falls below conventional bond yields (Karpf and Mandel, 2018[28]). Finally, Ando et al. (2022[29]) discovered an average greenium of 3.7 basis points for EUR-denominated government bonds and nearly 30 basis points for USD-denominated government bonds.

In contrast, Elhers and Packer (2017[30]) found no price premiums in their secondary market analysis, although they did identify a price premium for green bonds in the primary market. Similarly, Tang and Zhang (2018[31]) found no price premium when analysing the yield spread between the same issuing company within the same year. However, when assessing a broader sample, they found that green bonds were issued at a yield spread 6.94 basis points lower than corporate bonds issued by similar firms. A recent study by Doronzo et al. (2021[32]) compared bond prices in France, Belgium, Ireland, and the Netherlands. Results showed that yields from sovereign green bonds were nearly identical to those of conventional government bonds, consistent with previous findings for corporate and municipal green bonds. The findings in another paper (ESMA, 2023[33]) do not support the presence of a uniform or consistent pricing benefit across any category of sustainable bonds. Moreover, the study reveals that the pricing premiums experienced by some issuers can be attributed more to their issuer characteristics than their contractual commitments to sustainability.

These mixed findings suggest that if the greenium does exist as an incentive for issuers of sustainable bonds, it is generally minimal – with possible exceptions for some countries that are greatly vulnerable to the effects of climate change, transition and physical risks (Bolton et al., 2022[24]).

An analysis of a premium for sustainable bonds

The results from an empirical analysis in this report are consistent with the existing literature. The premium for a bond being labelled as sustainable is not statistically significant and may depend on several variables that are not entirely related to the nature of sustainable or conventional bonds per se. Using a data sample consisting of 69 718 corporate bonds and 63 022 official sector bonds, of which 5 563 and 270 are sustainable bonds respectively, and following the methodology in Bolton et al. (2022[24]), it has been possible to obtain two sets of quasi-exact matched bonds for both categories: 1 736 matched corporate bonds and 72 matched official sector bonds (see Annex 3.B for the descriptive statistics and the complete methodology). In these two sets, each sustainable bond matches with one conventional bond in all of the following seven variables: issuer, currency, issue date, maturity year, coupon, coupon class (fixed vs. floating coupon) and asset-linked security category (e.g., inflation-linked security).

Matching sustainable and conventional bonds issued by the same entity is essential because differences between issuers can affect the characteristics of sustainable bonds in ways that are not immediately observable. The main result of the empirical work, consisting of an application of a t-test and a basic linear regression model, found no statistically significant evidence of a premium, here expressed as the impact of being labelled as sustainable on the yield to maturity. However, for the official sector bonds the results must be interpreted with caution given the limited number of observations.

When looking at the difference in the yield to maturity between sustainable bonds and their matched conventional bonds, the trends do not show any particular and constant differences (Figure 3.18), but they do show a common trend with the difference in terms of yield of around 1 and 3 basis points (0.01% for official sector bonds, -0.03% for corporate bonds). Any differences, if they do exist, are neither statistically significant or consistent. Furthermore, when looking at the average premium calculated by currency and issuer's domicile, not only the constant absence of a premium for "sustainability" is confirmed, but a potential common trend is also missing (Figure 3.20).

Looking at the averages, for the official sector, for the 2016-19 period, the sustainable premium of 145 basis points (-1.45%) suggests that sustainable bonds had a meaningfully lower yield than conventional bonds. Conversely, for the 2020-23 period, sustainable bonds had yield that was on average 1 basis point (0.102%) higher than comparable conventional bonds. In the corporate sector, the premium is even less pronounced. During the 2014-18 period, corporate sustainable bond had a yield 6 basis points (0.06%) higher on average than comparable conventional bonds. This difference reduced to 4 basis points (0.038%) in the 2019-23 period, signalling a trend towards yield parity between conventional and sustainable bonds.

Figure 3.18. Average difference in yield-to-maturity of conventional vs. sustainable bonds for matched corporate and official sector bonds

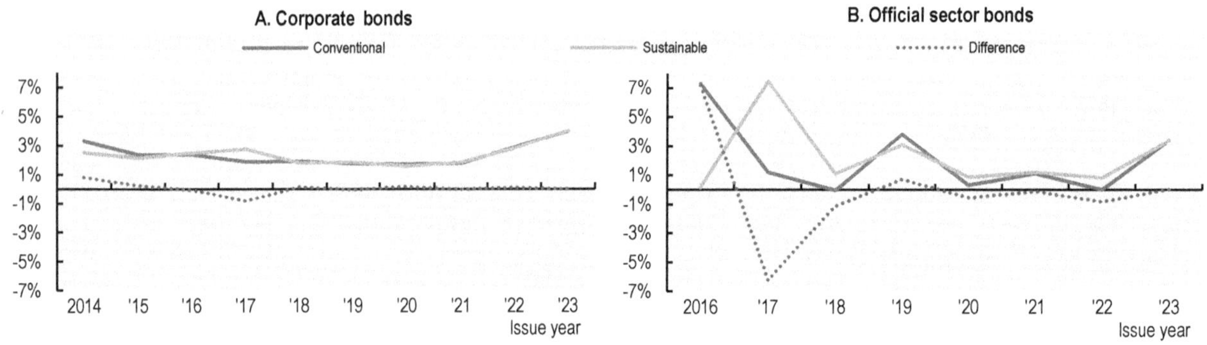

Note: Only pairs of matched bonds are considered. Matching procedures is based on an exact matching methodology (see 0) based on issuer, coupon type and currency, and the nearest matching for issue date, issue year, maturity year, and coupon.
Source: OECD Corporate Sustainability dataset, LSEG.

Figure 3.19. Yield-to-maturity of conventional vs. sustainable bonds for matched corporate and official sector bonds, 2014-23

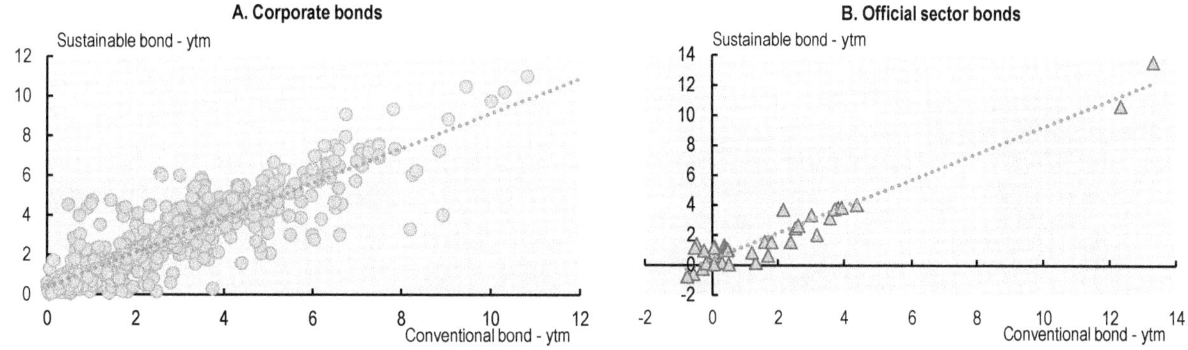

Note: Only pairs of matched bonds are considered. Matching procedures is based on an exact matching methodology (see 0) based on issuer, coupon type and currency, and the nearest matching for issue date, issue year, maturity year, and coupon.
Source: OECD Corporate Sustainability dataset, LSEG.

Figure 3.20. Average difference in yield-to-maturity of conventional vs sustainable bonds

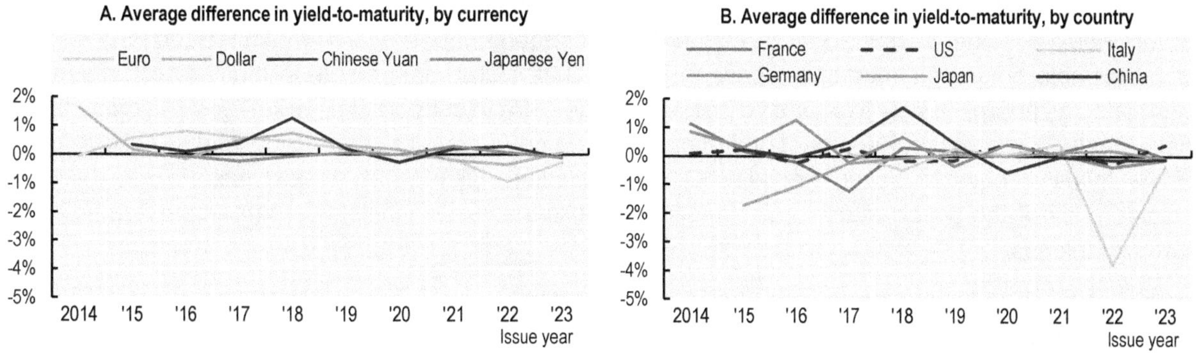

Note: Only pairs of matched bonds are considered. Matching procedures is based on an exact matching methodology (see 0) based on issuer, coupon type and currency, and the nearest matching for issue date, issue year, maturity year, and coupon.
Source: OECD Corporate Sustainability dataset, LSEG.

Trends in oversubscription

Large issuances of green bonds in EUR and USD during the past three years consistently showed slightly higher average oversubscription ratios (orders received over the value of the issuance) than conventional ones. The oversubscription ratios ranged from 2.6 to 5.4 for green bonds and from 2.3 to 3.3 for conventional bonds (Figure 3.21).

Figure 3.21. Average oversubscription of green and equivalent conventional bonds

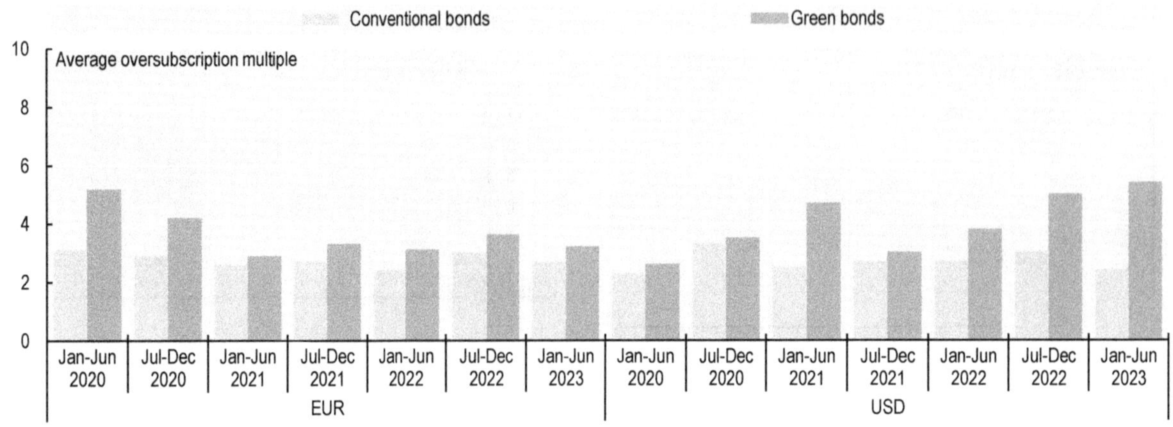

Source: Climate Bond Initiative, (CBI, 2023[34]).

Integration of sustainability factors in public debt management

According to a survey held in 2022 with OECD members and accession countries (OECD, 2023[35]), central governments consider sustainability factors in debt management operations, which includes the issuance of sustainable bonds, for numerous reasons (Figure 3.22). The most common motivations, which were mentioned by approximately two-thirds of these countries, are to support the market for sustainable finance instruments, align debt management operations with the government's ESG policy, and the diversification of the investor base of sovereign debt. Other motivations include improving the accountability and transparency of the government's sustainability and climate-related initiatives, and improving sovereign creditworthiness.

By exclusion, it is interesting to note that countries often do not issue sustainable bonds to minimise financing costs, as they do not observe a reliable greenium in sustainable bonds' issuances. In addition, among the main motivations frequently mentioned, only one (diversification of the investor base) is directly related to debt management, while all others are focused on supporting sustainability through capital market development, transparency or supporting government sustainability policy.

Figure 3.22. Motivation to consider sustainability factors in debt management operations in OECD and accession countries

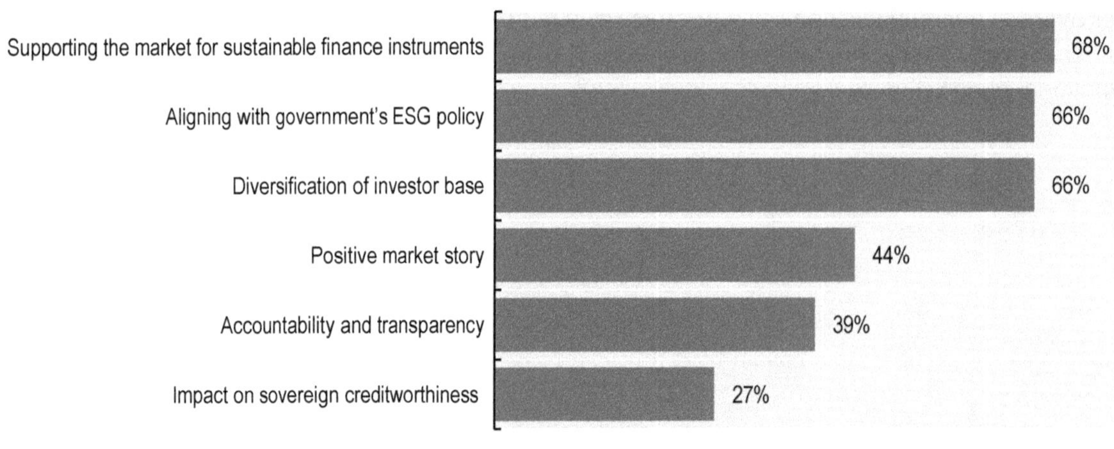

Source: 2022 OECD and accession countries Survey on Primary Market Developments (OECD, 2023[35])

3.3.3. Service providers

As in any bond issuance, the issuer typically needs to hire an underwriter to be responsible for the offering of the sustainable bonds and an independent trustee may be appointed to represent the interest of bondholders. Among other activities, underwriters may contact potential investors, fulfil filing obligations, and supervise whether the issuance complies with regulatory requirements. Trustees are commonly appointed when bonds will be offered to many investors, in which circumstance individual investors may not have the incentives to supervise whether the issuer is complying with all its obligations.

In the cases of both underwriters and trustees, there is no evidence their fees would be higher for sustainable bonds than they are for conventional bonds. In the OECD analysis presented in Section 3.3.4 below, there were two cases in which non-financial companies each issued both SLBs and conventional bonds. In the cases of both companies, the underwriter fees were slightly lower for the SLBs' offerings in comparison to the offerings of conventional bonds. This is unexpected, however, as, all other factors being equal, underwriters and trustees of sustainable bonds have a broader scope for their analyses and, therefore, a potential liability in the issuance of sustainable bonds. For instance, underwriters may need to assess whether a sustainable bond could effectively be labelled as such, and a trustee may be contractually required to check whether the issuer has complied with its disclosure obligations on the use of proceeds for GSS bonds. Both service providers may decide to charge more due to the greater scope of their activities and potential liability but, at least in the prospectuses analysed for this chapter (see a description of the sample in Section 3.3.4), underwriters often include disclaimers stating that there is a risk that the sustainable bond may not be considered as a "sustainable finance security" according to the relevant regulation for the investor. Moreover, it seems to be a relatively common practice to state that the "second party opinion" is not incorporated by reference into the prospectus, which may effectively mean that the underwriter is not liable if the "second party opinion" is not accurate.

What is clearly an extra cost for the issuance of sustainable bonds in comparison to the one of conventional bonds is the market practice of providing a second party opinion on whether the bond contract is aligned with a specific sustainable bond standard (the most common are the ICMA Principles, as analysed in Section 3.2.5) and/or a taxonomy for sustainable activities. The ICMA Principles recommend but do not require a second party opinion for issuers to claim alignment with the standard.

Figure 3.23. Sustainable bonds issuance with (without) the use of a second party opinion provider

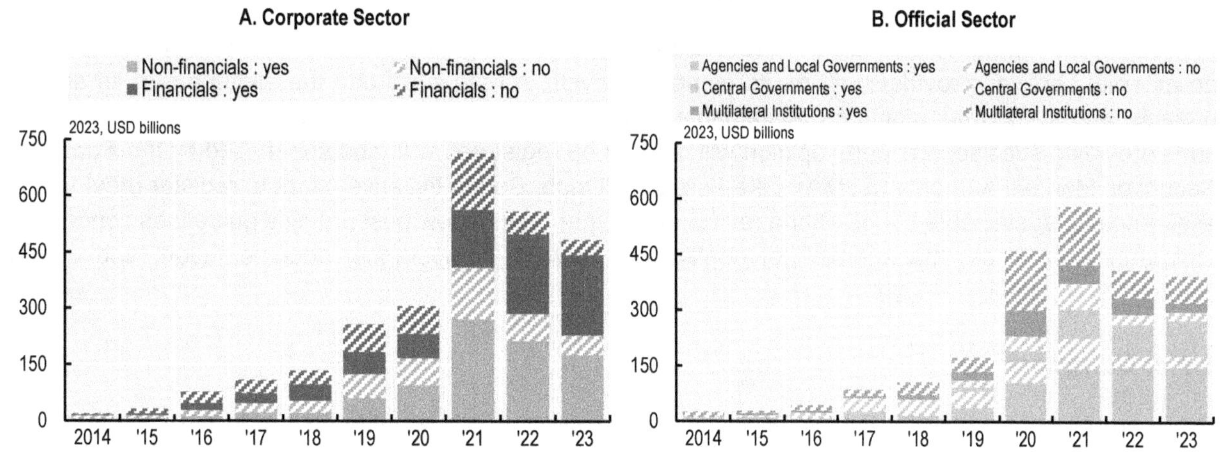

Source: OECD Corporate Sustainability dataset, LSEG.

Sustainable bonds have increasingly been assured by second party opinion providers. While in 2019 47% of the sustainable corporate bonds used a second party opinion provider, in 2023 81% did so. The official sector has also used second party opinion providers in their issuances. In 2023, 83% and 82% of the sustainable bonds issued by, respectively, agencies and local governments, and by central governments, used second party opinion providers. In contrast, multilateral institutions have used to a lesser extent second party opinion providers as part of their sustainable issuance, with only 26% of their sustainable bonds issued in 2023 using a second party opinion (Figure 3.23). Globally, the service providers with the greatest number of second party opinions developed include firms that belong to groups widely known for providing indices, credit ratings and proxy advice. Only to a smaller extent do auditing firms provide second party opinions.

Some of the same firms that provide second party opinions and other service providers offer assurance reviews of other aspects of the sustainable bonds before and after the issuance. *Pre-issuance assurance* can involve, for instance, a review of the processes followed to consider projects as eligible or an estimation of the expected social or environmental impact of the projects to be financed by the issuance. *Post-issuance assurance* can include, for example, an assessment of the effective impact of the projects financed by the issuance of GSS bonds or a review of the issuer's performance related to the KPIs selected in a SLB. As mentioned in Section 3.2.5, a post-issuance assurance of the performance related to KPIs is a condition for an issuer to legitimately claim alignment with the ICMA Sustainability-Linked Bond Principles.

Service providers that offer second party opinions, as well as pre- and post-issuance assurances, have some standards to guide their reviews. For instance, these standards include the International Standard on Assurance Engagements (ISAE) 3000 for assurance engagements other than audits or reviews of historical information, which is set by the International Auditing and Assurance Standards Board (the same organisation is currently developing the International Standard on Sustainability Assurance 5000). More specifically for sustainable bonds, there are also CBI's Climate Bonds Standard and ICMA Guidelines for Green, Social and Sustainability Bonds External Reviews.

The same conflicts of interest that exist for external auditors and credit rating agencies are also present for providers of second party opinion and other forms of assurance for sustainable bonds. The bond issuers may hire these service providers for several sustainable bond issuances, but they provide a service that is relevant to the public interest. While most external auditors and some credit rating agencies are regulated and supervised, providers of second party opinion and other forms of assurance for sustainable bonds do not – with some exceptions – face the same scrutiny.

In the approved framework for an EU Green Bond Standard, all green bonds will need to be reviewed by an external services provider both for its compliance with the standard and the alignment of its eligible projects with the EU taxonomy for sustainable activities (European Commission, 2023[36]). Notably, the firms providing such second party opinion will need to be registered with and supervised by the European Securities Markets Authority (ESMA). Likewise, the Climate Bonds Initiative offers to register providers of assurance for sustainable bonds after a review of whether they "follow best practice guidelines concerning ethics, independence, management of conflicts of interest, competence, documentation, and quality controls" (CBI, 2023, p. 11[12]).

3.3.4. Contracts

There are at least two explanations for the fact that issuers of sustainable bonds do not systematically benefit from a premium for the "sustainability" aspect of the bonds as analysed in Section 3.3.2. First, investors may not meaningfully prioritise the environmental and social impact of their investments, and some key issues raised in Section 3.3.1 may indicate that this hypothesis might be true for some institutional investors. Second, there is the possibility that, while some investors may significantly consider the environmental and social impact of their investments, market practitioners may still need to improve how sustainable bond contracts are designed to fulfil investors' expectations.

An analysis of a sample of 120 sustainable bonds issued between 2017 and 2022 can provide better clarity regarding the market practices for designing contracts. The sample is composed of the 60 largest issuances and 60 randomly selected issuances that have their prospectuses easily accessible in financial databases in English, and these issuances belong to the following categories: GSS bonds issued by financial corporations (23); GSS bonds issued by non-financial corporations (24); SLBs issued by financial corporations (18); SLBs issued by non-financial corporations (28); GSS bonds issued by official sector entities (23); SLBs issued by official sector entities (4). The sample includes issuers from jurisdictions such as Australia, Bermuda, Brazil, Canada, Chile, China, France, Hong Kong (China), Japan, Luxembourg, Mexico, New Zealand, South Africa, the United States, and Uruguay. The sample also includes multilateral institutions such as the African Development Bank and the European Union.

With respect to the "use of proceeds" of GSS bonds in the sample, three issues are worth noting: the possibility of refinancing; the existence of contractual penalties; and the commitment to provide annual assurance.

As allowed by the ICMA Use-of-proceeds Principles, two thirds (65%) of the GSS bonds' prospectuses mention that the refinancing of existing eligible projects with the proceeds is allowed, but, differently from what the mentioned principles recommend, the prospectuses do not provide an estimate of the share of financing versus re-financing. Notably, no prospectus in the sample specifically mentions that the proceeds would not be used for refinancing. The possibility of refinancing an eligible asset may incentivise the issuer not to sell it, but, evidently, no new investment will be made because the asset already exists. Actually, in some circumstances, it may even be negative for society to incentivise a company with access to the sustainable bond market to keep an asset instead of selling it to another company that may be able to operate the asset in a more efficient way but which does not have easy access to public capital markets (for instance, if the former is a listed company and the latter is not).

No GSS bond prospectus in the sample refers to a contractual penalty in case the issuer does not use all proceeds to finance or refinance eligible projects. As a matter of fact, the prospectus of a major non-financial corporate issuance defines that 70% of the proceeds would be invested in eligible green projects but the remaining would be used as working capital of the issuer. In 37% of the issuances, the prospectus notes that the non-compliance with the commitment to use proceeds for eligible projects would not be considered an event for the default of the GSS bond. Of course, this does not mean that issuers can simply disregard their obligation to use the proceeds of the issuance according to what is defined in the bond contract. Moreover, while symptomatic of their lack of importance for market participants, some prospectuses may have not included penalties that are indeed established in the bond contract. However, leaving a lawsuit for a damages award as the only recourse to investors may not offer them enough safety in some jurisdictions, especially because the effective damage may be difficult to assess in such a case.

Still in relation to the GSS bonds in the sample, only half of the prospectuses establish that the issuer will provide an annual assurance of the "use of proceeds". In two cases, the assurance of the "use of proceeds" will be published quarterly. If the chosen assurance provider is highly qualified and effectively independent from the issuer, the information could be valuable for investors. A smaller number of prospectuses (35%) establish that the issuer will provide an annual assurance – and, in two cases, a quarterly assurance – of the impact of the projects financed by the issuance of the GSS bonds (21 out of 60 issuances).

With regards to the SLBs in the sample, two issues are worth noting: the consequence of not reaching their sustainability performance targets; and the commitment to provide a report on the performance against the KPIs relevant to the targets.

All but three issuers in the sample face the same consequence if they do not meet the sustainability performance target(s) set in their SLB contract: an increase in the annual coupon rate after the predetermined date to reach the target (Figure 3.24). Increases range from 5 basis points (i.e., 0.05% per annum) to 85 basis points (i.e., 0.85% per annum). In 42% of the cases, the increase amounts to 25 basis points. Only in the case of three non-financial corporate issuances, the "penalty" for not reaching the target was a one-off payment of 10, 20, or 25, basis points. The money was to be donated either to eligible environmental organisations or local governments, or to be used to buy carbon credits and to fund green projects (and not paid to the bondholder as in all the other SLBs).

Interestingly, nearly half (42%) of SLBs in the sample had only one Sustainability Performance Target (SPT). Five corporate SLBs had three SPTs, and all the remaining bonds had two SPTs, including the two central governments SLBs in the sample. In Chile's SLB, the penalty for not reaching each target was 12.5 basis points; in Uruguay's SLB, there is a 15 basis points increase for not reaching each target (i.e., a penalty), but also a 15 basis points decrease for each target that is met (i.e., a premium). In the 26 SLBs included in the sample, the yield-to-maturity varied from 0% to 13.84% with the median at 5.36%.

Figure 3.24. Maximum coupon rate increase of sustainability-linked bonds

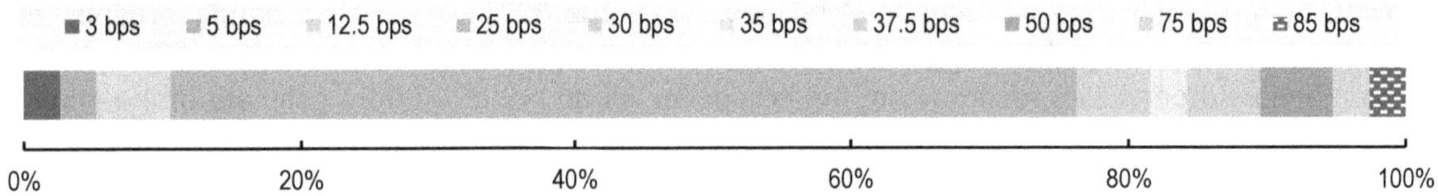

Source: SLB prospectuses, OECD analysis and calculations.

In nearly half (46%) of the corporate SLBs' prospectuses in the sample and in two out of the four of official sector SLBs, a report on the performance against the KPIs relevant to the targets would be provided annually to investors. In the other corporate SLBs in the sample, such a report would be provided only after the targets were supposed to be met, or the prospectus did not mention a commitment to issue a report on performance. In the case of the two sovereign SLBs in the sample, the frequency of reporting is not annual for all KPIs because, as explained in the prospectuses, the assessments depend on costly data collection (e.g., satellite images). The annual disclosure of the performance is effectively a requirement by the ICMA Sustainability-Linked Bond Principles for evident good reasons. In some cases, it was also promised that an assurance provider would be hired to assure the quality of mentioned reports. While accounting and reporting on the issuer's performance against relevant KPIs may be costly, in some cases the annual disclosure of this information – and not only when the target is supposed to be reached – may be material for investors. Particularly, this will be the case if targets are ambitious and the established penalties are relevant in relation to the yield of the issuance, because investors may incorporate the possibility of receiving a higher coupon in the future when pricing the SLB.

In any sovereign bond issuance, investors must be aware that it may be difficult for them to obtain or enforce judgements of foreign courts against a sovereign government. Specifically in the case of SLBs, it may even be challenging for investors to enforce the payment of the due coupon increase in the national judiciary of the sovereign issuer if a sustainability performance target has not been met. The existence of a bond contract may not be considered sufficient reason to limit the power of newly elected officials to legislate and to establish public policies that are different from the ones envisaged at the time of the bond issuance. Of course, a change in a SLB contract or the decision of not paying the coupon increase contractually due would probably harm the reputation of the sovereign issuer with investors, and this may be enough to deter any incompliance. Nevertheless, this legal and political uncertainty may explain why, as presented in Section 3.2, the issuance of SLBs among sovereigns is considerably less relevant than among corporate issuers.

3.3.5. The impact of sovereign sustainable bond issuance on the market

This section analyses whether the issuance of sovereign sustainable bonds has supported the development of a market of sustainable corporate bonds. It focuses mainly on green bonds, which is the most common type of bond issued by governments (OECD, 2023[35]), and on the non-financial corporate sector due to the fact that green bonds issued by financial companies have a different design: the proceeds are used for green loans instead of green projects. As a result, government green bonds are more comparable to those issued by non-financial corporations and, therefore, can arguably benefit more from government issuances.

Securities markets consist of a set of issuers requiring financing, investors looking to invest their savings and intermediaries that create a linkage between these investors and issuers. This occurs under a legal and regulatory environment that aims at facilitating price discovery, the secure ownership of holdings and the settlement of transactions. A developed market allows investors and issuers to trade with low transaction costs and assurances that minimise counterparty risk. The development of bond markets took years across OECD countries following the development of credible fiscal and monetary policy frameworks, the growth of government security markets, the design of sound legal and regulatory frameworks, and the evolution of the expertise of market intermediaries. While sustainable bonds are a relatively new instrument, they were developed in a period in which bond markets were already well developed, largely benefiting from the current market structure for conventional bonds.

Central governments, as typically the largest issuers of bonds in their respective jurisdictions, have had a notable market development role in bond markets. They aim at being a predictable and active provider of a large number of securities across the maturity spectrum, and at attracting a diversified base of investors to the domestic bond market. Additionally, these issuances allow market participants to use the yields paid by the government as a proxy for a benchmark yield curve of the "credit risk-free" interest rate. This curve is the main reference for the overall credit curve for non-sovereign bonds, greatly benefiting price discovery.

By issuing sustainable bonds, many governments aim to replicate their role in supporting the development of a conventional bond market to a sustainable bond market (refer to Figure 3.22). In the context of the sustainable bond market, such support may encompass the establishment of benchmarks for the framework, allocation, and impact reports, as well as raising awareness of sustainability issues.

The inception of a corporate sustainable bond market was largely neither driven by nor supported by central government issuances. In most cases, the opposite occurred – the government sector caught up with the private sector in the issuance of sustainable bonds. More specifically, of all the 79 countries that had at least one issuance of corporate sustainable bonds as of 2023, only in four countries (Hungary, Nigeria, Poland, and Togo) did the central government issue a sustainable bond before the private sector. Even when considering only green bonds and the non-financial sector, only in five countries did government issuance precede those from the non-financial corporate sector – namely in Belgium, Ireland, Hungary, Poland, and Nigeria.

Concerning the impact of government issuances on new corporate issuances, Figure 3.25 analyses trends in the growth rate of the amount issued in corporate green bonds four years before and after the first sovereign green bond issuance. Two observations can be made. First, only for the non-financial corporate sector is there a local peak in the amount issued in green bonds around the year of the first sovereign issuance. Second, there is no clear long-lasting effect of the issuance of sovereign green bonds on the growth of the issuance of corporate green bonds in either the corporate financial or the non-financial corporate sector, as in the subsequent year of the sovereign issuance the growth rate reduces.

Figure 3.25. Median and range of the annual growth rate of the amount issued in green bonds

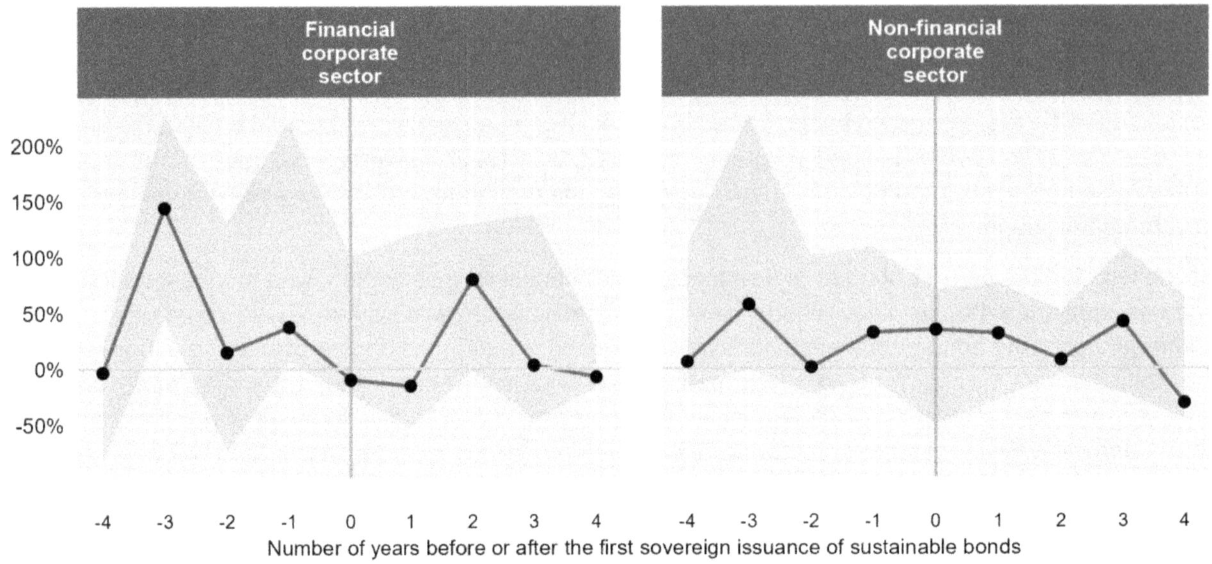

Note: This chart covers all countries with both corporate and sovereign green bond issuances. The trend line refers to the median growth rate of the amount issued in green bonds across these countries in the years before and after the issuance of the sovereign green bond issuance. The shaded area refers to the interquartile range – that is, the range between the 25% and the 75% percentiles of the growth rates.
Source: LSEG and Bloomberg, OECD calculations.

To complement the analysis above, Figure 3.26 compares the amount issued in green bonds as a share of all bond issuances by non-financial corporations across markets with and without sovereign green bond issuances. In the sample analysed, jurisdictions that issued sovereign green bonds before 2023 have always been in the top half portion of the chart. This means that the amount issued in green bonds as a share of all bonds issued by the corporate non-financial sector has grown more in these jurisdictions after the year of their first sovereign issuance compared to most other jurisdictions that have never issued sovereign green bonds. Nevertheless, a few jurisdictions that have not issued sovereign green bonds did experience even stronger growth (e.g. Finland and Norway), suggesting that the issuance of sovereign green bonds can help but is not a necessary condition to boost the growth of issuances.

Figure 3.26. Increase in the ratio between the amount issued in green bonds to all bonds issued by non-financial corporations

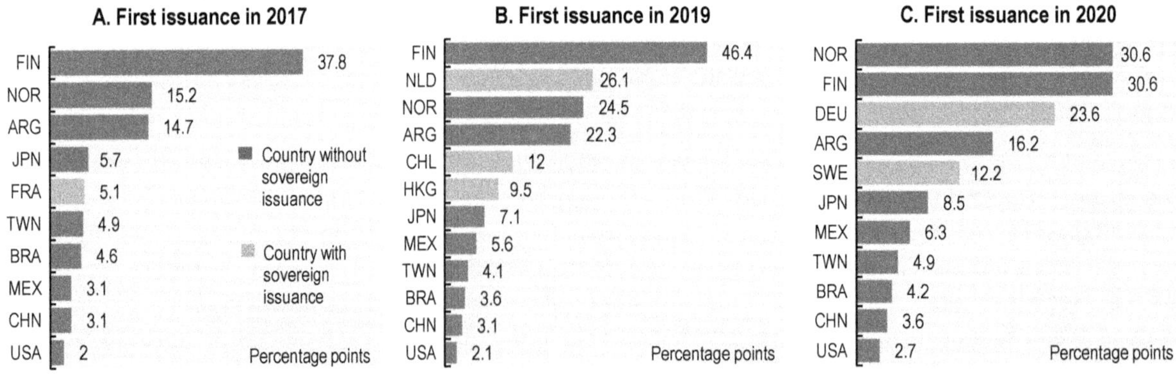

Note: The base year for each chart is the year of the first issuance of a green bond by sovereigns displayed. This chart covers only a selection of 18 jurisdictions with a frequent issuance of non-financial corporate bonds to avoid outliers in the ratio of green to all bonds. Mexico issued its first sustainability bond in 2020, while Argentina and Brazil did in 2023. However, none of them issued green bonds.
Source: LSEG and Bloomberg, OECD calculations.

Lastly, Figure 3.27 contrasts the trend in the ratio between the amount issued in green bonds to all bonds issued by non-financial corporations for four sets of countries within the same continent. Overall, it shows that many jurisdictions did experience an increase in this ratio after the first green sovereign issuances, but this growth is by and large comparable to those experienced by countries without sovereign green bond issuances. For instance, this share increased in France more substantially only after 2020, three years after its sovereign issuance. In this same period (between 2017 and 2020), this share rose more in Italy and the United Kingdom, even though their governments only issued a sovereign bond in 2021. Similarly, in Sweden, the strongest rise in this share occurred between 2017 and 2019, prior to its debut sovereign issuance in 2020. A comparable increase was experienced by its neighbour Finland, but Finland has never issued a sovereign green bond. Similar trends of jurisdictions experiencing a large growth in their corporate sustainable bond market without sovereign issuances occurred in Asia and South America.

Figure 3.27. Trends in the ratio between the amount issued in green bonds to all bonds issued by non-financial corporations in selected countries

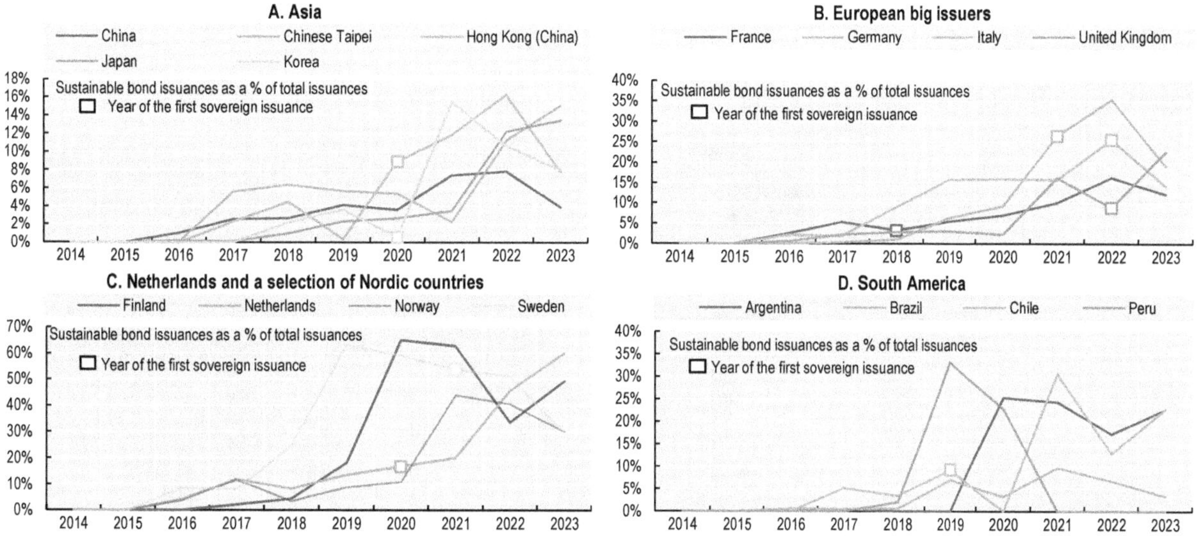

Note: Mexico issued its first sustainability bond in 2020, while Argentina and Brazil did in 2023. However, none of them issued green bonds.
Source: LSEG and Bloomberg, OECD calculations.

3.3.6. Liquidity

Although the sustainable bond market can benefit from the legal and regulatory environment for conventional bonds as well as the expertise of issuers and intermediaries, these elements can improve the development of the sustainable bond market only up to a certain point. Ultimately a market is only functional to the extent to which issuers and investors can find a counterpart to trade their security – that is, if markets are liquid. Market liquidity refers to the degree to which trading an asset impacts its value. The wider and deeper the issuer and investor base for an asset, the more likely it is for investors to buy and sell assets without meaningfully affecting the current price, which reduces the costs associated with entering or exiting a position in the market. Everything else held constant, there is a reinforcing loop in which the more issuers and investors are active in the market of an asset, the more attractive this market becomes for other investors and issuers due to the benefits of a liquid market. In that way, a diversified investor and issuer base is crucial for the development of markets.

This section assesses the liquidity of sustainable bond markets by comparing the bid-ask spread between a limited set of matched sustainable and conventional bonds for both the official and the corporate sectors. The set of bonds is the same as in the analysis in Section 3.3.2, and the matching controls for, among other variables, the issuer, currency, issue date, and maturity year. The bid-ask spread refers to the difference between the price at which participants offer to buy and sell a security, and it is the most used proxy for market liquidity and the one that conveys the most information in bond markets (Fleming, 2002[37]).

Figure 3.28 compares the weekly average bid-ask spread since issuance between sustainable and conventional bonds from the official sector. It shows that, out of the 19 matched bonds, in 14 of them the average bid-ask spread is higher for the sustainable bond compared to the matched conventional bond. This pattern was observed in multiple countries – namely France, Germany, Hungary, Lithuania, the Netherlands, Poland, Spain, Sweden, and the United Kingdom. Exceptions were observed in Poland and Serbia. Additionally, this trend also occurred over the maturity spectrum – it involves bonds maturing as early as 2025 and as late as 2051. The average difference was of 0.15 in the bid-ask price, which represents roughly half of the average bid-ask spread for the set of conventional bonds and 0.15% of the face value of 100 in the respective currency of denomination of the bond. It is worth noting that this difference in the average for the bid-ask spread over time for paired bonds reflects a persistent tendency for the bid-ask spread to be modestly higher for sustainable bonds (see Annex Figure 3.C.2, for bond-specific time series data).

Figure 3.28. Bid-ask spread in matched official sector sustainable and conventional bonds

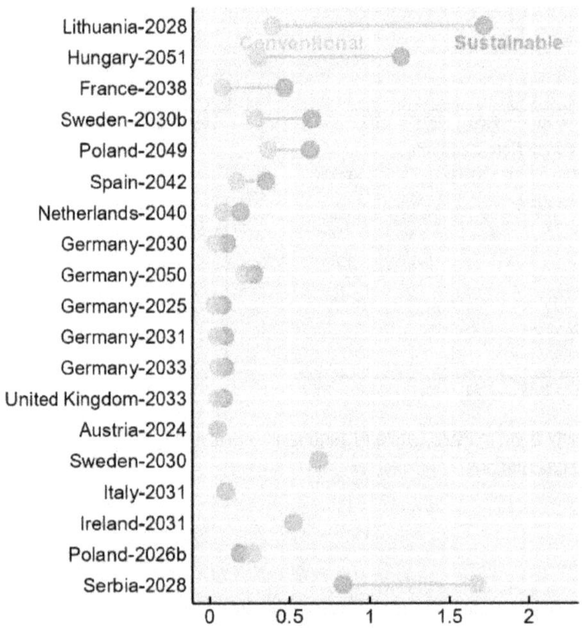

Note: The chart shows the difference in bid-ask spreads between bonds with 100 being the face value of the bond.
Source: LSEG and Bloomberg, OECD calculations.

For corporate bonds, there is also a small tendency for conventional bonds to have a lower bid-ask spread compared to their sustainable bond pair. Figure 3.29 shows the distribution of the average differences in the bid-ask spread between 214 pairs of sustainable and conventional corporate bonds. This set of pairs covers companies from various continents and sectors, and securities with varying maturities. Although the distribution of these differences is centred around zero, meaning that it is more likely to find a negligible difference in the bid-ask spread between the two types of instruments, a larger size of the distribution is on the right, which represents the cases in which the bid-ask spread is larger for sustainable bonds. A difference higher than 0.1 in the spread is nearly twice as likely to happen for sustainable bonds (22%) than for conventional ones (13%). On average the bid-ask spread is around 7% wider for sustainable bonds.

Figure 3.29. Bid-ask spread differences between matched sustainable and conventional corporate bonds

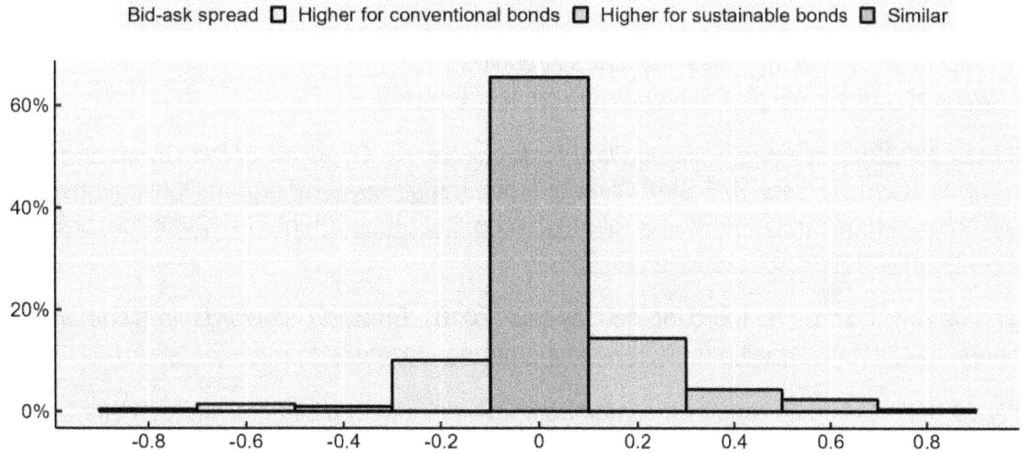

Source: LSEG and Bloomberg, OECD calculations.

Aside from differences in the investor base and the fact that there is a lower outstanding amount of sustainable bonds compared to conventional ones, one potential explanation for these results is that there are differences in the behaviour of climate-sensitive investors compared to conventional investors (Tang and Zhang, 2018[31]; Starks and Venkat, 2017[38]), with the former tending to have longer investment horizons than the latter. This means that climate-sensitive investors might be less willing to trade in times of asset depreciation to reduce their exposure, or in times of asset appreciation to profit from the short-term movement. If this is indeed the case, it is more challenging to find a counterpart to trade in a market with climate-sensitive investors than otherwise, which can affect the liquidity of the securities traded by them.

The challenge in pricing some of the characteristics of sustainable bonds may also explain their lower liquidity. For instance, for investors to adequately assess the value of an SLB, they will need to understand the likelihood of whether a sustainability performance target will be met and, therefore, the present value of the possible coupon rate increase. While this is feasible, it represents a cost for the investor that, all else being equal, does not exist for investors in conventional bonds.

References

Agence France Trésor (2023), *Press Releases Archives*, https://www.aft.gouv.fr/en/communiques-de-presse/archives. [5]

Ando, S. et al. (2022), *Sovereign Climate Debt Instruments: An Overview of the Green and Catastrophe Bond Markets*, IMF Staff Climate Note, https://www.imf.org/en/Publications/staff-climate-notes/Issues/2022/06/29/Sovereign-Climate-Debt-Instruments-An-Overview-of-the-Green-and-Catastrophe-Bond-Markets-518272. [29]

Associação de Investidores no Mercado de Capitais (2016), *Brazilian Stewardship Code and Principles*, https://amecbrasil.org.br/stewardship/amec-stewardship-code/?lang=en. [22]

Banca d'Italia (2021), *Annual report on sustainable investments and climate-related risks*, https://www.bancaditalia.it/pubblicazioni/rapporto-investimenti-sostenibili/index.html?com.dotmarketing.htmlpage.language=1 (accessed on 8 January 2024). [41]

Banca d'Italia (2021), *The Responsible Investment Charter*, https://www.bancaditalia.it/compiti/riserve-portafoglio-rischi/cis/index.html?com.dotmarketing.htmlpage.language=1&dotcache=refresh (accessed on 8 January 2024). [40]

Bolton, P. et al. (2022), *Climate and Debt, Geneva reports on the world economy*, Center for Economic and Policy Research, https://books.google.fr/books?id=ZU17zwEACAAJ. [24]

Bruckhaus, F. (2017), "SEC Issues Interpretations Relating to Rule 144A and Regulation S", *Oxford Business Law Blog*, https://blogs.law.ox.ac.uk/business-law-blog/blog/2017/01/sec-issues-interpretations-relating-rule-144a-and-regulation-s. [39]

Bundesrepublik Deutschland (2023), *Issuance Results in Syndication Process*, https://www.deutsche-finanzagentur.de/en/federal-securities/issuances/syndicates. [6]

CBI (2023), *Climate Bonds Standard Board*, https://www.climatebonds.net/standard/governance/board. [10]

CBI (2023), *Climate Bonds Standard V4.0*, https://www.climatebonds.net/climate-bonds-standard-v4. [12]

CBI (2023), *Reports*, https://www.climatebonds.net/resources/reports. [34]

CBI (2022), *Tax incentives for issuers and investors*, https://www.climatebonds.net/policy/policy-areas/tax-incentives. [20]

CBI (2021), *Climate Bonds Taxonomy*, https://www.climatebonds.net/standard/taxonomy. [14]

Dikau, S. and V. Ulrich (2021), "Central bank mandates, sustainability objectives and the promotion of green finance", *Ecological Economics 184*, https://doi.org/10.1016/j.ecolecon.2021.107022. [17]

Doronzo, R., V. Siracusa and S. Antonelli (2021), "Green Bonds: the Sovereign Issuers' Perspective", *Banca d'Italia, MISP*, Vol. 3, https://www.bancaditalia.it/media/notizia/green-bonds-the-sovereign-issuers-perspective/?com.dotmarketing.htmlpage.language=1&dotcache=refresh. [32]

Ehlers, T. and F. Packer (2017), "Green Bond Finance and Certification", *BIS, Bank of International Settlements*, https://www.bis.org/publ/qtrpdf/r_qt1709h.htm. [30]

Elderson, F. and I. Schnabel (2023), "How green is our balance sheet?", *The ECB Blog*, https://www.ecb.europa.eu/press/blog/date/2023/html/ecb.blog.230324~f417b719fd.en.html (accessed on 13 July 2023). [19]

ESMA (2023), "The European sustainable debt market – do issuers benefit from an ESG pricing effect?", *ESMA Report on Trends, Risks and Vulnerabilities Risk Analysis*, https://doi.org/10.2856/468709. [33]

European Central Bank (2022), *ECB climate agenda 2022*, https://www.ecb.europa.eu/press/pr/date/2022/html/ecb.pr220704_annex~cb39c2dcbb.en.pdf. [18]

European Commission (2023), *Regulation (EU) 2023/2631 of the European Parliament and of the Council on European Green Bonds and optional disclosures for bonds marketed as environmentally sustainable and for sustainability-linked bonds*, https://eur-lex.europa.eu/legal-content/EN/TXT/?uri=celex:32023R2631. [36]

Financial Reporting Council (2020), *UK Stewardship Code*, https://www.frc.org.uk/investors/uk-stewardship-code. [23]

Financial Services Agency (2020), *Principles for Responsible Institutional Investors ≪Japan's Stewardship Code≫ - To promote sustainable growth of companies through investment and dialogue*, https://www.fsa.go.jp/en/refer/councils/stewardship/. [21]

Fleming, M. (2002), "Measuring Treasury Market Liquidity", *Economic Policy Review*, Vol. 9/3, https://www.newyorkfed.org/medialibrary/media/research/epr/03v09n3/0309flempdf.pdf. [37]

Hinsche, I. (2021), "A Greenium for the Next Generation EU Green Bonds Analysis of a Potential Green Bond Premium and its Drivers", *Center for Financial Studies Working Paper* 663, https://doi.org/10.2139/ssrn.3965664. [26]

ICMA (2023), *Social Bond Principles*, https://www.icmagroup.org/assets/documents/Sustainable-finance/2023-updates/Social-Bond-Principles-SBP-June-2023-220623.pdf. [3]

ICMA (2023), *The Principles, Guidelines and Handbooks*, https://www.icmagroup.org/sustainable-finance/the-principles-guidelines-and-handbooks/. [11]

ICMA (2022), *Guidance Handbook*, https://www.icmagroup.org/assets/GreenSocialSustainabilityDb/The-GBP-Guidance-Handbook-January-2022.pdf. [1]

ICMA (2021), *Green Bond Principles*, https://www.icmagroup.org/sustainable-finance/the-principles-guidelines-and-handbooks/green-bond-principles-gbp/. [2]

ICMA (2020), *Governance Framework*, https://www.icmagroup.org/sustainable-finance/membership-governance-and-working-groups/governance-framework/. [9]

IPSF (2023), *The International Platform on Sustainable Finance – Annual Report 2023*, https://finance.ec.europa.eu/system/files/2023-12/231204-ipsf-annual-report_en.pdf. [15]

Italian Treasury Department (2023), *Risultati Aste e Collocamenti tramite Sindacato*, https://www.dt.mef.gov.it/it/debito_pubblico/emissioni_titoli_di_stato_interni/risultati_aste/. [7]

Karpf, A. and A. Mandel (2018), "The changing value of the 'green' label on the US municipal bond market", *Nature Climate Change*, Vol. 2/161e165, p. 8, https://doi.org/10.1038/s41558-017-0062-0. [28]

MacAskill, S. et al. (2021), "Is there a green premium in the green bond market? Systematic literature review revealing premium determinants", *Journal of Cleaner Production*, Vol. 280/124491, https://doi.org/10.1016/j.jclepro.2020.124491. [25]

OECD (2023), *OECD Sovereign Borrowing Outlook 2023*, OECD Publishing, Paris, https://doi.org/10.1787/09b4cfba-en. [35]

OECD (2022), "Climate Change and Corporate Governance,", *Corporate Governance, OECD Publishing, Paris*, https://doi.org/10.1787/272d85c3-en. [8]

Sierra Club (2023), *Lethal Investments: The Health Consequences of Cash Flows into Coal*, https://www.sierraclub.org/sites/default/files/2023-08/SierraClub-CoalUtilityFinancingReport.pdf. [16]

Starks, L. and P. Venkat (2017), "Corporate ESG Profiles and Investor Horizons", https://ssrn.com/abstract=3049943 or http://dx.doi.org/10.2139/ssrn.3049943. [38]

Tang, D. and Y. Zhang (2018), "Do shareholders benefit from green bonds?", *Journal of Corporate Finance*, https://doi.org/10.1016/j.jcorpfin.2018.12.001. [31]

The People's Bank of China (2021), *Green Bond Endorsed Projects Catalogue*, http://www.pbc.gov.cn/goutongjiaoliu/113456/113469/4342400/2021091617180089879.pdf. [13]

Ul Haq, I. and D. Doumbia (2022), "Structural Loopholes in Sustainability-Linked Bonds", *Policy Research Working Paper, World Bank Group*, https://doi.org/10.1596/1813-9450-10200. [4]

Zerbib, O. (2019), "The effect of pro-environmental preferences on bond prices: evidence from green bonds", *Journal of Banking Finance*, Vol. 98, p. 39e60, https://doi.org/10.1016/j.jbankfin.2018.10.012. [27]

Annex 3.A. Methodology for data collection and classification

OECD Corporate Sustainability dataset

Sustainable bonds are mainly collected from LSEG. This dataset contains deal-level information of nearly 14 400 bonds issued by both the corporate and official sectors from 103 jurisdictions since 2013. This dataset provides a detailed set of information for each sustainable bond issuance, including the identity, nationality, and industry of the issuer; the type, interest rate structure, maturity date and rating category of the bond, the amount of and "use of proceeds" obtained from the issue. The issuance amounts were adjusted by 2023 US CPI.

For sustainable bonds, values for corporations, agencies, local governments, and multilateral institutions correspond to the "gross proceeds" (i.e., the amount paid by investors to acquire the bonds) in most cases. Where the information on the gross proceeds could not be retrieved, the "original amount issued" (i.e., the face value of the bonds in their legal documentation) has been used as follows:

i. for corporates, 22% of the amount issued from 2013 to 2023 corresponds to the original amount issued, whereas the remaining 78% corresponds to the gross proceeds. For that 78% in which the gross proceeds are used, the original amount issued is 2.9% higher. However, the amount issued in "all corporate bonds", which includes conventional bonds, corresponds to the gross proceeds amounts in all cases.

ii. for agencies and local governments and multilateral institutions, 23% of the amount issued from 2013 to 2023 corresponds to the original amount issued, whereas the remaining 77% corresponds to the gross proceeds. For that 78% in which the gross proceeds are used, the original amount issued is 1.25% higher.

iii. for central governments, only the original amount issued (i.e., the face value of the bonds) is displayed for consistency with other OECD publications on sovereign debt markets.

Agencies and local governments include national government agencies (e.g., KFW, Transport for London), local governments (e.g., Prefecture of Shiga, Province of Ontario), and national development banks (e.g., China Development Bank, Brazilian Development Bank). This category does not contain US Municipals that are not readily available in LSEG. The category Central Governments includes governments, treasuries, and central banks. The category Multilateral Institutions includes organisations formed by three or more jurisdictions (e.g., Asian Development Bank, International Finance Corp), and the European Union.

The category "Asia excl. China and Japan" includes all jurisdictions in the continent excluding China and Japan (therefore this category includes Hong Kong (China), India; Korea, Singapore, and Chinese Taipei). "Latin America" includes jurisdictions both in Latin America and in the Caribbean. "Europe" includes all jurisdictions that are fully located in the region, including the United Kingdom and Switzerland but excluding Russia and Türkiye. "Other Advanced" includes all jurisdictions that are classified as advanced economies in IMF's World Economic Outlook Database but that are not represented in the other categories in the figure (e.g., Australia, Canada, and Israel). "Others" includes mostly jurisdictions that are classified as emerging market and developing economies in IMF's World Economic Outlook Database but that are not represented in the other categories in the figure (e.g., Saudi Arabia and South Africa).

LSEG data contains both Regulation S and Rule 144A sustainable bonds. Rule 144A presents a safe harbour from the registration requirements of the Securities Act for resales of securities not fungible with securities listed on a US securities exchange to qualified institutional buyers. Regulation S provides a safe harbour from the registration requirements of the Securities Act for offerings made outside the United States (Bruckhaus, 2017[39]). The calculations presented take account of this factor, and an exercise to eliminate the duplication when a single bond was issued both under Regulation S and Rule 144A was performed.

When calculating the outstanding amount of bonds in a given year, issues that are no longer outstanding due to being redeemed earlier than their maturity should also be deducted. Outstanding values refer to the "principal amount" or otherwise to the "original amount issued" (i.e., the face value of the bonds in their legal documentation) when the "principal amount" could not be retrieved. The early redemption data are obtained from LSEG and cover bonds that have been redeemed early due to being repaid via final default distribution, called, liquidated, put or repurchased. The early redemption data are merged with the primary bond market data via ISINs.

In Table 3.1, for the GSS bonds where more than one "use of proceeds" was disclosed by the issuer, the amount issued by the GSS bond was equally split for each of the use of proceeds. For example, if a GSS bonds amounting to USD 1 000 displayed *clean transport* and *energy efficiency* as promised use of proceeds, USD 500 was allocated into the category *clean transport* and USD 500 into *energy efficiency* one.

In Table 3.2, for the SLBs where more than one key performance indicator was disclosed by the issuer, the amount issued by the SLB was equally split for each of the key performance indicators. For example, if a SLB amounting to USD 1 000 displayed *renewable energy* and *sustainable forest management* as key performance indicators, half of that amount was allocated into the category *renewable energy* and half into the *sustainable and forest management* one.

In Figure 3.10, the values correspond to the sum of the amounts issued in 2022 and 2023. The five displayed categories stand for: *Large listed, advanced* (bond issuers that are MSCI World Index constituents as of September 2023), *Large listed, emerging* (bond issuers that are MSCI Emerging Markets Index constituents as of September 2023), *Smaller listed* (bond issuers that are listed on a stock exchange but that are not constituents of the MSCI World nor the MSCI EM indexes), and *Unlisted subsidiary with a listed parent* (bond issuers that were delisted prior to 2022, or that have never listed their equity, and which have their immediate or ultimate parent listed), *Other unlisted company* (other bond issuers that were delisted prior to 2022, or that have never listed their equity) . The bond issuer is categorised as listed if an ISIN exists and if it is associated with a valid LSEG Identification Code (RIC) made up of the bond issuer's ticker symbol and an exchange code (based on the name of the stock exchange). If the bond issuer does not display an ISIN coupled with a RIC or its RIC shows a delisting year prior to 2022 (e.g., SPS.N^H97), it is classified as unlisted.

Sustainable investment funds

Open-ended fund and ETF data have been retrieved from Morningstar Direct. Funds retrieved as "Sustainable Funds" in the case their names contain climate or ESG relevant acronyms and words such as "ESG", "sustainable", "responsible", "ethical", "green", "social", "environment", "Paris align" and "climate" (and their translation in other languages).

Funds without any asset value, as well as expired bond holdings, are excluded. USD (January 2024) is the portfolio currency for the holdings value.

Fixed Income funds are defined by Morningstar as open-ended funds and ETFs that have most of the holdings as fixed income assets.

A passive fund is defined by Morningstar as an open-end fund or exchange-traded fund whose portfolio managers do not choose specific investments but automatically invest in an index or part of a market. They often track stock or bond market indices.

Annex 3.B. An analysis of a premium for sustainable bonds

Annex Table 3.B.1. Paired GSS and conventional bonds for government primary issuances

	ISIN – GSS	ISIN – Conventional	Issuance – GSS	Issuance – Conventional	Maturity – GSS	Maturity – Conventional
France	FR0013234333	FR0013515806	2017	2020	2039	2040
France	FR0014002JM6	FR0013257524	2021	2017	2044	2048
France	FR001400AQH0	FR0013327491	2021	2018	2038	2036
Italy	IT0005542359	IT0005449969	2023	2021	2031	2031
Italy		IT0005436693		2021		2031
Italy	IT0005508590	IT0005496770	2022	2022	2035	2038
Italy	IT0005438004	IT0005530032	2021	2023	2045	2043
Germany	DE0001030757	DE0001102614	2023	2023	2053	2053
Germany	DE000BU3Z005	DE0001102515	2023	2020	2033	2035
Germany	DE0001030724	DE0001102614	2022	2022	2050	2053
Germany	DE0001030724	DE0001102572	2021	2022	2050	2052

Note: IT0005542359 is paired with a weighted average of IT0005449969 and IT0005436693.
Source: LSEG and Bloomberg.

Premium matching method

For this analysis, two datasets are used. One for corporate bonds and the other one for bonds issued by official sector entities. Both datasets include sustainable and conventional bonds, and the sample has been selected following (Bolton et al., 2022[24]), which considers whether the issuers had issued at least one sustainable bond and one conventional bond to ensure a balanced representation, to control for credit and exchange rate risk. To ensure data integrity and robustness in subsequent regression analysis stages, the focus is directed towards bonds with comprehensive data across specific variables. These variables include the issue date, yield-to-maturity (YTM), maturity date, coupon, coupon type and the amount issued in USD.

The *Nearest Neighbour Matching* technique was used for the matching process (using matchit command from R). This is a well-established method in propensity score matching analyses. A propensity score model was estimated using coupon, coupon class, issue year, maturity year and asset-linked securities type variables to estimate the probability of each bond being green. The matching was performed in a 1:1 ratio, meaning each green bond was matched to one conventional bond.

Propensity scores range between 0 and 1. In the context of propensity score matching, a propensity score is the probability of a unit (a bond, in this case) being assigned to a particular treatment given a set of observed characteristics. In other words, it is the conditional probability of receiving treatment (being a sustainable bond) as a function of observed characteristics. A score closer to 1 indicates a higher likelihood of being a green bond, given the observed features, while a score closer to 0 suggests a lower probability.

The objective of this technique is to achieve equilibrium in the distribution of observable characteristics between the treated group (sustainable bonds) and the control group (conventional bonds), thereby minimizing bias and enabling a more dependable comparison between the two groups. The aim is to simulate a randomized experiment, where the sole systematic difference between sustainable and conventional bonds is their "treatment" status, allowing any disparities in outcomes to be attributed to the "sustainable" status with a higher degree of conviction. The *nearest method*, also known as nearest neighbour matching, pairs a treated unit (sustainable bond) with a control unit (conventional bond) that has the closest propensity score.

Exact matching was executed on the two categorical variables, currency and issuer, to control for credit risk and exchange rate risk. This control ensured that the sustainable and conventional bonds matched were issued by the same entity and were denominated in the same currency, thus minimising potential sources of bias (Bolton et al., 2022[24]). The obtained dataset only includes bonds that have been matched based on their propensity scores and the exact match for issuer and currency, and thus have comparable characteristics, forming the basis for subsequent stages of analysis. The datasets include 72 government bonds (36 green and 36 conventional) and 1 736 corporate bonds (868 green and 868 conventional).

In summary, this methodology allows for a robust comparison between sustainable and conventional bonds, controlling for potential confounding variables. It ensures that possible differences observed in yield-to-maturity can be attributed mainly to the bonds' "sustainable" status.

Premium descriptive statistics

This section briefly presents the descriptive statistics of the data used for the regression performed following the methodology operated by Bolton et al. (2022[24]). The following descriptive statistics include 17 issuer's domiciles for 17 different issuers and 7 different currencies for official bonds. For corporate bonds, descriptive statistics include 41 issuer's domiciles for 419 different issuers and 24 different currencies.

Annex Table 3.B.2. Descriptive statistics – conventional matched bonds – official sector

	N	Mean	SD	Min	Max
Yield-to-maturity	36	1.8445	3.0878	-0.7472	13.3014
Coupon	36	1.6476	3.4468	0	7.1
Amount Issued in USD millions	36	3 308	3 346	26.36	10 192

Source: LSEG and Bloomberg, OECD calculations.

Annex Table 3.B.3. Descriptive statistics – sustainable matched bonds – official sector

	N	Mean	SD	Min	Max
Yield-to-maturity	36	2.0263	2.8278	-0.7601	13.5499
Coupon	36	2.9133	3.2413	0	7.29
Amount Issued in USD millions	36	3 935	3 969	27.70	14 592

Source: LSEG and Bloomberg, OECD calculations.

Annex Table 3.B.4. Descriptive statistics – conventional matched bonds – corporate sector

	N	Mean	SD	Min	Max
Yield-to-maturity	868	2.7310	2.0340	0.009	23.82
Coupon	868	2.7205	2.0309	0.01	23.82
Amount Issued in USD millions	868	238	447	0.948	5 293

Source: LSEG and Bloomberg, OECD calculations.

Annex Table 3.B.5. Descriptive statistics – sustainable matched bonds – corporate sector

	N	Mean	SD	Min	Max
Yield-to-maturity	868	2.7521	1.9617	0.001	17.52
Coupon	868	2.7361	1.9618	0.001	23.82
Amount Issued in USD millions	868	215	359	0.822	4 352

Source: LSEG and Bloomberg, OECD calculations.

Annex 3.C. The impact of sovereign sustainable bond issuance on the market

In Figure 3.26, the criteria are that a jurisdiction can only be selected if it had at least four years of green bond issuance by non-financial corporations. In addition, for issuers with sovereign green bond issuances, the country should have at minimum two issuances before and after the sovereign issuance with green bond issuances by non-financial corporations, which excluded countries whose first issuance was in 2021. This avoids the bias of using only one year to compute any ratio for the country. The ratio considers only the period between 2016 and 2023 and for years in this period with no green bond issuance but with conventional bond issuances by non-financial corporations, the ratio was set to zero.

Annex Figure 3.C.1. Bond-specific bid-ask spread time series for the official sector

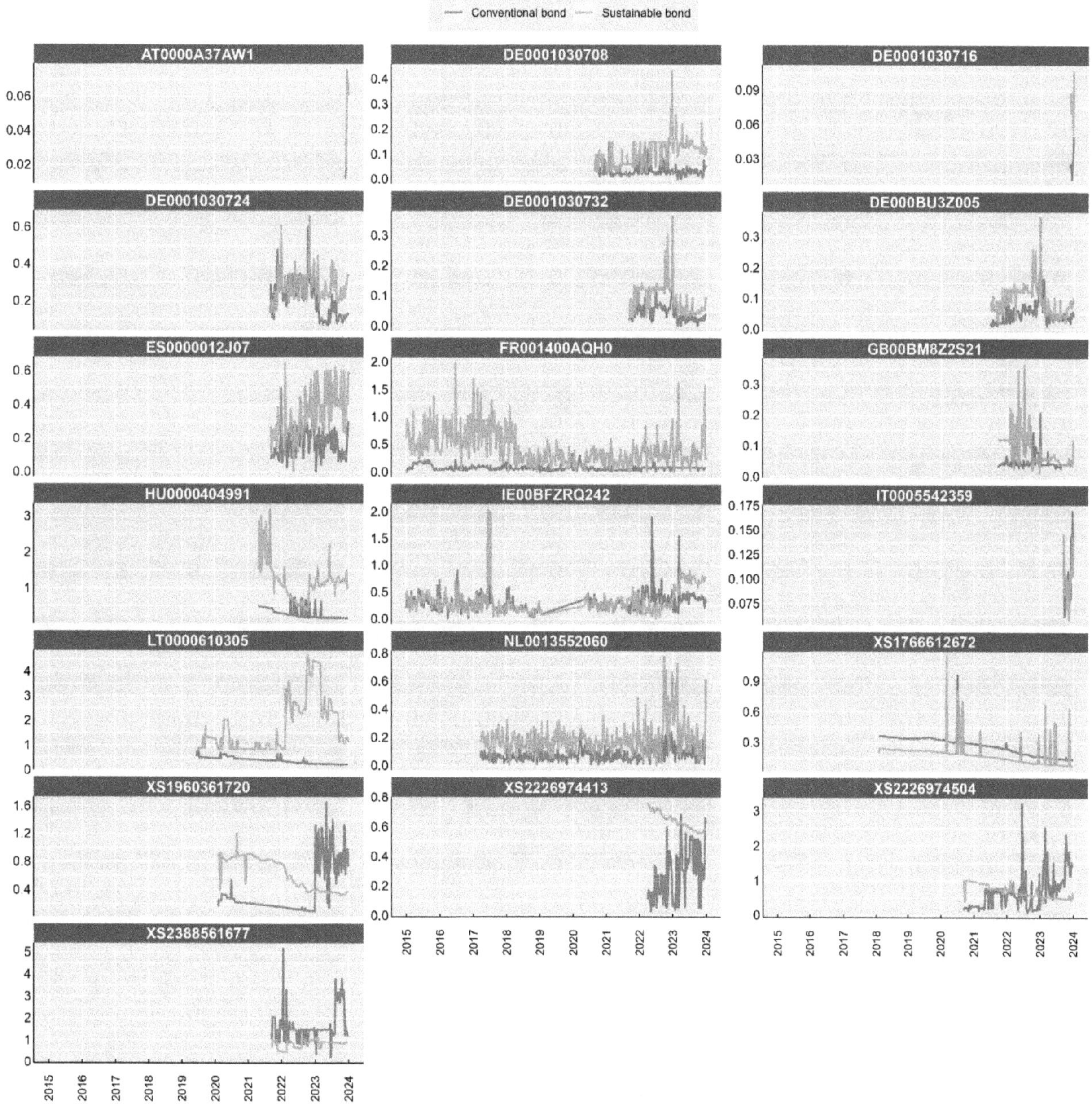

Source: LSEG and Bloomberg, OECD calculations.

Annex Figure 3.C.2. Bond-specific bid-ask spread time series for the corporate sector

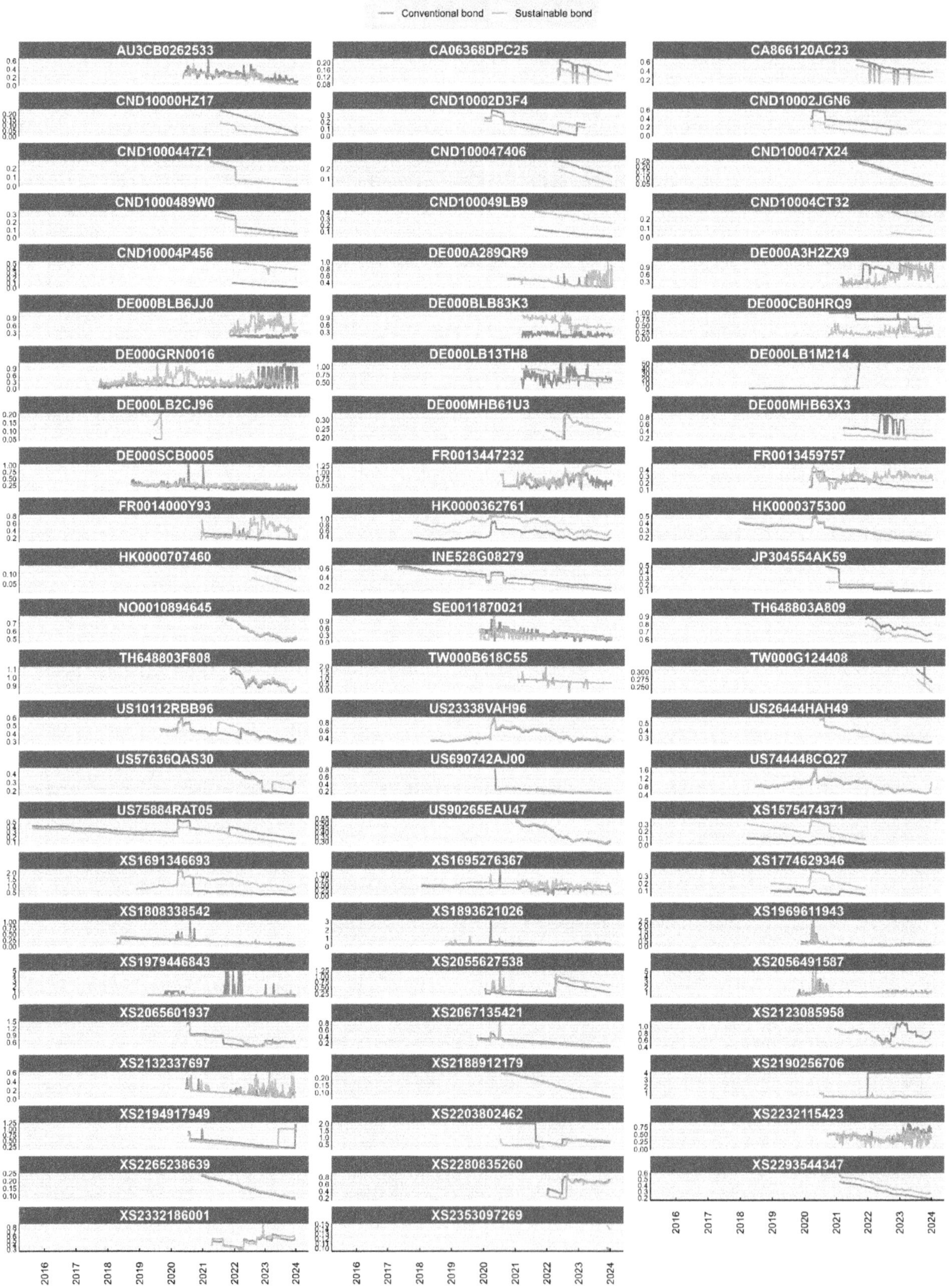

Note: Due to size constraints, only 72 bonds with a better matching statistic are displayed.
Source: LSEG and Bloomberg, OECD calculations.

Notes

[1] At the central government level, this reduction can be attributed to a scarcity of eligible expenditures for large issuers of sustainable bonds, such as Chile and France (OECD, 2023[35]).

[2] The sample encompasses both advanced economies and emerging market and developing economies for sovereign issuances, as well as corporations from varied sectors domiciled in multiple countries. The advanced economies for sovereign issuances include France, Germany, Italy, and the United Kingdom, while the emerging market and developing economies for sovereign issuances encompass Chile, Egypt, India, Mexico, and Türkiye. The corporate sector is represented by financial and non-financial entities.

[3] Banca d'Italia provides an example of a central bank integrating financial and sustainability criteria into its investment portfolio strategy. The Bank publishes a Responsible Investment Charter, which establishes principles for merging financial and sustainability assessments (Banca d'Italia, 2021[40]), and the Annual Report on Sustainability Investments and Climate-Related Risks (Banca d'Italia, 2021[41]).

[4] Other jurisdictions with repo-eligible government sustainable bonds are Thailand (2 securities), Hungary (2) and Hong Kong (China) (1).

[5] Other jurisdictions with repo-eligible corporate sustainable bonds are Chinese Taipei (54 securities), Australia (8), Russia (5), New Zealand (4), Brazil (1) and the United States (1).

[6] Other jurisdictions with repo-eligible agencies and supranational sustainable bonds are Australia (11 securities), New Zealand (7), Thailand (6), Indonesia (4), Russia (3), Chinese Taipei (3), the United States (1) and Viet Nam (1).

www.ingramcontent.com/pod-product-compliance
Lightning Source LLC
Chambersburg PA
CBHW061217240926
51846CB00006B/1262